VOCABULARY GROWTH
Strategies for College Word Study

Dorothy Grant Hennings
Distinguished Professor, Kean University

Prentice
Hall

Upper Saddle River, New Jersey 07458

Library of Congress Cataloging-in-Publication Data

Hennings, Dorothy Grant.
  Vocabulary growth : strategies for college word study / Dorothy Grant Hennings.
    p.   cm.
  Includes index.
  ISBN 0–13–022326–3
    1. Vocabulary—Problems, exercises, etc. I. Title.

PE1449.H4425 2001
428.2—dc21   99–054724

Editorial Director: *Charlyce Jones Owens*
Editor in Chief: *Leah Jewell*
Acquisitions Editor: *Craig Campanella*
Editorial Assistant: *Joan Polk*
Managing Editor: *Mary Rottino*
Production Liaison: *Fran Russello*
Project Manager: *Marianne Hutchinson (Pine Tree Composition)*
Prepress and Manufacturing Buyer: *Ben Smith*
Cover Director: *Jayne Conte*
Cover Designer: *Bruce Kenselaar*
Cover Image: *Paolo Koch/Photo Researchers, Inc.*
Marketing Manager: *Brandy Dawson*

The book was set in 10/12 Times Roman by Pine Tree Composition
and was printed and bound by Courier Companies, Inc.
The cover was printed by Phoenix Color Corp.

Prentice
Hall

© 2001 by Prentice-Hall, Inc.
A Division of Pearson Education
Upper Saddle River, New Jersey 07458

Printed in the United States of America

10   9   8   7   6   5   4   3   2   1

ISBN 0-13-022326-3

Prentice-Hall International (UK) Limited, *London*
Prentice-Hall of Australia Pty. Limited, *Sydney*
Prentice-Hall Canada Inc., *Toronto*
Prentice-Hall Hispanoamericana, S.A., *Mexico*
Prentice-Hall of India Private Limited, *New Delhi*
Prentice-Hall of Japan, Inc., *Tokyo*
Pearson Education Asia Pte. Ltd., *Singapore*
Editora Prentice-Hall do Brasil, Ltda., *Rio de Janeiro*

Brief Table of Contents

◆◆

Contents

◆◆◆

4   More Context Clues—Words from French   66

**Part III   Prefixes and Other Introductory
Elements That Matter   85**

**5   Word Elements—Prefixes That Tell "No," "When," "Where,"
or "More"   87**

Preface

◆◆

Purpose

The purpose of *Vocabulary Growth: Strategies for College Word Study* is to provide you—college students, prospective college students, and vocational-career students—with strategies to get meaning from context clues and word elements and in the process build your vocabulary. A related purpose is to help you perceive that words are great subjects to investigate. When you become a student of language, delight in discovering word relationships, and become aware of how you can make words work for you, you are more likely to stop when you encounter an unfamiliar word and consider its meaning. If you do this, you will become a master of words and your vocabulary will grow.

Because of its purpose, *Vocabulary Growth: Strategies for College Word Study* differs from vocabulary-building texts in which the emphasis is on memorizing words and their definitions. In *Vocabulary Growth* emphasis is on perceiving meaningful elements within words, making connections among words, and searching for words that are similar in some way. The aim is for you to develop strategies to conquer unfamiliar words when you find them in your college textbooks and on your learning to make words work for you. In short, through this text you will become a student of words.

General Organization

Vocabulary Growth: Strategies for College Word Study comprises fourteen chapters. Chapters 1 and 2—Part I—focus on general vocabulary-building strategies related to dictionary use and the use of word study notebooks and cards. Chapters 3 and 4—Part II—focus on strategies related to use of context clues. In addition, words featured in Parts I and II help you understand the most important sources of English words: words that language scholars trace back to Old English and to the Anglo-Saxons—early invaders of the British Isles; words derived from Greek; words derived from Latin; and words derived from French. Featured words also help you to review how words in English function as nouns, verbs, and adjectives. Readings relate to the history of English and explain the effects of an Anglo-Saxon migration, Greek myths, Latin legends, and a French invasion on Modern English. A supplementary skill taught in these chapters is the "Know-for-sure/Process-of-elimination" test-taking strategy that you will apply throughout the text as you complete related word study activities.

Chapters 5 through 7, grouped as Part III, introduce the importance of understanding word elements, or components. These chapters focus on basic prefixes, clarify strategies for working with prefixes, and feature words built from them. The readings in this block of chapters relate to prefixes and to ways in which new words enter the language—acronyms, modern-day coinages, and olden-day development of the calendar month names.

Chapters 8 through 10 (Part IV) offer strategies and word lists that help you work with word endings and begin to see words as units of meaning rather than strings of individual letters. The chapter readings expand your ability to perceive suffixes at the ends of words as well as your ability to spell words that incorporate suffixes.

Chapters 11 through 14 (Part V) focus on word-building roots and elements derived from Latin and Greek and help you visualize the basic structure of words by using word towers. Since many technical terms encountered in post–secondary school studies are constructed with these components, understanding of how to wrest meaning from them is vital for success in college, university, or advanced vocational-career programs. Readings in these chapters explain interesting ways in which writers use words and how words have developed: compound words, figurative language and clichés, professional jargon, literary allusion.

On the inside front cover of the text is an explanation of the symbols used in the text to indicate how to pronounce the featured words.

Features

Each chapter has these features:

- A statement of objectives to be achieved listed in the order presented in the chapter.

- An opening passage that introduces a word or group of words that relates in some way to the focus of the chapter and clarifies ideas about how words work. At the end of each passage is a segment called "Collaborative Search and Discover," which asks you to become a language investigator and think about word relationships.

- One or two strategy boxes that explain strategies that help you to wrest meaning from words. In chapters that deal with prefixes, suffixes, or roots, a table summarizes the word elements taught in the segment.

- Power words and expressions (with their derivations and pronunciations) as well as highlighted elements that are set off from the running text. These boxed segments add depth and breadth to your studies.

- Two modules—Module A and Module B. Each presents from twelve to fifteen words shown with pronunciation clues, part of speech, definition, related words, and contexts that model how the word functions in sentences. With each list of words are three to six practice activities.

- A final module. Module C offers a passage about an aspect of word building or use that relates to the focus of the chapter. In most instances, starting with Chapter 3, some words are presented in boldfaced type. In followup activities, you will have to explain the meanings of those words based on your growing ability to work with context clues and word elements.

- Confusing words box. English is filled with troublesome words such as *it's* and *its, eminent* and *imminent*. At the end of each chapter, you will have the opportunity to clear up misunderstandings you may have about such words.

Acknowledgments

I send my thanks to Maggie Barbieri, former Senior Editor, English, at Prentice Hall, who encouraged me to do a vocabulary development text. Without a chance communication with her via the Internet, I would probably not have taken the plunge at this time and *Vocabulary Growth* would still be an idea in my mind rather than a book on paper. Similarly, I send my appreciation to Craig Campanella, who took over for Ms. Barbieri during production, to Joan Polk of Prentice Hall for her efficiency in handling all my communications and getting anwers to my questions; and to Marianne Hutchinson of Pine Tree Composition, who skillfully guided my book through production.

I also say, "Thank you," to the three reviewers who commented on the first draft and supplied suggestions to strengthen it: Janet Cutshall, Sussex County Community College; Sue Hightower, Tallahassee Community College; and Elizabeth Semtner, Rose State College. In my more than twenty-five years of writing college-level texts, I have found that the key to a strong book is a cadre of reviewers who generously share their ideas.

Above all and once again, I send my husband George my love for the many days he did the shopping and other household chores so that I could stay glued to my computer. I thank my husband, too, for his thoughtful reading of the successive drafts and for his suggestions that are always on the mark. I am blessed!

Dorothy Grant Hennings
Distinguished Professor, Kean University
Warren, New Jersey
dhennings@advanix.net

PART **I**

THE DICTIONARY AND WORD ORIGINS

1

The Dictionary as the Book of Choice—Words about Words and Words from Old English

◆◆◆

Objectives: In Chapter 1, you will develop the ability to

- explain the Eurocentric nature of English by talking about the history of the word *orient;*

- interpret the parts of a dictionary entry;

- use the following words featured in Module 1-A to talk about words:

accent	derivatives	hyphen	root	synonym
affix	diacritical marks	homophone	schwa	
antonym	etymology	linguist	syllable	

- recognize and interpret the elements *syn-* (together) and *lingua-* (tongue), which are featured in Module 1-A;

- comprehend the following words featured in Module 1-B that show the Anglo-Saxon origins of English as well as the diverse origins of English words:

akin	decade	egocentric	oath	orb
conducive	decorous	lore	ominous	strut
contend	deem	migrate	onus	swarm
onerous (*power word*)				

- recognize and interpret the element *ego-* (self) featured in Module 1-B;

- explain the European antecedents (or beginnings) of modern English, especially the Anglo-Saxon influences, by using the word *ordeal* as an example; and

- handle the homophone pair *who's* and *whose* and recognize and interpret the elements *homo-* (same) and *phone-* (sound).

> **A**s sheer casual reading matter, I still find the English dictionary
> the most interesting book in our language.
>
> —Albert Jay Nock, *Memoirs of a Superfluous Man,* 1942

◆◆◆

Interesting Words to Think About— *Orient* and *the Orient*

English is a Eurocentric language. By *Eurocentric,* we mean that English grew up centered not in Asia, Africa, Australia, or the Americas but in Europe, more specifically in the British Isles. As a result, other European languages (both ancient—such as old Germanic and Latin—and modern—such as French) have had major roles in determining the English language we speak today. Non-European languages have had an impact on English but a significantly lesser one.

Another result of the Eurocentricity of English is that some words in the language incorporate a decidedly European point of view. For example, in English we call the countries of Asia, as distinguished from those in Europe and the Americas, "the Orient." The word *orient* comes from the Latin word *orientem,* meaning "east." Why do we call the Asian countries "the Orient" when we must fly west to get there if we live in San Francisco?

The answer is simple. The English-speaking people of the past who lived in the British Isles had to travel eastward to reach the Orient. For them, the Orient was the East. They even included the word *Orient* in the name of a train that they took to go east to Istanbul in Turkey—the Orient Express. *Orient* was used for the Asian areas of the world before English-speaking people lived in the Americas.

Orient still retains the more general meaning of the Latin word *orientem*—"the east." Sometimes we also use *orient* as an adjective to mean "bright or shining," but we do not apply that meaning very often today. Sometimes, too, we use it as a verb meaning "to place in a particular direction" as in the sentence, "The traveler oriented her map so that the direction in which she was going was at the top." At other times we talk about "orienting ourselves"; in this case, we mean that we are adjusting ourselves to and learning about a new situation. When you first came to college, you probably had to participate in freshmen orientation. During orientation week, you found out about the institution in which you had enrolled and learned what you had to do to adjust to this new environment.

Collaborative Search and Discover

- A must-do is to get yourself a dictionary. If you do not have a dictionary, head to a local bookstore and select one with the word *college* or *advanced* in its title. Get a dictionary that provides pronunciations of words, definitions, some sample phrases with the listed words, and the origin, or etymology, of them. Bring your dictionary to class each session. You might also want to buy a pocket-sized dictionary that fits in your notebook or briefcase.

- Working with a partner, find the word *occident* in a dictionary. What does it mean? From what Latin word is it derived?

- English has borrowed words from European languages. Use your new dictionary to check the origins and meanings of these words: *baloney, fjord, dandelion, cruise, macaroni.*

- English has borrowed words from non-European languages. Use your new dictionary to check the origins and meanings of these words: *bazaar, calico, maverick, tycoon, zombie, toboggan, raccoon, igloo, shampoo.* Do this cooperatively with a partner or two.

- Hypothesize with a partner: Why are some carpets called "Oriental rugs"?

Strategy Box 1-A—Interpreting a Dictionary Entry

A typical dictionary entry includes these parts:

- the word or phrase broken into syllables.
- the word or phrase with the pronunciation indicated through the use of *diacritical marks*—marks that indicate the vowel sounds such as a long vowel or a vowel affected by other sounds, accent marks, a mark called the *schwa* (ə) that tells you that the vowel is in an unaccented syllable of the word. On the front inside cover of this book is a list of diacritical marks that you will find useful in pronouncing new words.
- the part or parts of speech the word functions as—for example as a noun (*n.*), verb (*v.*), adjective (*adj.*), or adverb (*adv.*).
- related forms of the word, such as the plural form of nouns and the past tense of verbs.
- the definition or definitions of the word or phrase. Generally dictionaries group the definitions according to a word's use as a noun, verb, adjective, and/or adverb.
- the origin, or etymology, of the word or words, such as from the Latin, Old French, Middle English, Hebrew, the name of a person. Some dictionaries use the symbol < to mean "came from." For example, the origin of the word *flank* is given as " < Old French *flanc* < Germanic." This tells us that *flank* came from the Old French word *flanc*. The French word in turn came from the German language. Some dictionaries use abbreviations to tell you where the item came from: *OE* for Old English, *L* for Latin, and so forth.

Here is an entry for the word *orgy*, marked to show you its components:

pronunciation   *part of speech*   *definitions*

or gy (ôr′ jē), *n.,* 1. drunken, wild activity; 2. time of complete overindulgence, such as a drinking orgy; 3. **orgies,** *pl.,* secret rites, especially those carried on as part of some religious celebrations during the worship of some Greek gods, such as the god of wine. During orgies much wild dancing and drinking take place. [< Greek *orgia,* secret rites]

sample sentence

etymology

Interpret the entry step-by-step in this way:

- Step 1: Pronounce the word in syllables using the diacritical marks as a guide. (In this case, there are two syllables; the ^ over the letter *o* tells us that the letter *r* that follows controls the sound of the vowel; the vowel in the second syllable is the long ē; the accent is on the first syllable.)

- Step 2: Note the part or parts of speech of the word and any related words. (Here we learn that *orgy* functions as a noun. Its plural is spelled *orgies,* just as we expect.)

- Step 3: Read the definitions. (Note here that there are three definitions and that one is for the plural form. Note, too, that some phrases [*a drinking orgy*] and a sentence demonstrate two contexts in which we use the word.)

- Step 4: Check the etymological reference to see if you can find remnants of the meaning of the originating word in the meaning of the entry. (In this case *orgy* comes from a Greek word meaning secret rites. This meaning is retained in the meaning of the English word *orgy.*)

- Step 5: Use the word in a sentence that has a clue in it as to the meaning of the word.

Collaborative Search and Discover

- With a partner, study the dictionary entries for these words: *ordeal, nobelium, impart, gulch, guitar, cashmere, tuxedo, moccasin, goober.* Decide what each component of the entry tells you; be ready to explain your discoveries.

- Flip through your dictionary and locate a word you think has an interesting etymology. Be ready to share your discovery—its meaning and origin. You may do this collaboratively.

- Internet Search: The Internet has many dictionaries. You can access some of these by going to a general dictionary clearinghouse site: http:/www.onelook. com. From this site, you can go to general dictionaries as well as more specific references in such areas as sports, technology, and science. If you have access to the Internet, explore the site.

Word Study Module 1-A—Words about Words

Read each boldfaced word using the diacritical marks to help you to pronounce the sounds and accent the syllables. Then read the definition of the featured word and the sample sentences. Construct a sentence in your head using each word following the pattern of the model sentence.

✦   1.   **de rive** (di rīv′), *v.,* **derived, deriving,** trace to a point of origin; get, obtain; figure out by reasoning.

      Related words: **de ri va tion,** *n.;* **de ri va tive,** *n.;* **deriv.,** *abbreviation for derivation.*

      Contexts: The word *derive* was derived from, or can be traced back to, the Latin word *derivare,* meaning "to lead off," which in turn was derived from the prefix *de-* and the root *rivus,* meaning "stream." In studying words, at times we consider their derivations, or origins. The word *derive* is a derivative of the Latin word *derivare.* A *derivative* is a word formed from another word.

✦   2.   **et y mol o gy** (et′ ə mol′ ə jē), *n., pl.* **etymologies,** the derivation of a word; explanation of the history of a word; study of language changes, especially study dealing with the evolution of individual words.

      Related words: **et y mo log i cal,** *adj.;* **et y mol o gist,** *n.*

      Contexts: My English professor is a lover of etymology; he always has a dictionary in hand and is checking on the etymological background of words. I guess he is an etymologist at heart.

✦   3.   **di a crit i cal mark** (dī′ ə krit′ ə kəl), a small mark such as ‾ or ′ that indicates pronunciation.

      Contexts: By looking at the diacritical marks placed on or by the letters of the word *etymology,* I was able to pronounce it correctly.

✦   4.   **root** (ro͞ot), *n.,* base part of a word, especially a word derived from Latin and Greek words. An example of a root based on a Latin word is *fort-* (meaning "firm or strong"); an example of a root based on a Greek word is *cardi-* (meaning "heart").

      Contexts: In studying a word, you will find it is helpful to look for a root with which you are familiar.

✦   5.   **af fix** (af′ iks), *n.,* prefix or suffix added to a word or a root; (ə fiks′), *v.,* attach.

      Contexts: Pre- is an affix—in this case a prefix—added to the word *fix; -ist* is an affix—in this case a suffix—added to the Latin root *lingua* to form the word *linguist. Lingua* in Latin means "language."

Before mailing a letter, you must affix a postage stamp if you want the United States postal service to deliver it.

✦ 6. **hy phen** (hī′ fən), *n.,* mark (-) used to divide parts of a word at the end of a line; mark placed at times between the two parts of some compound words as in the name of the one-time chairman of the Chinese Communist party Mao Tse-tung. Note the use of the hyphen in the compound adjective *one-time.*

Related words: **hy phen ate,** *v.;* **hy phen a tion,** *n.*

Contexts: When I got married, I decided not to hyphenate my name. Instead I decided to affix my husband's family name after my own.

✦ 7. **syl la ble** (sil′ lə bəl), *n.,* word or part of a word pronounced as a single unit and containing a vowel sound.

Related words: **syl lab i cate,** *v.;* **syl lab ic,** *adj.;* **mo no syl lab ic,** *adj.*

Contexts: The word *name* has one syllable, whereas the word *context* has two. Sometimes we talk about a multisyllabic word—one having many syllables.

✦ 8. **ac cent** (ak′ sent), *n.,* force, or emphasis, put on a syllable when pronouncing a word, usually indicated through the diacritical mark ′; characteristic way, or manner, of speaking often associated with speakers from particular areas of the country; *v.,* put force or emphasis on a syllable or trait.

Related words: **ac cen tu ate,** *v.;* **un ac cent ed,** *adj.*

Contexts: Multisyllabic words generally have two accents, a primary or strong accent shown as ′ and a secondary or weaker accent shown as ′.

He was a believer in accentuating the positive; as a result, he had many lifelong friends.

✦ 9. **schwa** (shwä), *n.,* vowel sound found in an unaccented syllable of a word, shown as ə.

Contexts: In the word *hyphen,* the vowel in the last syllable has the sound of the schwa. Because the schwa sound is so nondescript, many people make errors when they spell words containing that vowel sound.

✦ 10. **syn o nym** (sin′ ə nim), *n.,* word having the same or nearly the same meaning as another; expression accepted as another name for something.

Related words: **syn on y mous,** *adj.;* **syn on y mous ly,** *adv.*

Contexts: A synonym for the word *dissimilar* is *disparate.*

Mother Teresa's name became a synonym for goodness.

◆◆◆

Highlighted Word Element

syn- or **sym-,** a prefix from Greek meaning "together, united"; see Chapter 6 for more on this word element.

Words with the element: *symbol, symmetry, synchronize.*

◆◆◆

◆ 11. **ant o nym** (an′ tə nim), *n.,* word having the opposite or nearly the opposite meaning as another.

  Contexts: The word *evil* is an antonym for the word *good.*

◆ 12. **hom o phone** (hom′ ə fōn), *n.,* word having the same pronunciation as another word but differing in origin and meaning.

  Contexts: Write and *right* are homophones. *There* and *their* are also homophones. Some people find the spelling of homophones difficult to master. It is easy to confuse homophones.

◆ 13. **lin guist** (ling′ gwist), *n.,* person who is an expert about languages.

  Related words: **lin gual,** *adj.;* **lin guis tic,** *adj.;* **lin guis tics,** *n.;* **mul ti lin gual,** *adj.*

  Contexts: The woman was a talented linguist who had dedicated her life to the study of languages. Her linguistic skills were unmatched, for she had begun her study of linguistics when she was in her teens. By the age of twenty she was multilingual; she could speak English, Arabic, and Russian.

◆◆◆

Highlighted Word Element

lingua-, a root from Latin meaning "tongue."

Words with the element: *linguist, lingual, bilingual, multilingual.*

◆◆◆

Word Study Module Activities 1-A—Making Meaning with Words

1-A-1 Words in Meaningful Sentence Contexts: From the list, select the featured word that best fits into the overall meaning of each sentence. Write that word in the blank.

Use each option only once. (Clue: Use a Know-for-sure/Process-of-elimination test-taking strategy: Scan the sentences for items you "know for sure." Cross out options as you use them. In this way you leave difficult items until last and tackle them through the "process of elimination.")

a. accent   d. derivatives   g. hyphen   j. root
b. affix   e. diacritical marks   h. homophone   k. schwa
c. antonym   f. etymology   i. linguist   l. syllables
                                                        m. synonym

1. The printer had to use a/an _____ to break the word *multilingual* at the end of the line because it was too long to fit on one line and had to be carried over to the next.

2. A suffix is a/an _____ attached at the end of a word or root.

3. My composition teacher suggested that I find a/an _____ to substitute for the word *good* because I had used *good* too often in my essay.

4. There is a relationship between the study of _____ and the study of history, for both deal with tracing what has happened in the past and drawing conclusions about those events.

5. Some words have many _____ all of which trace their origins to the same Latin root.

6. The word *happy* is a/an _____ of *sad*.

7. I have trouble spelling the unaccented vowel sound, or the _____, in the middle syllable of the word *separate*.

8. In the English department of our university, we have a/an _____ who is a specialist in the study of languages.

9. When I am uncertain how to pronounce a word, I study the _____ given with the word in the dictionary entry.

10. I sometimes find it difficult to decide how to break words into _____. This becomes a problem for me when I must hyphenate a word at the end of a line of type.

11. When I do not know what syllable to _____ in pronouncing a word, I run a dictionary check.

12. The words *brake* and *break* are _____.

13. *Mal(e)-* in the word *malignant* is a Latin _____.

1-A-2 Synonym Study: Star the word or words that mean the same or almost the same as the given word or word element. (Clue: Again, use the process of elimination to solve each problem. Cross out the options you are certain are not correct. That narrows the field from which you must choose.)

1. **homophone**   a. word of opposite meaning

   b. word of similar meaning

   c. word with the same pronunciation as another but of different origin and meaning

   d. word that comes from another

2. **affix**   a. a prefix or suffix

   b. an accented syllable

   c. a word of unknown origins

   d. the main part of a word

3. **linguist**   a. ability to speak many languages

   b. person skilled in languages

   c. person able to use language to tell a lie with ease

   d. person who has lived in many countries.

4. **hyphen**   a. an accent mark

   b. the sound of the vowel in an unaccented syllable

   c. a diacritical mark used to separate two parts of a compound-type word

   d. a zero

5. **schwa**   a. an accent mark

   b. the sound of the vowel in an unaccented syllable

   c. a diacritical mark used to separate two parts of a compound-type word

   d. a zero

6. **synonym**   a. word of opposite meaning

   b. word of similar meaning

   c. word with the same pronunciation as another but of different origin and meaning

   d. word that comes from another

7. **antonym**   a. word of opposite meaning

   b. word of similar meaning

   c. word with the same pronunciation as another but of different origin and meaning

   d. word that comes from another

8. **syllable**   a. part of a word pronounced as a single unit
                    b. word with many units of pronunication
                    c. derivative
                    d. affix

9. **derivative**   a. word of opposite meaning
                    b. word of similar meaning
                    c. word with the same pronunciation as another but of different origin and meaning
                    d. word that comes from another

10. **example of a diacritical mark**
                    a. letter of the alphabet, such as *A*
                    b. û
                    c. numeral
                    d. abbreviation *v.* (standing for verb) given as part of a dictionary entry

11. **accent mark**   a. diacritical mark showing emphasis in a word
                      b. schwa
                      c. part of the etymology of a word
                      d. part of the derivation of a word

12. **etymology**   a. origin   b. stress   c. part of speech   d. linguist

13. **root**   a. prefix   b. suffix   c. base   d. etymology

14. **syn-**   a. self   b. tongue   c. together   d. opposite

15. **lingua-**   a. self   b. tongue   c. together   d. opposite

1-A-3 Examples: Next to the word, phrase, or sentence, write a term such as *diacritical mark* or *affix* that best characterizes the aspect of word study highlighted in that example. In some instances, more than one term may apply. The same term may apply more than once. Use the words listed in 1-A-2 as the options from which to choose.

1. The word *frankfurter* comes from the German word *frankfurter,* which in turn comes from the city of Frankfurt. _____

2. high/low ___ant._____

3. hit-and-run ___hy_____

4. ə _____

5. sale/sail _____

6. lin' guist ___accent_____

7. frank/open ___Syn._____

8. raise/lift _____

9. *pre-* as in the word *preview* _____

10. *-ment* as at the end of the word *government* _____

11. evil/good _____

12. peak/peek _____

13. lingua- _____

1-A-4 Dictionary Search and Discover: Use a dictionary to discover the answers.

1. What is the derivation of the word *salad?*   *Lat Greek It?*

2. On what syllable do we place the primary accent in the word *salivation?*

   _____

   What is the vowel sound in that strongly accented syllable? _____

   On what syllable do we place the secondary accent in the word *salivation?*

   _____

   What is the vowel sound in that syllable? _____

   Where is there a schwa in the word *salivation?* _____

   What do you do when you salivate? _____

3. List two meanings that your dictionary gives for the word *sad.*

   Meaning 1:

   Meaning 2:

4. Use your dictionary to discover how to divide these words into syllables: *cosmopoli-tan, foreshadow, hypocritical, indistinguishable, mystify.* Based on the definitions

you find in your dictionary, devise a sentence using each as the part of speech given. Write your answers here:

Word Written in Syllables   Sentence with the Word

a.

b.

c.

d.

e.

5. Use your dictionary to check the meaning of each of these words; then record their definitions and decide whether the words are synonyms or antonyms.

   a. extinct

   b. extant

   c. Are the words synonyms or antonyms? Give a reason for your answer.

Word Study Module 1-B—
Old English Words, as Well as Some Others

The English language came into Britain in the fifth century A.D. when the Angles and the Saxons invaded Britain. Here are some words that linguists trace back to that time. Pronounce each featured word and use it in a sentence. Write your sentence in your word study notebook.

Words Derived from Old English

1. **a kin** (ə kin′), *adj.,* of the same kind, of the same family.

    Related words and phrases: **kin,** *n.;* **kin dred,** *adj.;* **next of kin; kin folk.**

    Contexts: She felt more akin to her best friend than to her sister because she and her friend shared many of the same interests.

    English is more akin to the Germanic languages than to the Romance languages.

    Because I have kith and kin (friends and relatives), my life is one of joy. My next of kin is my son. We are kindred souls, alike in so many ways; we both enjoy travel and books, and we love to discuss issues of the day. I look forward to the holidays because then I see my kinfolk.

2. **oath** (ōth), *n., pl.* **oaths,** solemn promise.

    Related words or phrases: **take an oath,** meaning "to promise"; **under oath,** meaning "sworn to tell the complete truth."

    Contexts: The president of the United States takes an oath of office when he or she is sworn in on January 20.

    As a witness in the case, I had to swear under oath to tell the truth.

3. **lore** (lôr), *n.,* traditional knowledge, facts, stories, beliefs; learning or knowledge.

    Related word: **folklore.**

    Contexts: Marinda knows the lore of her native American culture.

    Our common folklore includes home remedies that sometimes are effective.

4. **swarm** (swôrm), *n., pl.* **swarms,** great number; group of bees led by a queen bee that flies together to form a new hive; *v.,* **swarmed, swarming,** fly off together; move about in great numbers.

    Contexts: Swarms of people watched the display.

    The bees swarmed around the cavity in the tree searching for a place to form a new hive.

5. **strut** (strut), *v.,* **strutted, strutting,** walk in a self-important way; *n.,* a way of walking that communicates, "I have a big ego."

    Related noun: **strut,** supporting beam or brace.

    Contexts: The emperor strutted around as if to say, "I own this world."

6. **deem** (dēm), *v.,* **deemed, deeming,** believe, consider, think.

    Contexts: The professor deemed it important that students turn in their papers in a timely fashion.

Words Derived from Other Languages

7. **e go cen tric** (ē′ gō sen′ trik), *adj.,* self-centered, egotistic.

> *Related words:* **e go,** *n.;* **e go tist,** *n.;* **e go tis tic,** *adj.;* **e go tis ti cal,** *adj.;* **cen tral,** *adj.;* **Eur o cen tric,** *adj.;* **Af ro cen tric,** *adj.*

> *Contexts:* The king was the most egocentric person I had ever met; he believed the world revolved around him. His ego was bigger than life itself. He was the ultimate egotist.
> A Eurocentric theory centers on Europe; an Afrocentric theory centers on Africa.

✦✦✦

Highlighted Word Element

ego-, a word element from Latin meaning "self."

Words with the element: *ego, ego-trip, egomania.*

✦✦✦

8. **mi grate** (mī′ grāt), *v.,* **migrated, migrating,** move away from an area to settle somewhere else.

> *Related words:* **mi grant,** *adj.* and *n.;* **mi gra tory,** *adj.;* **im mi grant,** *n.;* **im mi grate,** *v.*

> *Contexts:* What makes a person want to migrate? A desire for a better life is a major factor accounting for people's migratory behavior. Massive immigration to America from Europe occurred during the eighteenth and nineteenth centuries. As a result, during that period, America was home to many immigrants.

9. **de cade** (dek′ ād), *n.,* a period of ten years.

> *Contexts:* The 1990s are considered to have been a decade of general prosperity in the United States.

10. **con tend** (kən tend′), *v.,* **contended, contending,** say to be true; assert as the truth.

> *Related words:* **con ten tion,** *n.;* **con ten tious,** *adj.*

> *Contexts:* My friend contended that the best professor is one who entertains. I had to disagree with her contention for I believe that the best professor is one who has organized the material in an interesting and logical way and presents it clearly. I did not mean to be contentious or argumentative, but my friend thought I was when I criticized her position.

11. **orb** (ôrb), *n.,* anything round or ball-like, sphere, globe.

> *Related words:* **or bit,** *n.* and *v.;* **or bi tal,** *adj.*

> *Contexts:* The sun, the planets, and the moons of our solar system are orbs. The planets travel in orbital paths around the sun.

12. **om i nous** (om′ ə nəs), *adj.,* threatening, very unfavorable.

> *Related words:* **o men,** *n.;* **om i nous ly,** *adv.;* **om i nous ness,** *n.*

> *Contexts:* To some people, a black cat walking in front of them is an omen of bad times ahead.
> Dark clouds hung ominously low in the sky, threatening a storm later that day.
> The disagreement was an ominous sign that relationships in her family were disintegrating.

13. **dec or ous** (dek′ ər əs, di kôr′ əs), *adj.,* acting with good taste and with dignity.

> *Related words:* **dec or um,** *n.;* **dec or ous ly,** *adv.*

> *Contexts:* We expect the participants to act decorously. Lack of decorum will not be tolerated. So be forewarned! Be decorous.

14. **con du cive** (kən dū′ siv), *adj.,* favorable, helpful.

> *Related word:* **con duct,** *v.* or *n.*

> *Contexts:* Loud noise is not conducive to productive study; what is conducive is a quiet place where one can concentrate.
> His conduct left much to be desired. "Try to conduct yourself with a modicum of decorum," his teacher told him.

15. **o nus** (o′ nəs), *n.,* something that is a burden, especially that which is a great responsibility; blame.

> *Contexts:* Just remember! If this fails, the onus will be on you, for you contended that we must operate in this manner.

♦♦

Power Word

on er ous, (on′ ər əs), an adjective meaning "troublesome, burdensome, hard to take." The word can be traced to the Latin word onus meaning "burden," and came into Middle English via the Old French word *oneros.*

Contexts: My friend found that repeating her college algebra course was particularly onerous because she felt that she had persevered the first time around.

♦♦

Word-Study Activities Module 1-B—
Making Meaning with Words

1-B-1 Words in Meaningful Sentence Contexts: From the list given, select the word that best fits the overall meaning of each sentence. Write that word in the blank. Use each option only once. Apply your Know-for sure/Process-of-elimination test-taking strategy.

a. akin	d. decade	g. egocentric	j. oath	m. onus
b. conducive	e. decorous	h. lore	k. ominous	n. orb
c. contend	f. deem	i. migrate	l. onerous	o. strut
				p. swarm

1. The supervisor admonished, "I must admit that the situation was an extreme one, but we still expect _____ behavior from our employees."

2. It is very hard to be friends with someone who is very _____ because such a person wants everything his or her way.

3. The senator took a/an _____ that she would uphold the Constitution.

4. The poet wrote, "The golden _____ in the sky filled me with internal warmth."

5. I _____ that everyone who attends must perform with at least a modicum of respect for others.

6. His love of books is _____ to my love of music.

7. Eating a diet low in fats is _____ to good health.

8. This was a/an _____ of great turmoil. As a result, that ten-year period seemed to creep by.

9. I _____ it inappropriate for anyone to attend who has not handed in his or her assignment.

10. At the end of the decade, many people decided to _____ ; times were harsh, and the people wanted to get a fresh start in a new place.

11. Participants in the cakewalk dance must _____ across the floor with a sense of pride in who they are.

12. The chief administrator took the _____ upon himself. He felt responsible for the error, and so he stayed many nights to correct it.

13. His failure to attend seemed _____, for it showed that he had little interest in this important pursuit.

14. A _____ of locusts flew overhead. There were so many that the sun was blocked out for just a moment.

15. The task the house husband found the most _____ was cleaning the oven.

16. I believe that children should become familiar with the _____ that is part of their cultural heritage.

1-B-2 Synonym Study: Star the word or phrase that means the same or almost the same as the given word. Use the process of elimination to help you.

1. **swarm**   a. blame   b. sworn statement   c. ball   d. great number

2. **orb**   a. blame   b. sworn statement   c. ball   d. great number

3. **onus**   a. blame   b. sworn statement   c. ball   d. great number

4. **oath**   a. blame   b. sworn statement   c. ball   d. great number

5. **migrate**
   a. walk in a self-important way
   b. go to and settle somewhere else
   c. assert as the truth
   d. consider, or believe

6. **contend**
   a. walk in a self-important way
   b. go to and settle somewhere else
   c. assert as the truth
   d. consider, or believe

7. **deem**
   a. walk in a self-important way
   b. go to and settle somewhere else
   c. assert as the truth
   d. consider, or believe

8. **strut**
   a. walk in a self-important way
   b. go to and settle somewhere else
   c. assert as the truth
   d. consider, or believe

9. **ominous**   a. helpful   b. in good taste, tasteful
             c. threatening   d. self-centered

10. **decorous**   a. helpful   b. in good taste, tasteful
             c. threatening   d. self-centered

11. **conducive**   a. helpful   b. in good taste, tasteful
             c. threatening   d. self-centered

12. **egocentric**   a. helpful   b. in good taste, tasteful

c. threatening   d. self-centered

13. **decade**   a. a period of one year

b. a period of ten years

c. a period of twenty years

d. a period of one hundred years

14. **lore**   a. trap   b. yoke   c. stories   d. pull

15. **akin**   a. related   b. unrelated   c. positive   d. negative

16. **onerous**   a. alone   b. hard to take

c. related to one's possessions

d. related to activity done rapidly

17. **ego-**   word element meaning   a. self   b. alone   c. earth   d. edge

1-B-3 Truth or Falsity: Write True or False on the line after each statement to indicate the correctness or lack of correctness of the statement. (Test-taking strategy: Ask yourself, "What evidence do I have that lets me know this is not true?" If you have any evidence that contradicts the statement, it must be false.)

1. Most adults would want to invite to their homes a person lacking in decorum.

_____

2. An egocentric person is more likely to strut about as compared to someone who is shy. _____

3. A decade is shorter than a century. _____

4. Research shows that smoking is conducive to good health._____

5. When you see a swarm of butterflies in the sky, you are seeing lots of butterflies.

_____

6. People who migrate to another area are more than likely to be those who are very, very content with what they already have._____

7. Migrant workers tend to work in one location for long periods of time.

_____

8. To have the onus put on you generally makes you very uncomfortable.

_____

9. To have someone contend that you are the best qualified for a particularly great job is more likely to make you happy than sad. _____

10. Most men and women tell the truth when they are under oath. _____

11. Some people of days gone by considered an eclipse to be a bad omen.

   _____

12. Contentious individuals are easy to get along with. _____

13. Egocentric people are typically ones whom you would choose as your best friends.

   _____

14. We deem those with loving kith and kin as fortunate human beings.

   _____

15. Storytellers generally are familiar with the folklore of their culture.

   _____

Reading with Meaning Module 1-C— Learning about the Beginnings of the English Language

Read the following account of how the English language developed. Ask yourself, "How did the English language come to Britain?"

The Anglo-Saxons Bring Their Language to Britain: An Historical Account

"Wow, what an ordeal that was!" we remark as we exit an algebra exam. Yet, what we call an ordeal today is far from what the early Anglo-Saxon residents of England would have described as one. For them, an ordeal was a test to determine the truth within a situation. Their word *ordal* from which our word *ordeal* is derived meant "judgment." In Anglo-Saxon days, the guilt or innocence of a person suspected of a crime was determined by having him or her attempt a dangerous deed, such as walking through glowing embers or carrying a red hot poker. If the person survived the ordeal, he or she was deemed innocent; if he or she did not survive, he or she was guilty.

   The word *ordal/ordeal* came into the English language in the later decades of the fifth century A.D., when Germanic peoples migrated from Europe and swarmed into what is today the southern part of England. (See Figure 1.1 for a language tree that shows the relationship between English and the Germanic languages.) These immigrant hordes—the Angles and the Saxons—were really invading conquerors: They took over the land from

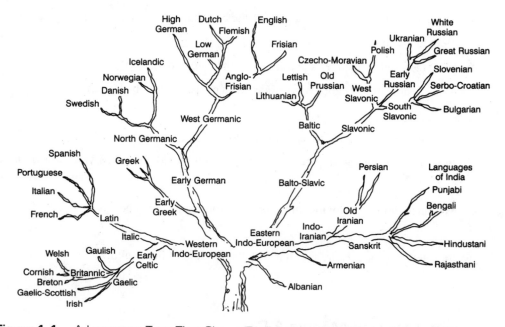

Figure 1.1   A Language Tree That Shows English As a Twig Off the Germanic Branch of the Indo-European Language. (*Source:* Dorothy Grant Hennings, *Communication in Action: Teaching Literature-based Language Arts,* 7th ed., © 2000. Reprinted by permission of Houghton Mifflin Publishers, Boston, MA.)

the Celtic peoples who lived there and made their own language the language of the land. Today the English language retains only a few words that can be traced back to the language of the people who lived in England before the mass migration of the Germanic tribes. We do, on the other hand, have many words like *ordeal* that are derived from the Angles and the Saxons—words that we use to describe everyday actions and things such as *stool, stone, stork, strut, stride, stun,* and *storm,* and words that start with the *th* sound such as *thank, thaw, that, then, there.* Because modern-day English had its beginnings in the language of the invading Anglo-Saxon tribes, linguists contend that English is more akin to German than it is to other European languages such as Italian, Spanish, or French.

Word Study Activities Module 1-C— The Dictionary and Word Origins

1-C-1 Dictionary Search and Talking Points: Check the dictionary entry of these words for their derivation: *the, deep, man, wife, woman, theory, conclusion.* What are the characteristics of words that are derived from Old English words? How do these characteristics contrast with the characteristics of words that come from the classical languages—Greek and Latin? Write your responses in your word study notebook.

1-C-2 Writing Points: Use the word *ordeal* in a sentence that shows its meaning. Then write a paragraph in which you describe a real-life ordeal you have had. Record your sentence and paragraph in your word study notebook.

Confusing Words—*Who's* and *Whose*

English has a feature that can cause confusion: Some words in the language are pronounced exactly or almost the same although they are spelled differently from one another and differ in meaning. These words are called *homophones—homo-* meaning "same" and *phone-* meaning "sound." An example of a homophone set is *who's* and *whose*. To deal with homophones successfully, you must focus attentively on the spelling of the members of a set for the spelling is the clue to the meaning.

Think about these two sentences and the meaning of *who's* and *whose* in them:

- "Who's coming with me?" my friend asked.
- Whose book is this?

In the first example *who's* is a contraction that takes the place of the two words *who is*. Contractions are relatively informal forms of expression, generally restricted to oral communication; however, you may see them from time to time in letters, memos, and the like. Other contractions include *don't* for *do not, can't* for *cannot*, and *wouldn't* for *would not*. In each case, the apostrophe takes the place of letters that we omit in the contractional form. You can check that the word is a contraction by substituting the original two-word phrase. For example, you can say, "Who is coming with me?" rather than, "Who's coming with me?"

In contrast, in the second example given above (Whose book is this?), *whose* is a possessive pronoun. You can figure that out by flipping the expression: the book of whom. Although a possessive noun carries an apostrophe, possessive pronouns do not. That is where the confusion comes in.

Fill in the blanks of the following sentences with either *who's* or *whose*.

1. "___Whose___ father is coming to the station to meet us?" she asked.

2. "___Who's___ taking us home?" she continued.

At the end of each chapter of this book are boxed segments dealing with homophones and other confusing word sets. These boxes are designed to help you comprehend the differences between words that sometimes can trip you up.

◆◆

Highlighted Word Element

homo-, a word element from Latin meaning "like" or "same."

Words with the element: *homograph, homogeneous, homosexual.*

phone-, a word element from Latin meaning "sound."

Words with the element: *telephone, megaphone, phonograph.*

◆◆

Collaborative Search and Discover

• Check your dictionary for the meanings of *homograph, homogeneous,* and *homosexual.* In what way is the meaning of each of these words similar?

• In your dictionary find one or more other words that include *homo-.* Be ready to share your word finds and their meanings.

• Check your dictionary for the meaning of *megaphone* and *telephone.* What meaning is shared by both words?

2

Word Study Notebooks and Cards— Words from Greek

◆◆◆

Objectives: In Chapter 2, you will develop the ability to

- explain the influence of the Greek language and Greek myths on modern English, using the myth about the Titans and the word *hubris* as examples;

- maintain a word study notebook;

- comprehend the following words that have Greek origins and that are featured in Module 2-A:

acme	dogma	epoch	stratagem
antithesis	enigma	phobia	stoic
chaos	epitome	stigma	theoretical

- recognize and interpret the element *phobia-* (abnormal fear of) when it appears in other words;

- use word study cards to improve your vocabulary;

- recognize some commonly found adjective endings and comprehend and use the following adjectives featured in Module 2-B:

ambiguous	frugal	incongruous	prudent
cosmopolitan	grandiose	ludicrous	transparent
ephemeral	incessant	meticulous	universal

cataclysmic (*power word*)

- recognize and interpret the element *cosm-* (universe, order) when it appears in words;

- explain how such words as *chaos, cosmos, cosmetics,* and *hubris* came into the English language; and

- distinguish between the homophones *it's* and *its* and among *their, there,* and *they're.*

> Every living language, like the perspiring bodies of living creatures, is in perpetual motion . . . ; some words go off, and become obsolete; others are taken in, and by degrees grow into common use; or the same word is inverted to a new sense and notion.
>
> —Richard Bentley, *Dissertation upon the Epistles of Phalaris*

◆◆

An Interesting Word to Think about— *Titanic* and the Greek Myths

The ancient Greeks took their myths seriously. Through myths, the early Greeks explained happenings in nature that they did not understand because of their limited ability to investigate natural events (such as lightning, the seasons, and death). The Greeks relied on myths filled with supernatural incidents involving gods, goddesses, and demons to explain their world.

In Greek mythology, Gaia (the earth goddess) and Ouranos (the god of the sky) were the first goddess and god to emerge from the original, confused material, or chaos, that made up the world. In the Greek language today, *chaos* still means "open gulf." Today in English, we use the word *chaos* when we talk about a situation of utter, complete, and hopeless disorder.

The ancient Greeks believed that Gaia (pronounced Jee′ uh in English) and Ouranos (spelled Uranus in English and pronounced U rā′ nəs) were wife and husband who gave birth to huge, powerful beings, or Gigantes. Based on that myth, in English today, we use the word *gigantic* to mean huge. The most important and tremendous of the giants were the Titans and Titanesses. That is why in English we use *titan* as a synonym for *giant* and as a way to talk about a person or thing of enormous size or power.

Because of the film *Titanic,* most of us know the true story of the ill-fated ship by that name. Filled with **hubris,** or unshakable, almost insolent, pride, those who built and owned the Titanic did not take adequate safety precautions. They failed to put enough lifeboats aboard the Titanic for all 2206 passengers and crew that the ship carried, and the captain went full steam ahead through a dark, iceberg-filled sea. The outcome was chaotic, with 1600 people lost in a disaster that was one of the most deadly and gigantic of history.

Most of us, however, do not know about the element titanium. Titanium is an element of super strength, although it and its alloys are relatively light. Its name is most appropriate, don't you think? We may not know, too, about Titan, the largest of the ten moons of Saturn, and about Titania, the largest of the five known moons of Uranus.

Words such as *titanic* and *titan* as well as names such as *Uranus, titanium, Titan,* and *Titania* demonstrate the influence that the ancient Greek "mythos" continue to have on the English language. Based on the myths surrounding Gaia, Ouranos, and the Titans and Titanesses, here is a summary list of words or word parts we use today:

Uranus: a planet in the solar system far out in the sky;

Gaia: the word-building part written *geo-*, meaning "earth," from which we get *geography, geology, geode;*

titan: a giant of power and/or strength, especially used in reference to powerful people of industry such as John D. Rockefeller and Bill Gates;

titanic: an adjective used to describe anything large and/or powerful;

chaos: a noun meaning complete disorder and confusion; also **chaotic,** a related adjective.

Notice, too, in the above discussion, the use of the word *hubris*—boastful pride that the Greeks believed led to ultimate destruction. You might want to consider why the word *hubris* is a rather appropriate one to use in reference to the builders and owners of the great ship *Titanic*.

Collaborative Search and Discover

- Look up the following words or phrases in a dictionary to discover the Greek myth from which each is derived and its meaning when used today: *Procrustean bed, Herculean strength, Achilles' heel, Adonis, Amazon, Cassandra.*
- Internet Search: If you have Internet access, go to www.randomhouse.com/jesse and log onto "Jesse's Word of the Day." This is a fun site where someone poses a question about a word each day, and in conversational tone, Jesse explains its meanings and etymology. At the site is also an alphabetical, linked list of words from previous days.

Word Study Module 2-A—Words from the Greek

After pronouncing each featured word, use it in a sentence following the model in the sample sentence. *All 12*

- 1. **ac me** (ak′ mē), *n.,* highest or greatest point; culmination. The best

    Contexts: At the acme of his career, he resigned from his high-powered job to spend more time with his family.

- 2. **an tith e sis** (an tith′ ə sis), *n., pl.* **antitheses,** total opposite.

    Related word: **an ti thet i cal,** *adj.*

Strategy Box 2-A—Word Study Notebook

Your knowledge of words and your ability to understand words as you read them determine how fully you comprehend college reading assignments. One strategy to build your vocabulary for success in college is keeping a word study notebook. For example, suppose you encounter an unfamiliar word such as *hubris* as you read. Because the word is defined in the sentence where you read it, you know *hubris* means "excessive, even arrogant, pride." However, you recognize that this is a new word that will be useful in reading and writing. In your word study notebook, you record *hubris* with its definition and perhaps the sentence from the text where you met the word. Periodically you flip through your notebook, review the words you have recently recorded, and think of instances in your life where you could have used some of the words. Doing this, you bring your newly "owned" words to the forefront of your mind; as a result you are more likely to use them in talking, writing, and thinking.

To this end, label several pages of the notebook you are keeping for your reading course or activities "Word Study Notebook." Record the word *hubris,* its definition, and a sample sentence. Also record the power word from Chapter 1— *onerous.* During the next week, review those words from time to time. Add at least two other words from your reading.

Contexts: The end result was the complete antithesis of what I had expected; what sadness I felt!

✦ 3. **cha os** (kā′ os), *n.,* complete and utter confusion.

Related word: **cha o tic,** *adj.*

Contexts: Europe was in chaos as World War II came to a close; cities and factories lay in ruins, food was almost impossible to secure, and the young men were gone. In those chaotic times, everyone who was left had to pitch in and clean up.

✦ 4. **dog ma** (dôg′ mə), *n.,* doctrine; belief taught, especially as part of formal religion.

Related words: **dog ma tic,** *adj.;* **dog ma tism,** *n.;* **dog ma tist,** *n.*

Contexts: I could not accept the dogma of that particular religious sect; my beliefs are far different.
Her dogmatic attitude completely turned me off.

✦ 5. **e nig ma** (i nig′ mə), *n.,* puzzle, riddle.

Related word: **e nig ma tic,** *adj.*

Contexts: Until I reached the final chapter, the character's motivation was an enigma to me; only at the end did I realize what the meaning of the novel was.

My friend has an enigmatic personality. I find it difficult to figure out "where she is coming from."

6. **e pit o me** (i pit′ ə mē), *n.,* someone or something that is typical or representative of something.

    Related words: **e pit o mize, e pit o mized,** *v.*

    Contexts: The professor was the epitome of scholarliness; brilliant, she researched her topics thoroughly and presented with clarity. In every way, she epitomized the best in academia.

7. **ep och** (ep′ ək), *n.,* period of time, age.

    Contexts: The development of the computer opened a new epoch in which technology reigned supreme.

8. **pho bi a** (fō′ bi ə), *n.,* obsessive, morbid fear, often beyond that which is reasonable. abnoramal free

    Related words: **claus tro pho bi a,** *n.,* fear of enclosed places; **An glo pho bi a,** *n.,* intense fear of anything English; **hy dro pho bi a,** *n.,* morbid fear of water.

    Contexts: Her fear had advanced beyond anything normal; it had become a full-blown phobia. Because she suffered from claustrophobia, she refused to get into an elevator or an airplane.

◆◆◆

Highlighted Word Element

-phobia, a combining form from the Greek meaning "abnormal fear of."

Words with the element: *claustrophobia, hydrophobia.*

◆◆◆

9. **stig ma** (stig′ mə), *n.,* stain on one's reputation; a mark of disgrace or dishonor.

    Contexts: He could never erase the stigma attached to his name despite all that he did thereafter.

10. **sto ic** (stō′ ik), *n.,* one who controls his/her feelings and is indifferent to pleasure or pain.

    Related word: **sto i cal,** *adj.*

    Contexts: Because of his stoical approach to living, he was able to get on with his life despite the continuous pain that he suffered. Only a true stoic could keep going given everything that had occurred.

11. **strat e gem** (strat′ ə jəm), *n.*, scheme—often complex—for deceiving an enemy, especially a political opponent.

> *Related words:* **stra te gic**, *adj.;* **strat e gy**, *n.*

> *Contexts:* The senator's clever stratagem worked because his opponents failed to analyze his ambiguous words and his crafty actions.
> Most of us need to develop a strategy for saving money for our future. That country is in a strategic location in central Europe.

12. **the o ret i cal** (thē′ ə ret′ ə kəl), *adj.,* dealing with theory or that which is hypothesized rather than factual—based on theory, not on fact.

> *Related words:* **the o rize**, *v.;* **the o ret i cal ly**, *adv.;* **the o rist**, *n.;* **the o ry**, *n.*

> *Contexts:* I did not understand his theoretical position. Of course, he could understand the theory behind his work for he was a noted theorist.
> Theorizing was his greatest delight in life.

Word Study Activities Module 2-A—
Making Meaning with Words from the Greek Language

2-A-1 Words in Meaningful Sentence Contexts: From the list, select the featured word that best fits into the overall meaning of each sentence. Write that word in the blank. Use each option only once. Apply your Know-for-sure/Process-of-elimination test-taking strategy. Cross out options as you use them.

a. acme	d. dogma	g. epoch	j. stratagem
b. antithesis	e. enigma	h. phobia	k. stoic
c. chaos	f. epitome	i. stigma	l. theoretical

1. During that _____, scientific progress was limited by dogma that supported a geocentric view of the universe.

2. My friend is a/an _____ who believes in a philosophy of grin and bear it.

3. Even to this day it remains a/an _____ as to what happened to the original settlers in that region of Virginia.

4. The heretic contended that church _____ did not allow for any freedom of thought.

5. _____ ruled in the South after the Civil War since so much of the infrastructure had been destroyed.

6. The general was uncertain as to what _____ was necessary to win the battle; in the end, his indecisiveness led to a chaotic defeat.

7. The scientist had extensive _____ understanding, but he lacked practical means to test the equations with which he was working.

8. The first lady was the _____ of charm and graciousness.

9. Gershwin reached the _____ of his career at a very young age; unfortunately, he died very young, so his career was cut short.

10. The outcome of the revolution was the _____ of the freedom for which the people had fought; the people ended up being ruled by a dictator who had little concern for their rights.

11. I see no _____ in failing if a person has worked hard and given his or her best. Where I see one is in failing to try in the first place.

12. My friend's fear of falling was beyond reason; it was a true _____.

2-A-2 Synonym Study: Match the words in the left-hand column with their synonyms at the right. Write the correct option on the line before each word in the right-hand column. Apply your Know-for-sure/Process-of-elimination test-taking strategy. Cross out options as you use them.

1. **acme**	_____	a. puzzle
2. **antithesis**	_____	b. plan
3. **chaos**	_____	c. not factual
4. **dogma**	_____	d. time period
5. **enigma**	_____	e. indifferent to pain
6. **epitome**	_____	f. unreasonable fear
7. **epoch**	_____	g. disgrace
8. **phobia**	_____	h. complete opposite
9. **stigma**	_____	i. set of beliefs
10. **stratagem**	_____	j. representative of
11. **stoic**	_____	k. complete confusion
12. **theoretical**	_____	l. top

2-A-3 Collaborative Search and Discover: Find the answers to these questions by checking a dictionary and a thesaurus—a book that lists related words, especially synonyms.

• *Roget's International Thesaurus* lists sixty-nine kinds of phobias. Look up the word *phobia* in the back section of the thesaurus; this will tell you where in the book to look for the list of phobias. Select two or three from those listed, record them here, and check their meanings and etymologies in your dictionary.

The Phobia	*The Meaning*	*The Etymology*
1.		
2.		
3.		

- The word *criterion* comes from the Greek. Look up its meaning in your dictionary. Record the meaning here, along with its plural form. Try to write a sentence using the word.

- The word *mania* is derived from the Greek. Look up its meaning in your dictionary. Write a sentence here that contains the word in a way that shows its meaning.

2-A-4 Crossword Puzzle: Use your knowledge of the Greek words you have been studying to solve the puzzle in Figure 2.1.

Strategy Box 2-B—Word Study Cards

A strategy for keeping recently encountered words at the forefront of your mind is making word study cards and keeping them handy to study from time to time. Simply record words you want to learn on index cards. Then keep your words-to-own in a place where you can access them, such as in your briefcase or backpack. Periodically glance at and think about one of the words and invent a sentence with it. In this way you will begin to make the words your own. Begin by making a study card on which you print the words *hubris* and *onerous*. Refer to your card several times during the day.

Word Study Module 2-B—
Words We Use to Describe People, Places, and Things

We use adjectives to describe people, places, and things. For example, we can say that the teacher asked an ambiguous question or that her ideas were grandiose. In these contexts, *ambiguous* and *grandiose* are adjectives that describe things. Notice also the relative position of the two adjectives. *Ambiguous* comes before the word *question,* which is a noun.

Figure 2.1 Crossword Puzzle of Greek Words

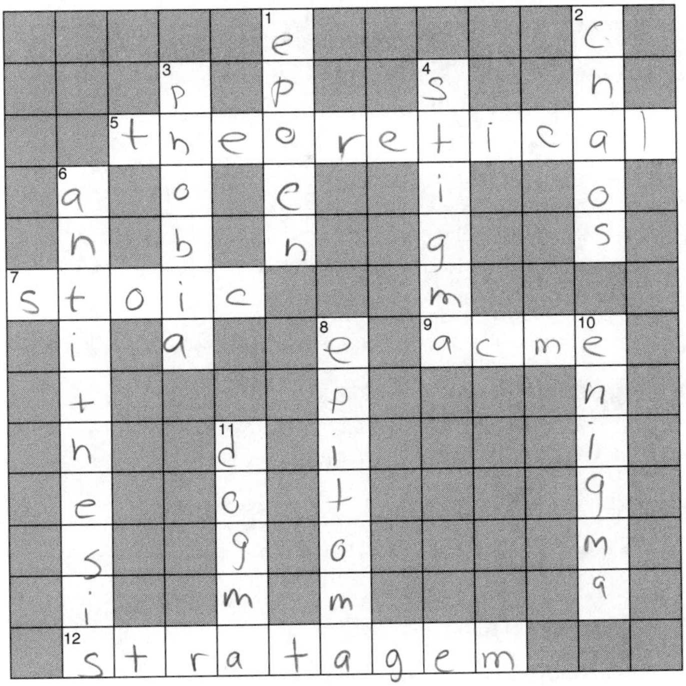

ACROSS
5 Unproven
7 Indifferent to pain
9 Top
12 Plan

DOWN
1 Time period
2 Complete confusion
3 Irrational fear
4 Disgrace

6 Opposite
8 Representative of
10 Puzzle
11 Doctrine

Grandiose comes after a verb of "being." (For example, *is, are, was, were* are verbs of "being.") It modifies the noun *ideas* and tells us what kind of ideas.

- The teacher asked a/an _____ question. (Note that any adjective that fits in the blank describes the word *question,* which is a noun.)
- Her ideas were _____. (Note that any adjective that fits in the blank describes the noun *ideas.*)

As these sentences demonstrate, we use adjectives in reference to nouns. Here are some words that can function as adjectives. Pronounce each featured word, and in your notebook write a sentence using it as an adjective.

1. **am big u ous** (am big′ yŏŏ əs), *adj.,* liable to be interpreted in more than one way; uncertain, or unclear in meaning.

   Related word: **am bi gu i ty,** *n.*

All 12 + power word

Contexts: I am afraid I do not do well in ambiguous situations, for I am a person who likes things to be clear-cut. To be absolutely truthful, ambiguity in any form frightens me.

✦ 2. **cos mo pol i tan** (koz′ mə pol′ i tn), *adj.,* at home at any place in the world; not local; common to the entire world. Also used as a noun to mean one who feels comfortable anywhere in the world.

> *Related word:* **cos mos,** *n.;* **cos mo naut,** *n.*

> *Contexts:* The senator's cosmopolitan outlook helped him to become an expert highly respected for his knowledge of foreign affairs.
> A cosmonaut is a Russian astronaut, one who goes into space.

◆◆

Highlighted Word Element

cosm-, a Greek root, or base, meaning "universe, order."

Words with the element: *cosmos, cosmic, cosmonaut.*

◆◆

✦ 3. **e phem er al** (i fem′ ər əl), *adj.,* lasting but a short time, lasting only a day, transitory.

> *Related word:* **e phem er al ly,** *adv.*

> *Contexts:* The man's influence was ephemeral; he appeared in the news one day, but he was gone the next.

✦ 4. **fru gal** (frōō′ gəl), *adj.,* careful in the use of money, thrifty.

> *Related words:* **fru gal i ty,** *n.;* **fru gal ness,** *n.;* **fru gal ly,** *adv.*

> *Contexts:* The young couple lived frugally because they were saving their funds for a new house. Their frugality was rewarded for by the time they were thirty-five, they had paid off their mortgage. The moral of the story is that frugal living has its rewards.

✦ 5. **gran di ose** (gran′ dē ōs′), *adj.,* grand, marked by great scope and grandness, sometimes even to the extent of being pompous.

> *Contexts:* His plans for his own future were grandiose. I doubted whether he could ever achieve them.

✦ 6. **in cess ant** (in ses′ ənt), *adj.,* going on endlessly, occurring without interruption, continuous.

> *Related word:* **in cess ant ly,** *adv.*

> *Contexts:* The incessant ringing of the bells eventually got on my nerves. "Enough!" I shouted.

He talked incessantly to the point that I came to believe that his tongue was connected to a nonstop motor.

7. **in con gru ous** (in kong′ groo əs), *adj.,* not corresponding with, disagreeing with; inconsistent with what is logical.

   Related words: **in con gru ous ly,** *adv.;* **in con gru i ty,** *n.;* **con gru i ty,** *n.*

   Contexts: To me his physical appearance was incongruous with his manner of speaking. He, on the other hand, was not even aware of the incongruity.

8. **lu di crous** (loo′ di krəs), *adj.,* silly, or absurd, as to be laughed at.

   Related words: **lu di crous ly,** *adv.;* **lu di crous ness,** *n.*

   Contexts: The man looked ludicrous dressed in a red coat, yellow tie, and orange pants. His attire gave him an overall appearance of ludicrousness that I can only believe must have been intentional.

9. **me tic u lous** (mə tik′ yə ləs), *adj.,* extremely careful, sometimes to the point of excessive concern for details.

   Related words: **me tic u lous ness,** *n.;* **me tic u lous ly,** *adv.*

   Contexts: The man was a meticulous housekeeper; he seemed to catch the specks of dust before they landed on a surface. He approached each task he did with a meticulousness that I knew I could never achieve.

10. **pru dent** (prood′ nt), *adj.,* using good judgment; especially careful with one's own affairs and interests.

    Related words: **pru dence,** *n.;* **pru dent ly,** *adv.;* **im pru dent,** *adj.;* **im pru dent ly,** *adv.;* **im pru dence,** *n.*

    Contexts: The student prudently left herself plenty of time to study for her final exams. Previously, she had been imprudent and had partied during the week of exams. She had learned from her imprudence, and henceforth she was more prudent in her use of time.

11. **trans par ent** (trans pâr′ ənt), *adj.,* able to transmit light so that you can see through to the other side; readily understandable, clear.

    Related word: **trans par ent ly,** *adv.*

    Contexts: Glass is transparent; as a result, we can see through it. Some people, too, are transparent; we can see right through them and understand their motives and actions. A person's behavior can be transparently obvious.

12. **un i ver sal** (yoo′ nə vûr′ səl), *adj.,* extending to and including the entire world or all members of a group; of or related to the universe or to the cosmos.

    Related word: **un i verse,** *n.*

    Contexts: I believe in universal suffrage—the vote for everyone.

During that epoch of history, there was universal hunger.
We are part of the universe—the vastness of space and the bodies therein.
An idea that has universal appeal is one that is acceptable to many people.

◆◆◆

Power Adjective

cat a clys mic (kat′ ə kliz′ mik), an adjective from the Greek meaning "related to violent upheaval or disaster." *Cataclysmic* can be traced to two Greek words, *kata* meaning "down" and *kluzeim* meaning "to wash." It came into English from Latin by way of French.

Contexts: When the large company located in our town went into bankruptcy and fired its employees, we expected cataclysmic changes within the community.

◆◆◆

Word Study Activities Module 2-B—
Making Meaning with Adjectives

2-B-1 Words in Meaningful Sentence Contexts: From the list, select the adjective that best fits into the overall meaning of each sentence. Then write that word in the blank. Use each option only once. Apply your Know-for-sure/Process-of-elimination test-taking strategy. Cross out options as you use them.

a. ambiguous	d. frugal	g. incongruous	j. prudent
b. cosmopolitan	e. grandiose	h. ludicrous	k. transparent
c. ephemeral	f. incessant	i. meticulous	l. universal
			m. cataclysmic

1. Her _____F_____ chatter drove me to distraction, for I need quiet, not noise, when I study.

2. "It would be _____J_____ to call ahead before going to be sure your friend is there," my brother advised me.

3. Because the directions the service station operator gave me were _____A_____, I lost my way again.

4. With the light shining from behind, the dress became _____K_____; it appeared as if she had on no dress at all.

5. The successful student was a/an _____I_____ note taker. She was able to get down every detail from the professor's lecture.

6. Because my mother was so _____D_____, by the end of the week she still had half of her paycheck money in the bank.

7. That belief is almost _____G_____ in this country; few people do not believe that way.

8. My sister's _____ plans fell through because she had not thought through each part step-by-step.

9. I was struck by how _____C_____ life really is; it is as though each of us is simply "passing through."

10. He perceived himself as a/an _____B_____ man-about-town, a jet-setter who was at home in any country of the world.

11. I really do not know how I got myself in such a/an _____ situation. Here I—a college senior—was dressed up as a New Year's Eve baby.

12. It seemed _____C_____ to me that a man of his great theoretical ability had so little common sense.

13. The earthquake resulted in _____M_____ changes in the surrounding area.

2-B-2 Antonym Study: Match the adjectives in the left-hand column with their antonyms at the right. Put the appropriate option on the line before each word in the right-hand column.

1. **ambiguous**   _____   a. not funny

2. **cosmopolitan**   _____   b. messy

3. **ephemeral**   _____   c. logical

4. **frugal**   _____   d. opaque

5. **grandiose**   _____   e. intermittent

6. **incessant**   _____   f. small

7. **incongruous**   _____   g. limited

8. **ludicrous**   _____   h. careless

9. **meticulous**   _____   i. free with money

10. **prudent**   _____   j. everlasting

11. **transparent**   _____   k. nonviolent, without disaster

12. **universal**   _____   l. provincial

13. **cataclysmic**   _____   m. clear

2-B-3 Sort and Discover

- Look at the dozen adjectives you have been studying in this module. Sort and list them here according to their endings, or suffixes. Can you think of other adjectives with the same suffixes to add to your lists? If so, add a couple here.

  -ous   **-al**   **-ent**   **-an**   **-ose**   **-ic**   **-ant**

- Based on your sorting and listing, decide: Which of these are the most common adjective endings, or suffixes? Which are the least common adjective suffixes?

- What do we mean by the phrase *universal suffrage?* Record the meaning here in sentence form.

✔ **2-B-4 Crossword Puzzle:**   Use your knowledge of the adjectives you have been studying to solve the puzzle in Figure 2.2.

Reading with Meaning Module 2-C— Learning about the Greek Origins of Some English Words

Read the following short passage, and note how the words you have been studying are used in telling a story. Ask yourself, "How has the English language been influenced by the Greek language and the myths of the ancient Greek people?"

Order Out of Chaos

Before **sallying** forth for the day, many women apply their cosmetics—lipstick, eyeliner, and perhaps a bit of rouge or powder. They do this without thought as to the word they use to talk about their beauty products—*cosmetics*—or the fact that the word and the idea of using such preparations go far back in history.

The ancient Greeks devised a myth to explain the origins of the universe. They proposed that originally the universe was a swirling, transparent mass of disordered nothingness. What existed was a vast emptiness where there was only confusion, or shall we say with the Greeks, "chaos"? This, of course, was before the birth of the Titans and Titaneses, for the Greeks believed that even their gods and goddesses could not exist amid chaos.

Figure 2.2 Crossword Puzzle of Adjectives

ACROSS
3 Using good judgment
4 Clear
6 Large
10 Worldly
11 Careful with money
12 Attentive to details

DOWN
1 Continuous
2 Inconsistent
5 Funny

7 Unclear
8 Short-lived
9 Worldwide

What began to form out of chaos, the ancient Greeks called *kosmos,* meaning "order" and "good arrangement." That is why you and I today use the word *cosmos* when referring to the universe and why we talk of "cosmic rays" that bombard the earth from everywhere in the universe. That is why, too, we use the word *cosmic* not only to refer to the universe but to mean "vast and grandiose," for *vast* and *grandiose*—after all—are two words we use in describing our universe. In this context, also, we are inclined to talk of things being "of cosmic proportions," or of extreme size and/or importance. In like vein, we describe someone who is not bound by local habits and prejudices and is at home in varied countries and cultures as being "cosmopolitan" in outlook.

"So, how do cosmetics fit into the picture?" you ask. Remember that the Greek word *kosmos* means "good arrangement." The lipstick, eyeliner, and rouge with which people make up their faces result in a good arrangement, perhaps creating order out of chaos. As a result, the Greeks developed the word *kosmetikcos* from their word *kosmos* to talk about preparations used to beautify the face.

Word Study Activities Module 2-C—
Learning about Word Relationships

2-C-1 Dictionary Investigation: Search the part of your dictionary where words related to *cosmos* are located. (Clue: Look up words starting with the letters *cosm.*) Locate at least six other words that share an etymological relationship with *cosmos*. Sort your findings into two lists that you record in your word study notebook—one labeled "related to universal," the other "related to cosmetics." Next to each record a brief definition.

2-C-2 Word Relationships: The Greeks use the letter *k* to represent the hard *c* sound at the beginning of *cosmos*. What has happened to the spelling of some Greek words such as *kosmos* when they entered the English language? Why do you think this has happened? Respond in your notebook.

Some other English words use the letter *k* to represent the hard *c* sound. Familiar examples are *kite, kiss,* and *kitchen.* Why do English words differ in this way? Check a dictionary for the etymology of these words. That will give you a clue.

2-C-3 Context Clues: In the first sentence in the passage, you saw the word *sallying.* Based on how *sallying* is used in that sentence, predict its meaning. Record your prediction in your notebook. Then check the prediction you figured out from the context clues with the dictionary definition. In the next chapter, you will be considering how to figure out the meaning of a word based on its use in a sentence or paragraph you are reading.

Confusing Words—*There, Their,* and *They're; Its* and *It's*

Some people tend to misuse two sets of short words: *their, there,* and *they're; its* and *it's.* Do you know the difference? Let's talk about them.

Their and *its* are possessive pronouns just as *his, her,* and *our* are. We talk about his books, her house, our lives, their computers, its paws. Although we use an apostrophe with possessive nouns such as the girl's book (the book of the girl) and the boys' father (the father of the boys), as you learned in Chapter 1, we do not need an apostrophe with possessive pronouns.

They're and *it's* are contractions; they stand for *they are* and *it is.* It's simple to test for *they're* and *it's.* We just substitute the words *they are* or *it is.* If the substitution makes sense, we use the contraction. Incidentally, some people use *its'* in their writing. No such word exists in the English language!

There is the opposite of *here*. We talk of going there just as we talk of coming here. There is also one rather bland way of using *there*. Some people start sentences with "There is . . ." or "There are . . ." as I just did with the previous sentence. We can do this from time to time, but we should not overly rely on this structure.

Fill in the blanks in these sentences:

1. _____ a beautiful morning.

2. The bird tucked _____ head beneath its wings.

3. _____ is considerable doubt in his mind about the feasibility of my plan.

4. When I went _____, I met my prospective father-in-law.

5. The authors came to talk about _____ books.

6. Because _____ my friends, I can rely on them when trouble comes.

PART II

CONTEXT CLUES AND MORE ABOUT WORD ORIGINS

3

Context Clues—Words from Latin

◆◆◆

Objectives: In Chapter 3, you will develop the ability to

- explain the influence of the Latin language on modern English, using the root *verb-* and the word *verbatim* as examples;

- figure out word meanings based on context clues—synonyms, definitions, and antonyms;

- recognize and attach meaning to three word elements featured in Module 3-A that come from Latin: *bene-* (good), *male-* (bad), and *mort-* (death);

- comprehend and use the following Latin phrases and power word featured in Module 3-A:

mea culpa	per annum	status quo	terra firma
modus operandi	per diem	sub rosa	vice versa
acumen (*power word*)			

- comprehend and use the following words derived from Latin roots featured in Module 3-A:

  | hiatus | benefit | malignant | moral | mortal |

- figure out word meanings based on context clues by using a substitution strategy;

- recognize some commonly found verb endings and comprehend the following verbs derived from the Latin language featured in Module 3-B:

accelerate	correlate	emulate	rationalize
admonish	demolish	liberalize	subsidize
clarify	diminish	pacify	verify

- recognize and attach meaning to the element *pax-* (peace) featured in Module 3-B;

- explain the influence on modern English of the Roman legends, especially the legend about Romulus and Remus; and

- distinguish among the confusing homophones *site, cite,* and *sight.*

Interesting Words to Think about—*Verbatim* and *Verboten*

The word *verbatim* (vər bāt′ əm), which today functions in English as either an adjective or an adverb, has an interesting origin. *Verbatim* came into the English language during medieval times and can be traced back to the old Latin word *verbum,* meaning "word."

You can use *verbatim* adverbially as in this sentence: "The newspaper printed the president's speech verbatim, so that I could read what he had said word for word." The context of this sentence provides the meaning of *verbatim*—"word for word, in the same words as spoken or written."

You can also find *verbatim* used as an adjective: "I read a verbatim report of her legal testimony to be certain that I understood her position." Again the context in which *verbatim* is found supplies a clue to its meaning, although the clue is not so clear as in the prior example. If a person is to understand someone's position, he or she should study the exact words spoken.

In English, we have numbers of words that trace their origins to the Latin *verbum* and in some way carry the meaning "word." A *proverb* is a short, wise saying, one that usually has been around a long time. Think of some of the proverbs you heard as a child: Waste not; want not. Haste makes waste. A stitch in time saves nine. The early bird catches the worm. Derivatives of the word *proverb* are *proverbial* (*adj.*) and *proverbially* (*adv.*), meaning "expressed like a proverb, in the manner of a proverb." We tend to use *proverbial* in sentences like this one: "He was like the proverbial bird—always on time; in contrast, she was like the worm—always late."

Think about the following words and their meanings; they also trace their origins to the Latin *verbum:*

- **verb** (*n.*), the part of speech that shows action or being;
- **verbal** (*adj.*), in words; and the derivative **verbally** (*adv.*), using words;
- **verbalize** (*v.*), express with words;

- **verbalization** (*n.*), the process of expressing in words;
- **verbalism** (*n.*), overattention to mere words, an expression that has little meaning.

Look at the sentences given next. Can you figure out the meanings of the words written in boldfaced type from the way they are used? Underline the clues that provide the meaning right there in the context of each sentence.

- A **verb** is a word that changes form to indicate time change.
- The minister was gifted **verbally;** words flowed from her mouth as easily as water flows over a falls.
- Try to **verbalize** your understanding of the subject. By putting your ideas into words you will gain control over them.
- **Verbalization** is an important study strategy. Telling yourself what you know will help you later when you must take a test on the material.
- The teacher was inclined to use **verbalisms** in explaining; as a result, her explanations were not clear to me.

Now consider the word *verboten* (fer bōt′ n), *adj.,* as it is used here: "Smoking in this lounge is *verboten.* You will be fined if you do it." Obviously from the use of *verboten* in the sentence, you can tell immediately that although there appear to be aspects of the word *verbum* in the word *verboten, verboten* means something completely different. The reason relates to the etymology, or the origin, of *verboten. Verboten* is really not an English word; it is a present-day German word that means "strictly and absolutely forbidden by an authority." It has slipped into English speech because of the mixing of cultures and the interaction among peoples. English speakers use this German word so often that English dictionaries list it. Some dictionaries, however, write the word *verboten* in italics to show that it is a foreign word, not fully assimilated into the English language.

The outward similarity between *verbatim* and *verboten* combined with the difference in meaning indicates that you must take care in concluding that two words are closely related. Sometimes words that seem to incorporate common meanings do not. Again this shows how important it is to use context clues in figuring out the meanings of words that are new to you.

Collaborative Search, Sort, and Discover

- In a dictionary, check the meanings and origins of these phrases: *in memoriam, esprit de corps, in situ, in absentia, bon appetit, in extremis, en masse.* In your word study notebook, organize the words into two lists based on their Latin or French origins.
- If your dictionary lists foreign words in italics, thumb through it and locate other foreign words to add to your word lists.
- What is a context clue? What is the general meaning of the word *context?* Write your ideas in your notebook.

- Use the context of the quotation that opens Chapter 2 to predict the meanings of the words *obsolete* and *perpetual* used there. Write your prediction in your notebook.

- If you have Internet access, go to http://ablemedia.com/ctcweb/showcase/roots.html for "Roots of English: An Etymological Dictionary," a Windows® software program that emphasizes etymologies from Latin and Greek that you can download. This program lets you explore the origins of words. You may want to use it in reference to this chapter as well as later chapters of this book.

Strategy Box 3-A—Context Clues: Definitions, Synonyms, and Antonyms

A basic strategy for unlocking the meaning of an unfamiliar word is to search the context of the sentence in which a new word appears for clues. Sometimes this can be easy to do because the author may have provided a definition or a synonym right there next to or near a term that you can use to unlock its meaning. A definition is a statement giving the meaning of a word. A synonym is a word that means almost the same as another.

Consider how you can use synonyms and definitions within a sentence to understand a new word by studying this sentence: "Don't think of words as separate, discrete items, or entities." What is the meaning of the word *entities?* No hassle! The definition is right there—separate, discrete items. "Ah," you ask, "but what is the meaning of *discrete?*" The meaning of that word is right there, too—separate.

So when in doubt about the meaning of an unfamiliar word, look around in the sentence; check to see if there is a definition or synonym clue to help you unlock meaning. Actually there are definitions of the words *definition* and *synonym* embedded in the first paragraph of this Strategy Box. Underline them and be on the lookout for other places in this textbook—especially within the sentences used to introduce new vocabulary—where words are defined in context.

Another kind of context clue (in addition to definitions and synonyms embedded in sentences) is a word or words of opposite meaning set somewhere near a word that is unfamiliar. If you find a word or words of opposite meaning and you recognize it or them, you are "home free." You can unlock the meaning of the unfamiliar word.

For example, read the following sentence: "I was not exactly enamored of the travel plans my agent made for me; my lack of enthusiasm was triggered by the eight-hour layover required between flights that turned a relatively easy trip into an endurance test." What is the meaning of the word *enamored?* You can use the context of the sentence to reason in this way: *Enamored of* means just the opposite of *lacking in enthusiasm for*. Reasoning from that fact we know that to be enamored is to feel strongly about in a positive way. A dictionary definition of *enamor* is "to inflame with love," so that the context allows you to come rather close to that definition. Go back now and **wrestle** the meaning of the phrase *endurance test* from the context of the sentence. What words in the sample sentence suggest the opposite of *endurance test?*

First steps in a strategy for figuring out the meaning of an unfamiliar word or phrase from the context in which it appears are as follows:

- Step 1: Check for synonyms or definitions embedded right there. (I like to call this the "Right-there strategy.") If you find a synonym or definition, reread the sentence with the new term keeping that synonym or definition in mind. Then tell yourself in your own words what the sentence is saying to you.
- Step 2: Check for an antonym clue. If you find one, think about its meaning, actually telling yourself the opposite meaning. Then reread the sentence and rephrase it in your own mind.

Collaborative Search and Discover

What is the meaning of the word *wrestle?* Decide based on the way the word is used in this section, write a definition in your notebook, and check your definition in a dictionary.

Word Study Module 3-A—Words and Phrases of Latin Origin

Pronounce each featured word or phrase. Then, based on the definition, create a sentence in which you use it following the pattern offered in the sample sentence. Using the context of the sample sentences, decide on the meanings of any related words or phrases.

Commonly Used Phrases Taken Directly from Latin

1. **me a cul pa** (mē ə kul′ pə), *n.,* confession of guilt, apology [*culpa-* in the Latin is a root meaning "guilt"].

    Contexts: The chairperson's speech was a mea culpa in which she explained her behavior and asked forgiveness from those whom she had harmed.

2. **mo dus op e ran di** (mō′ dəs op ə ran′ di), *n.,* method of working or operating [literally in Latin—modus = method; operandi = operating].

    Contexts: I was aghast at his modus operandi; his way of doing things had no logic at all.

3. **per di em** (pər dē′ əm), *adv.,* by the day, for each day [literally in Latin—per = for; diem = day].

Related expression: **per an num,** *adv.*

Contexts: My job paid on a per diem basis; I got $25 per day. My sister earned $25,000 per annum. She had to stretch that across the full twelve months.

4. **sta tus quo** (stāt′ əs kwō), *n.,* the existing state of affairs.

Related word: **sta tus,** *n.*

Contexts: My mother is a believer in the status quo; she is always saying, "I like things exactly as they are." Within the community her status was very low, for people knew that they could not trust her word. In contrast, my uncle held a high status because of his wealth and position.

5. **sub ro sa** (sub rō′ zə), *adv.,* in great confidence, secretly, literally in Latin "under the rose" [*sub* indicating "under," the rose being an ancient symbol of high secrecy].

Contexts: The invasion was planned sub rosa with only those immediately involved being aware of what was to happen.

6. **ter ra fir ma** (ter′ ə fûr′ mə), *n.,* solid ground, dry land [*terra* in Latin means "earth or land"; *firma* in Latin means "fixed"].

Related words: **ter race,** *n.;* **ter rain,** *n.;* **ter rar i um,** *n.*

Contexts: After having been at sea for more than two weeks, I was happy to get my feet back on terra firma.
We constructed a terrace at a point where the terrain was even.
The young boy kept his toad in a terrarium.

7. **vice ver sa** (vīs′ vûr′ sə), *adv.,* with the order changed; conversely.

Contexts: I never can remember whether Mary was born before Fred, or vice versa.

✦✦

Power Word

a cu men (ə kyo͞o′ mən), a noun from the Latin meaning "clear thinking, keen insight, quick perception."

Contexts: The man moved ahead in the business world because of his financial acumen. (Note: Add *acumen* to a word card that you can look at from time to time.)

✦✦

Words from the Latin Language

8. **hi a tus** (hi ā′ təs), *n.,* gap, empty space.

Contexts: Some people hasten to fill any hiatus in conversation with talk or chatter; they abhor a vacuum.

✦ 9. **ben e fit** (ben′ ə fit), *n.,* something that is to the advantage of a person, something for the good; also *v.,* be good for.

> *Related words:* **be nef i cence,** *n.;* **ben e fac tor,** *n.;* **ben e fic i ar y,** *n.;* **bene dic tion,** *n.;* **ben e vo lent,** *adj.;* **ben e vo lence,** *n.;* **ben e fi cial,** *adj.*

> *Contexts:* I see a benefit in studying over an extended period of time rather than cramming before a test. Taking notes in a systematic way will benefit you.
> Mother Teresa was known for her beneficence.
> I did not know who my benefactor was, but I know that without him or her I could not have survived. I was the primary beneficiary of his will; he left me everything he had.
> After the benediction, we left the church. The rabbi was a benevolent person, respected for all he gave to others. His benevolence was recognized through a prestigious award.
> What would be most beneficial at this time would be help in getting the job done.

✦✦

Highlighted Word Element

bene-, a Latin root, or base, meaning "well, good."

Words with the element: *beneficial, benefactor, benefit.*

✦✦

✦ 10. **ma lig nant** (mə lig′ nənt) [from the Latin *malus,* meaning "bad, evil"], *adj.,* very hateful, very harmful; very dangerous.

> *Related words:* **ma lig nan cy,** *n.;* **ma lign,** *v.;* **ma lign er,** *n.;* **mal ice,** *n.;* **ma li cious,** *adj.;* **ma li cious ness,** *n.*

> *Contexts:* Raymond had a malignant growth on his forehead that could have been deadly. It was that malignancy that caused his death.
> He maligned his ex-wife to their children, speaking evil against her, which caused suffering in the family.
> She seemed to act with malice toward everyone she encountered.
> The youngster had a malicious streak that was frightening to behold; he was cruel to people and animals alike.

✦✦

Highlighted Word Element

mal(e)- or **malign-,** a Latin root, or base, meaning "bad or evil."

Words with the element: *malign, malfeasance, malcontent.*

✦✦

✦ 11. **mor al** (mor′ əl) [from the Latin *mores*, meaning "manners"], *adj.,* having to do with standards of right and good as they apply to general behavior and character; *n.,* a lesson, especially one stated at the end of a fable.

> *Related words:* **mor al i ty,** *n.;* **im mor al,** *adj.;* **im mor al i ty,** *n.*

> *Contexts:* The father had a moral responsibility to tell the truth to his family. The moral of the story is "Don't bite off more than you can chew."
> I question the morality of the woman's actions; she should have told the truth at the beginning.
> The governor was basically an immoral person who had no sense of right or wrong. His immorality showed in every major action that he took.

✦ 12. **mor tal** (mor′ tl), *adj.,* sure to die at some point; causing death; of human beings; *n.,* a being that is certain to die; a human being.

> *Related words:* **mor tal i ty,** *n.;* **im mor tal i ty,** *n.;* **im mor tal,** *adj.;* **mortal ly,** *adv.;* **mor tu a ry,** *n.;* **mor ti cian,** *n.;* **mor ti fied,** *adj.;* also note the expression *post mortem,* an expression directly from Latin, meaning "after death."

> *Contexts:* All mortals see death in their future. They never question their mortality because they know that death comes to all. As humans, our only hope for immortality is our reputation that lives after us and the mark we make on the future.
> The ancient Greeks believed that their gods and goddesses were immortal.
> The soldier was mortally wounded during the Normandy landing.
> His funeral was held at a local mortuary. The mortician at the mortuary had a somber look as he opened the door for us. The medical examiner conducted a post mortem examination to find out the cause of death.
> I was mortified that everyone had heard of my mistake; I was simply embarrassed to death.

◆◆

Highlighted Word Element

mort-, a Latin root, or base, meaning "death."

Words with the element: *immortal, immortality, mortician.*

◆◆

Word Study Activities Module 3-A— Making Meaning with Words

3-A-1 Discovering Other Expressions from Latin: Check the meanings of these expressions in your dictionary: *persona non grata; in toto; ad hoc.* Then, in your notebook, create a sentence using each expression. Using all three phrases, you may be able to write a paragraph that makes sense.

3-A-2 Phrases in Meaningful Sentence Contexts: From the list, select the Latin expression that best fits into the overall meaning of each sentence. Write it in the blank. Use each option only once. Then circle the word or phrase in each sentence that was the clue that "set you wise."

a. mea culpa
b. modus operandi
c. per annum

d. per diem
e. status quo
f. sub rosa

g. terra firma
h. vice versa
i. acumen

1. When the astronauts set their feet on _____ after a particularly harrowing space trip, they breathed a sigh of genuine relief.

2. Although my father earns a hundred thousand dollars _____, he never seems to have enough to last the year.

3. The professor's _____ was to start his class each day with a brief review quiz.

4. Is your name Mary Elizabeth, or is it _____?

5. Her _____ did not ring true; I had trouble believing that she really had repented.

6. Most of her money was earned _____; she operated this way to avoid taxes—which is not an ethical thing to do.

7. I was a _____ worker; I came in from time to time to work for a day or so.

8. The chairperson of the Federal Reserve must have strong business _____ if he or she is to set interest rates in the country.

9. Soon I got bored with the _____, with doing the same thing in the same way every time.

3-A-3 Related Words in Meaningful Sentence Contexts: In each case, select the form of the word that best fits into the sentence slot. Write that word in the blank. Use each option only once. Use the process of elimination to help you.

a. malignant adj
b. malignancy noun

c. malign verb
d. maligner noun

e. malice noun
f. malicious adj.

g. maliciousness noun

1. The dictator was a _____adj._____ person, out to do the most for himself and nothing for his people.

2. Such ____noun.____ I had never seen in action in another human being. It was beyond comprehension that anyone could be that evil.

3. The neighborhood gossip took every opportunity to _____*verb,*_____ others living nearby.

4. His motto seemed to be: "With _____*noun*_____ toward everyone; with good toward no one."

5. The growth on his ear was not _____*adj.*_____. As a result, the doctors were able to give him a good report.

6. If they had discovered a _____*noun*_____ in his brain, the prognosis could have been far different. His life could have been shortened considerably.

7. I am glad that I do not live next to a _____*noun*_____. Such a person is too eager to spread evil rumors.

3-A-4 More Related Words in Meaningful Sentence Contexts:

In each case, select the form of the word that best fits into the sentence slot. Write that word in the blank. Use each option only once. Use the process of elimination.

a. mortal *adj*   c. immortality *noun*   e. mortally *adj verb*   g. mortuary *noun*
b. immortal *adj.*   d. mortality *noun*   f. mortified *adverb*   h. mortician *noun*

1. Another name for an undertaker is a/an _____*H*_____.

2. Another name for a funeral parlor is a/an _____*G*_____.

3. We are all _____*adj. A*_____ beings; we know that some day we must die.

4. Some people believe that their souls are _____*adj B*_____ and will live on after they are gone.

5. When the young man realized that he had gone around all morning in an unzipped state, he was _____*adverb F*_____.

6. None of us will be blessed with _____*noun C*_____. There is an eventual end to life for each individual.

7. My friend was _____*adverb E*_____ wounded when her husband left her for another woman.

8. Our own _____*D*_____ becomes more strikingly apparent as we grow older.

3-A-5 Other Related Words in Meaningful Sentence Contexts:

In each case, select the form of the word that best fits into the sentence slot. Write that word in the blank. Use each option only once. Cross out options as you use them.

a. hiatus   d. moral   g. benevolent   j. beneficial
b. immoral   e. morality   h. benediction   k. beneficiary
c. immorality   f. benefactor   i. benevolence

1. My ___benefactor___ was a kindly schoolteacher who gave me the money to go to college.

2. Jonah was the primary ___beneficiary___ under the terms of his father's will, which accounted for the large amount of money he had.

3. I never forgot his _____, and I remembered him many years later as the most generous person I had ever met.

4. The nurse was recognized for her many _____ deeds by being awarded the title "Most Generous Person of the Year."

5. At the end of the church service, the priest gave the _____.

6. If you will tell others about the kinds of things our organization does, it will be _____ to our cause.

7. During the _____ before a new group of doctors came on duty, my friend Mary jumped in to take charge and make decisions.

8. My father was an exceptionally _____ person; he had a code of ethics and he practiced what he believed.

9. In contrast, my uncle was an exceptionally _____ person; he did not know right from wrong.

10. Many people believe that we are seeing a decline in the overall _____ of our country, with people doing whatever they want without concern for the welfare of others.

11. _____ in that country was the norm; no one considered the welfare of others. What a disaster it was!

3-A-6 Synonym Study: Match the words in the left-hand column with their synonyms at the right. Write the appropriate option on the line before the word in the right-hand column to which it belongs.

1. **mortal**   _____   a. extremely embarrassed

2. **immoral**   _____   b. without values

3. **moral**   _____   c. kindly, generous

4. **malicious**   _____   d. must die

5. **benevolent**   _____   e. everlasting

6. **mortified**   _____   f. ethical

7. **immortal**   _____   g. evil

3-A-7 Definitional Study: Match the words in the left-hand column with their definitions at the right. Write the appropriate option on the line before the word in the right-hand column to which it belongs.

1. **beneficiary**   _____   a. a blessing at the end of a service

2. **benefactor**   _____   b. one who inherits under a will

3. **benediction**   _____   c. undertaker

4. **mortuary**   _____   d. state or quality of being evil

5. **maligner**   _____   e. keen insight

6. **morality**   _____   f. one who helps another, especially financially

7. **immorality**   _____   g. one who pulls down another verbally

8. **mortician**   _____   h. state or quality of being good

9. **acumen**   _____   i. funeral parlor

3-A-8 Truth or Falsity: Write True or False after each statement.

1. An immoral person is likely to be beneficent. _____

2. Human beings are immortal. _____

3. A maligner is a malicious person. _____

4. Often parents make their children beneficiaries under their wills. _____

5. Where there is a hiatus, you find much activity going on. _____

6. Most people are extremely upset when they learn they have a malignancy in their body. _____

7. A person offering a benediction should be an immoral individual. _____

8. Most benefactors are malicious people. _____

9. A mortician generally works in a mortuary. _____

10. Most people are mortified when something wonderful happens to them.

_____

Word Study Module 3-B—Verbs of Latin Origin

By traditional definition, verbs are words that show action or state of being. For example, you can say that the instructor clarified the assignment for you. You can also say that he is an excellent instructor. In the first example, *clarified* is a verb. In the second example, *is*

Strategy Box 3-B—Context Clues: Substitution

At times, rereading a sentence that contains an unfamiliar term and substituting a word or phrase for it that makes sense can help you to unlock the meaning of the unfamiliar word. To understand the Substitution strategy, read this sentence:

> When we stayed at the military base, each Saturday we went to the commissary to buy the food and supplies we would need for the next week.

Although you may never have visited a commissary, given the use of the word in this sentence, you immediately can substitute the word *store* for the word *commissary*. You probably can wrestle an even more complete meaning for *commissary* from the overall context of the sentence: a store for food and supplies that is located on a military base.

Steps in the Substitution strategy are as follows:

- Step 1: When you read a sentence that you have trouble understanding because of an unfamiliar word in it, reread the sentence and substitute a word that seems to make sense in the context.
- Step 2: Read on. If the word you substituted does not make sense in the context of the rest of the paragraph, try again.
- Step 3: If the sentence still does not make sense to you and you do not understand the main point the author is making in the paragraph, look for synonym, definition, and antonym clues. If you are still uncertain, check a dictionary.

is a verb. Notice some typical positions of verbs in sentences as shown in the following models. In each, only a verb can fit in the blank:

- The car will _____.
- The teacher _____ you to _____ harder.
- He _____ a man.

Pronounce each of the following featured verbs. Then, in your notebook write sentences that follow the pattern of the sample sentences.

✦   1. **ac cel e rate** (ak sel′ ə rat′), *v.,* speed up.

> ***Related words:* ac cel e ra tion,** *n.;* **ac cel e ra tor,** *n.;* **ac cel e ra tive,** *adj.*

> ***Contexts:*** I plan to accelerate my progress through college so that I graduate in three years. Such an acceleration will jump-start my career. I have always taken an accelerative route in life; I do not like to go slowly. I guess you could say that I am an accelerator of progress.

✦   2. **ad mon ish** (ad mon′ ish), *v.*, warn against; scold in a gentle way; urge to do something.

> *Related words:* **ad mon i tion**, *n.;* **ad mon ish er**, *n.;* **ad mon i tory**, *adj.*

> *Contexts:* My teacher admonished me to try harder; however, I did not listen to her admonition. I really would not have listened to any admonisher, for I was at a time of life when I thought I knew it all. Now when I receive an admonitory suggestion, I think about it.

✦   3. **clar i fy** (klar′ ə fi), *v.*, make clear, explain.

> *Related words:* **clar i fi ca tion**, *n.;* **clar i ty**, *n.;* **clar i fi er**, *n.*

> *Contexts:* In his lecture, my professor clarified the relationship between cause and effect in history. He spoke with such clarity that I understood the point immediately. I really needed clarification on the topic for I had been confused.

✦   4. **cor re late** (kôr′ ə lāt), *v.*, show the connection or relationship between, place in proper relationship to.

> *Related words:* **cor re la tion**, *n.;* **cor re la tion al**, *adj.*

> *Contexts:* I tried to develop a correlation between the two events to determine which was the cause and which was the effect. I failed to correlate the two. Correlational studies have proved that a relationship does exist.

✦   5. **de mol ish** (de mol′ ish), *v.*, tear down; destroy.

> *Related word:* **dem o li tion**, *n.*

> *Contexts:* The explosion practically demolished the building. As a result, a crew was brought in to complete the demolition.

✦   6. **di min ish** (də min′ ish), *v.*, lessen, reduce, make or get smaller.

> *Contexts:* Your assets will diminish very quickly if you spend more money than you take in, for you will have to dip into your savings.

✦   7. **em u late** (em′ yə lāt), *v.*, strive to be the same as, copy to equal or exceed.

> *Related words:* **em u la tion**, *n.;* **em u la tor**, *n.;* **em u la tive**, *adj.*

> *Contexts:* My friend always was trying to emulate what I did. His emulative behavior got on my nerves. It is difficult to live with an emulator in one's shadow. As a result I broke up with him.

✦   8. **lib er al ize** (lib′ ər ə līz), *v.*, make or become more open, free, tolerant.

> *Related words:* **lib er al i za tion**, *n.;* **lib er ate**, *v.;* **lib er al**, *adj.*

> *Contexts:* In voting for Jack Thomas for governor, Ruth hoped that she would see a liberalization of the rules related to free speech. However, when Thomas became governor, he did nothing to liberalize the rules. She had believed

him to be very liberal, but instead he turned out to be very a close-minded man. In no way did he try to liberate the state from the shackles of the past.

◆　9.　**pac i fy** (pas′ ə fī), *v.*, quiet down, calm down, bring peace to.

> *Related words:* **pac i fist,** *n.;* **pac i fism,** *n.;* **pac i fi er,** *n.;* **pac i fi able,** *adj.*

> *Contexts:* Jeff's father tried to pacify him by telling him that success would sooner or later come his way. However, the boy was not pacifiable. Nothing would calm him down after he had suffered such a great loss.
>
> A pacifist is antiwar—someone totally against aggression. A pacifist believes in pacifism—the idea that all disagreements should be settled peaceably.

◆◆◆

Highlighted Word Element

pax-, a Latin root meaning "peace."

Words with the element: *peace, Pacific Ocean, pacify.*

◆◆◆

◆　10.　**ra tion al ize** (rash′ ə nə līz), *v.*, treat or explain in a reasoned way; find an excuse for.

> *Related words:* **ra tion ale,** *n.;* **ra tion al i za tion,** *n.;* **ra tion al,** *adj.*

> *Contexts:* Many people try to rationalize their inappropriate actions by concocting excuses in their minds. Such rationalizations can lead to disaster because eventually the truth catches them up.
>
> A rational person is a thoughtful person who reasons out the actions he or she will take. This kind of person often has a logical rationale to support his or her actions.
>
> I never can seem to rationalize my checkbook at the end of a month.

◆　11.　**sub si dize** (sub′ sə dīz), *v.*, support with a grant of money.

> *Related word:* **sub si dy,** *n.*

> *Contexts:* His mother offered to subsidize his graduate work at the university, but he did not like the idea of living off his mother. Instead, he got a subsidy from the government.

◆　12.　**ver i fy** (ver′ ə fī), *v.*, confirm or prove to be true and accurate, check the accuracy of.

> *Related words:* **ver i fi ca tion,** *n.;* **ver i fi a ble,** *adj.*

> *Contexts:* I had to verify my identity by showing a valid driver's license. Some people use a passport as verification of their identity.
> Some facts are hard to verify. Other facts are verifiable.

Word Study Activities Module 3-B— Making Meaning with Verbs

3-B-1 A Verb Sort According to Suffixes: In your reading notebook, sort the twelve verbs you have just studied into four piles based on the suffixes they bear. Just list the verbs in four columns according to their suffixes. Then brainstorm one or two other verbs that carry each of these suffixes. You may do this cooperatively with a friend.

3-B-2 Words in Meaningful Sentence Contexts: From the list, select the verb that best fits into the overall meaning of each sentence. Write it in the blank. Use each option only once. Then circle the word or phrase in each sentence that was the clue that "set you wise."

a. accelerate	d. correlate	g. emulate	j. rationalize
b. admonish	e. demolish	h. liberalize	k. subsidize
c. clarify	f. diminish	i. pacify	l. verify

1. My mentor tried to _____ me to get to class on time, take good notes, and participate actively. I failed to take his warning.

2. I hoped that the university would _____ its requirements, but the administrators held fast.

3. My church agreed to _____ my studies at the university.

4. Before granting me the subsidy, the elders had to _____ my status as a student.

5. I also had to _____ for them how I would spend the money.

6. My explanation seemed to _____ my parents, for they calmed down immediately.

7. Because my older sister had done so well at the school, I tried to _____ her behavior. I did everything just as she had.

8. Try to _____ the characteristics of the two events so that you can see how they are similar.

9. No matter what my husband did and how often he failed, he always tried to _____ his behavior. Then I would scream at him, "Excuses! Excuses! That is all you have to offer!"

10. The contractors decided that they would have to _____ the building because the ground beneath was insecure.

11. My repeated lies began to _____ me in his eyes. I learned then that honesty was the way to proceed.

12. In order to _____ my progress, I took 18 credits per semester and then attended summer session.

3-B-3 Definitional Study: Match the words in the left-hand column with the definitions at the right. Write the appropriate noun on the line before the definition in the right-hand column to which it belongs.

1. **acceleration**   _____   a. the act of checking on the accuracy of

2. **admonition**   _____   b. the act of supplying an excuse for one's behavior

3. **clarification**   _____   c. the act of making more open and free

4. **correlation**   _____   d. the act of speeding up

5. **emulation**   _____   e. the act of copying

6. **liberalization**   _____   f. the act of warning

7. **rationalization**   _____   g. the act of making clearer, an explanation

8. **verification**   _____   h. the act of interrelating

3-B-4 Truth or Falsity: Write True or False after each statement.

1. The word element *pax-* means "peace." _____

2. An accelerator slows us down. _____

3. An emulator is a copier. _____

4. A subsidizer takes away. _____

5. A rationalizer makes up excuses to support his or her unwise actions. _____

6. A demolisher builds things up. _____

7. An admonisher gives a warning. _____

8. A liberalizer opens things up and allows more freedom. _____

9. A verifier checks things out. _____

10. A clarifier makes things more complicated. _____

11. A diminisher builds other people up. _____

12. A correlator identifies relationships between two things. _____

13. A pacifier stirs up trouble. _____

Reading with Meaning Module 3-C— Learning to Rely on Context Clues as You Read a Legend

Read the following passage, paying particular attention to the meanings of the words in boldfaced type:

Romulus and Remus: A Legend That Explains the Founding of Rome

People have **legends**—stories coming down from the past—to explain early happenings in the history of their nation. These stories generally incorporate elements of fact but also include a **fictional** event as part of the explanation. For example, legend tells of the founding of the Italian city of Rome by Romulus in 753 B.C.

As tradition explains it, Amulius **usurped** the throne of his brother Numitor and forced Numitor's daughter, Rhea Siva, to become a vestal virgin and tend the **eternal** flame in honor of the goddess Vesta at her ancient temple. Amulius did this to **ensure** that Rhea Siva would not conceive or bear any children, who in turn might take the throne away from him. However, according to legend, Rhea Siva bore twin sons **sired** by the god Mars. The twins were Romulus and Remus.

When Amulius discovered what had happened, he imprisoned his niece, put the twins in a basket, and set the basket **adrift** on the river Tiber. A fast current carried the basket ashore where **fortuitously** a she-wolf found them. She **suckled** the boys until eventually Romulus and Remus were discovered by a shepherd and his wife who reared them until they became adults. At that point—as the legend tells us—Romulus and Remus learned of their true identity and of the **infamous** act of their great-uncle Amulius. Seeking revenge, they killed Amulius and restored their grandfather Numitor to his throne.

Having righted the wrongs of the past, the twins went on to **found** the city of Rome at the very **site** along the river Tiber where they had floated ashore. **Discord** arose between Romulus and Remus, however, when through an omen Romulus was named as the one and only founder of the city—the one whose name the city would bear. The strife was so extreme that Romulus ended up killing Remus.

Legend further **recounts** that fugitives from other cities and city states came to Rome and helped to build it. Needing wives in order to populate Rome, these men raided the nearby Sabine region and **abducted** the women, carrying them off to Rome. Until this day, this abduction has been known as "The Rape of the Sabine Women." The event has been memorialized in painting and sculpture.

Remember, of course, that all this is legend—a legend that grew up to explain an event that happened over 2,753 years ago. A bit may be fact, but most is fiction.

Word Study Activities Module 3-C— Learning to Rely on Context Clues

Activity 3-C-1 Wrestling Meaning from Context: Answer the questions in the space provided. Just use the way the words work in the story to decide on their meaning.

1. What is a **legend?**

2. What event in the Romulus/Remus legend most certainly was **fictional?** What event might have been **factual?**

3. What happens when someone **usurps** the throne or position of another person?

4. What is an **eternal** flame?

5. What phrase can be substituted meaningfully for the phrase **to ensure?**

6. What word can be substituted meaningfully for the word **sired?**

7. What do you do when you set something **adrift?**

8. What words make sense when substituted for the word **fortuitously?**

9. Give a synonym for **suckled.**

10. What meaning can you make with the word **infamous?**

11. Romulus **founded** a city. What is the meaning of the word **founded** in this context?

12. Substitute a word for the word **site** as used in the legend.

13. What synonym can you find in the selection that means almost the same as **discord?**

14. Substitute a word for the word **recounts** as used in the legend.

15. What word or phrase can you substitute for the word **abducted** in the legend?

Activity 3-C-2 Definitional Study: Match the words on the left with the meanings on the right by writing the correct word on each line. Start with the ones you know for sure; cross out items as you use them.

1. abduct   _____   a. story

2. adrift   _____   b. take for oneself without having the right to

3. discord   _____   c. everlasting

4. ensure   _____   d. be certain of

5. eternal   _____   e. fathered

6. fictional   _____   f. explain

7. fortuitously   _____   g. location

8. founded   _____   h. not based totally on fact

9. infamous   _____   i. nurse with milk

10. legend   _____   j. evil to the point of having a bad reputation

11. recount   _____   k. strife

12. sired   _____   l. carry off

13. site   _____   m. started up

14. suckle   _____   n. cast off without guidance

15. usurp   _____   o. by lucky chance

Confusing Words—*Site, Cite,* and *Sight*

You met one of a set of homophones in Module C of Chapter 3—*site* meaning "location." *Site* is a relative of *situate* and *situation,* both of which also deal with the idea of location or position. Once you make this correlation, you will have little trouble handling the word *site* as you read.

A problem may arise for you, however, when you are writing the word in an essay. Pronouncing it in your head, you may be uncertain whether to spell the word *site, cite,* or the more familiar *sight.* The easiest way to proceed is to make connections with related words. *Cite* is a verb meaning "to quote, especially to quote an authority in speaking or writing." It also can mean "to bring before a court of law for an offense." *Cite* is related to *citation*—that is what we call the quotation you use in your paper or the summons you get for speeding. If you connect *cite* to *citation,* you are less likely to use *site* for *cite* as you spell the word in a composition.

Of course, you know that the word *sight* refers to eyesight—the process of seeing with the eyes.

To deal with homophones successfully, you really must focus attentively on the spellings of the members of a set such as *site, cite,* and *sight.* You must try to make connections between one member of a set and other words that are related structurally and etymologically. Complete these sentences:

1. When my family toured Washington, D.C., I visited the _____ where Abraham Lincoln was shot.

2. In my term paper, I had to _____ the references that I had consulted.

3. What a magnificent _____ it was—a rainbow that touched the earth at each of its ends!

4

More Context Clues—Words from French

◆◆

Objectives: In Chapter 4, you will develop the ability to

- recognize and make meaning with the element *commun-*;
- interpret words that have multiple meanings;
- comprehend and use the following French words and expressions featured in Module 4-A:

carte blanche	coup d'état	de rigueur	détente
double entendre	en masse	faux pas	debacle
façade	gauche	malaise	cliché
hors d'oeuvre (*power word*);			

- interpret abbreviations, especially such common ones as *etc., et al., i.e.,* and *e.g.;*
- comprehend and use the following nouns from the French language featured in Module 4-B:

bourgeoisie	debut	melee	rapport
connoisseur	entrepreneurs	milieu	rendezvous
debris	liaison	protégé	résumé

- explain the influence of the French language on modern English, especially starting with the Norman invasion of Britain in A.D. 1066;
- use context clues to figure out meanings of words as part of actual reading; and
- distinguish between the homophones *principal* and *principle*.

Language is a city to the building of which every human being brought a stone.

—Ralph Waldo Emerson, *Quotation and Originality*

◆◆

An Interesting Word to Think about—*Common*

The word *common* is a commonly used word in the English language because, as Raymond Williams in *Key Words* (Oxford Press, 1976) explains, *common* has "an extraordinary range of meanings." Pick up any dictionary and you will see that this is true. One dictionary, for example, offers eleven definitions for *common* as used as an adjective, four definitions when *common* serves as a noun, and four definitions when *common* functions as a verb. All these uses can be traced to the Latin word *communis* meaning "common" or "general." Other words that contain the root *commun-* also communicate the meaning of the Latin source word in some way.

Consider the ways you use *common* today. At some point you probably have talked about something being a "common occurrence." By that you may have meant that the event was one that you often encountered, not anything extraordinary. In your studies of history, you may have talked about "the common people." By that, you may have meant those without great rank or wealth—just ordinary folk. At another time, you may have seen someone do something that you thought was gross or vulgar and said to yourself, "How common!"

Still another use of *common* is to mean belonging to two or more people: We talk of "common property," which is property owned by two people. Similarly, we use *common* to mean belonging to the entire community, as when we speak about a "common carrier"—meaning an aircraft on which anyone can travel. In the same vein, we use *common* to mean belonging equally to two or more things. You may remember in mathematics when you learned about "common denominators." Also you may remember learning about "common nouns" in contrast to "proper nouns," common nouns being names of those belonging to a category, such as girl, professor, or student, and proper nouns being names of specific things or people, such as Glenn, Puerto Rico, or the House of Representatives. Note the use of capital letters at the start of proper nouns but not at the beginning of common nouns. Note also that all the uses we have discussed so far are ones in which *common* functions as an adjective.

Now let us think about *common* (plural, *commons*) when it serves as a noun. Especially in past times, people talked about "the commons," meaning an area set aside that belonged to all the people and often was located in the middle of a town. Today on university campuses, some areas in which people meet to talk, relax, and eat are called "the commons." And, of course, you know about the British House of Commons, the lower legislative house within the British government to which people are elected; *commoners,* or untitled men and women, sit in the lower legislative house while titled men and women sit in the House of Lords. Another political use of the word *common* is seen in the term *commonwealth,* or the total body of people in a state. At times, too, *commonwealth* is used to mean a nation that is a self-governing democracy. Clearly, the meaning of *common* depends on the precise way it is used in a sentence.

A number of words are derived from the word *common.* We talk of a *commonality*—a quality common to or shared by two or more things—as when we remark, "We were struck by the *commonalities* we shared. We were born in the same year, on the same day, and in the same state." We might say that a person is *uncommonly* handsome, meaning that he or she is extraordinarily handsome. We also talk of *uncommon* events, which are events that are out of the ordinary and generally unexpected. Everyday events, in contrast, are said to be *commonplace.*

Some phrases rely on the word *common:*

- **common cold:** a simple cold such as has plagued most of us from time to time.
- **common-law marriage:** a living together as wife and husband but without benefit of an official marriage ceremony; in this instance, the wife is a common-law wife, and the husband is a common-law husband.
- **common sense:** good sense in everyday activities.
- **common stock:** ordinary stock in a company, as distinct from preferred stock.

So although *common* appears to be a simple word, it has multiple meanings and it shows up in a variety of contexts.

◆◆

Highlighted Word Element

commun-, a word element from Latin meaning "common."

Words with the element: *communicate, communism, communist, community.*

◆◆

Collaborative Search and Discover

- Here are some other words with multiple meanings: *break, compound, composition, consideration, round, step, throw.* Working with a partner, search a dictionary for the multiple meanings of one of these words, and in your notebook make a word wheel that shows several of the meanings, as in Figure 4.1. Be ready to explain your findings.

- Thumb through your dictionary and discover another word with multiple meanings. Select one. In your notebook, make a word wheel with it on the order of the one in Figure 4.1 that shows a word with its many meanings.
- Check the meanings of the words *communicate, communism,* and *communist* in a dictionary. In what way does each express the idea of "commonness"? Be ready to explain this.
- Internet Search: If you have Internet access, go to www.m-w.com where you will find a number of links to sites such as the following:
    1. "Word of the Day" with a definition of the word, an example sentence, and information about the word and related words at www.m-w.com/<gi-bin/mwwod.pl
    2. "Cool Words Site" that includes "Flappers2Rappers," a source on American Youth Slang at www.m-w.com/lighter/flap/flaphome.htm
    3. "Today's Word Puzzle" at www.m-w.com/cgi-bin/get_puzzle.pl/game

Log on and find out more about words.

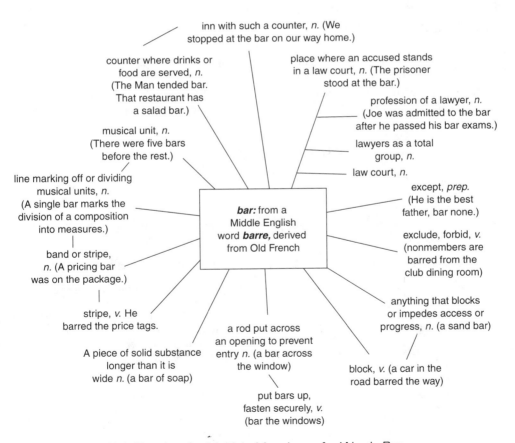

Figure 4.1   A Web Showing the Multiple Meanings of a Word: *Bar*

Strategy Box 4-A—Context Clues: Multiple Meanings

As you have learned in Chapter 3, a basic strategy for unlocking the meaning of an unfamiliar word is to search the context of the sentence in which a new word appears for clues. This is especially important when a word has multiple meanings that you already know and you must decide the particular one that applies.

The strategy to use here is simple—exactly what you have been learning to do in Chapter 3:

Step 1: Check the context for clues: definitions and synonyms given "right there" as well as words of opposite meaning—antonyms.

Step 2: Substitute each meaning you know in the context of the sentence until you find one that makes good sense there.

Word Study Module 4-A—
Words and Expressions Coming Directly
from the French Language

Pronounce each featured expression or word. Then try to think how you could use it in a sentence. Each expression or word comes to us from the French language. (Note: The spelling of the French words has been generally anglicized—that is, most of the diacritical marks over vowels have been eliminated in English [example: mêlée → melee]).

French Expressions We Use in English

1. **carte blanche** (kärt′ blänch′), *n.,* full authority, freedom to do as one feels is right; literally, a "white paper."

    Contexts: The professor gave her students carte blanche in selecting topics for their research papers.

2. **coup d'é tat** (ko͞o′ dä ta′), *n.,* sudden overthrow of government, usually by force.

    Contexts: The military staged a coup d'état in which the duly elected president was killed.

3. **de ri gueur** (də rē gûr′), *adj.,* required absolutely by custom, etiquette, or fashion.

    Contexts: Formal dress is no longer de rigueur aboard most cruise ships in the evening.

4. **dé tente** (dä tänt′), *n.,* easing of tensions between countries.

    Contexts: After the Berlin wall fell, the U.S.A. and the U.S.S.R. entered a period of détente.

5. **dou ble en ten dre** (dub′ əl än tän′ drə), *n.,* expression or word that can be interpreted with two meanings, one usually with a risqué meaning.

   Contexts: Every sentence the speaker uttered prompted snickers as members of the audience picked up on his double entendres.

6. **en masse** (ən mas′), *adv.,* as a group, all together.

   Contexts: The people in the audience rose to their feet en masse and gave the tenor a standing ovation.

7. **faux pas** (fō pä′), *n., pl.* **faux pas,** a slipup in manners, actions, or speech; literally, a "false step."

   Contexts: I felt embarrassed because I had made a social faux pas; I had worn formal attire to an informal party.

Other Words Coming Directly from French

8. **cli ché** (klē shā′), *n.,* trite expression that has become meaningless from overuse—for example; "sadder but wiser," "stir up a hornet's nest," "face the music," "absence makes the heart grow fonder," "bull in a china shop." (Note: For more on clichés, see Chapter 12.)

   Contexts: The student writer was inclined to use clichés, so his writing lacked sophistication.

9. **de ba cle** (da bä′ kəl), *n.,* complete disaster, sudden collapse.

   Contexts: The battle proved to be a debacle for the inexperienced troops.

10. **fa çade** (fə säd′), *n.,* the outer side of a building, the side facing the street; the general outward appearance.

    Contexts: The statues on the front façade of the cathedral are beginning to decay. Her smile was only a façade that she put on to cover her embarrassment.

11. **gauche** (gōsh′), *adj.,* awkward, lacking in grace.

    Contexts: I felt gauche in their presence; they seemed to know just what to say, whereas I stumbled over my words and even at one point over my feet.

12. **ma laise** (mal āz′), *n.,* vague bodily discomfort; disturbed, disoriented condition.

    Related words: **mal a droit,** *adj.* (also from the French and meaning clumsy); **ma la dy,** *n.* (Reminder: Remember that *mal-* means "bad.")

    Contexts: After returning from Europe, I suffered from a general feeling of malaise as a result of jet lag. On another occasion, I suffered a far more serious malady—intestinal disorder.

◆◆

Power Word

hors d'oeuvre (ôr dûrv′), a French expression meaning "an appetizer served before the main meal and often before diners have been seated at the table." The plural form is *hors d'oeuvres* (ôr dûrvz′).

Contexts: When my husband and I attended the reception, waiters offered us hors d'oeuvres before we went into the main dining room for dinner.

◆◆

Word Study Activities Module 4-A—
Making Meaning with Words
That Come to Us Directly
from the French Language

4-A-1 Words in Meaningful Sentence Contexts: From the list, select the word that best fits into the overall meaning of each sentence. Then write that word in the blank. Use each option only once. Use the process of elimination to help you with the more difficult items.

a. carte blanche	d. coup d'état	g. de rigueur	j. détente
b. double entendres	e. en masse	h. faux pas	k. debacle
c. façade	f. gauche	i. malaise	l. clichés
			m. hors d'oeuvres

1. The _____ on the front of the Lincoln Memorial is really striking.

2. The students went _____ to the president of the university to protest the higher tuition rates.

3. Before the gala, we were served _____ that were absolutely delicious.

4. I ate so much that I awoke in the night with a feeling of general

   _____.

5. How _____ I felt when I realized that I had overdressed for the occasion.

6. The woman's husband gave her _____ to decorate their home as she saw fit.

7. During the late sixties, green kitchen applicances were _____. Everyone had to have them.

8. Martha made a severe _____ when she commented about the chair-person's hair arrangement. She discovered later that the hair arrangement was really a wig.

9. After the conflict, there was a period of _____ between the two countries that all the people appreciated.

10. The comedian was known for the _____ that he offered his audience one after another.

11. When the generals' _____ failed, they were jailed for their attempt to overthrow the legitimate government.

12. Some students rely on _____ to express their thoughts; since these expressions have been overused, the students' papers are less effective than if they had used more original phrases.

13. The army suffered a great _____ when the soldiers tried to cross the open field.

4-A-2 Search and Discover: Here are some other expressions and words from the French language that we use "as is" in English: *bon appétit, bonbon, filet mignon, boutonniere, boudoir, boutique.* Search your dictionary for several of these for their meanings and pronunciations. Then check the section of your dictionary that lists expressions starting with *bon.* Locate two other expressions and record their meanings and pronunciations in your notebook.

4-A-3 Truth or Falsity: Mark each statement True or False, based on the likelihood of its being true or false.

1. Some people are mortified when they make a faux pas. _____

2. People tend to eat bonbons for breakfast. _____

3. If you were giving a speech and members of your audience walked out en masse, you would be rather satisfied. _____

4. Often there is loss of life associated with a coup d'état. _____

5. When something is de rigueur, one has the freedom to do what one desires.

_____

6. Détente among nations is something to be avoided at all costs. _____

7. When you are given carte blanche in a situation, you can do what you want.

_____

8. If your behavior is a façade that you put on to cover your true feelings, you are acting honestly._____

9. A person whose writings are filled with clichés is considered a great author. _____

10. Given a feeling of general malaise, you should probably take a rest to prevent a more serious malady from developing. _____

11. You probably will feel gauche when you are in a social situation for which you are unprepared. _____

12. Most people are gratified when a debacle occurs. _____

13. A person is generally happy to be the butt of a double entendre. _____

14. Before going to a formal ball, a man pins a boutonniere on his top hat. _____

15. People tend to eat hors d'oeuvres after a meal. _____.

4-A-4 Crossword Puzzle: Complete the puzzle in Figure 4.2 based on your knowledge of the words in this module.

Figure 4.2 Crossword Puzzle of French Words and Expressions

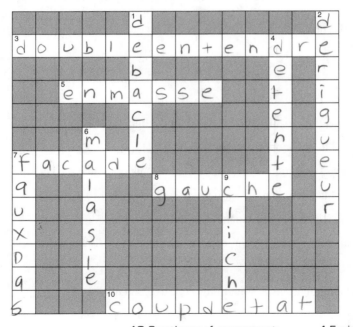

ACROSS

3 Expression with two interpretations, one being a bit off-color (two words)
5 As a group (two words)
7 Side facing outward
8 Awkward
10 Overthrow of government (two words)

DOWN

1 Complete disaster
2 Required by custom (two words)
4 Easing of tension
6 General feeling of being under the weather
7 Social slipup (two words)
9 Overworked expression

Strategy Box 4-B—Abbreviations

As you read, you may encounter abbreviations some of which are very familiar, others of which are more difficult to handle. The clue to abbreviations is the period that typically follows one. Common abbreviations include these: *Dr.* that stands for the word *Doctor; Mr.* that stands for the word *Mister; Hon.* that stands for the title *Honorable.* When writing abbreviations such as these, just remember the period after each.

Less common abbreviations include these: *e.g.,* which stands for the words *for example; i.e.,* which stands for the phrase *in other words; et al.,* which stands for the phrase *and others;* and *etc.,* which stands for the phrase *et cetera* and which means "and so forth."

Since these four abbreviations are used so frequently in college texts, you probably would do well to commit them to memory. In other cases, where you encounter a rather sophisticated abbreviation, your best strategy is to consult a dictionary and record its meaning in your word study notebook or on a word card for future reference.

Word Study Module 4-B—Nouns from the French Language

Nouns are words that we use to name persons, places, or things. We talk about a *connoisseur,* some *debris,* one *liaison.* The italicized words are nouns. The words *a, some,* and *one* are clues that *connoisseur, debris,* and *liaison* serve as nouns. We sometimes call these little words that come along before a noun "noun markers." They mark the noun, or tell you that a noun is coming. Remember, however, that adjectives like to sit before a noun as in the phrase "a wealthy connoisseur." This pattern is typical of the way we handle nouns:

a	wealthy	connoisseur
noun marker	adjective	noun

Pronounce each of the nouns in this module. Then in your mind, create sentences in which you use the words as nouns. Remember that in writing sentences with nouns, you are wise to start with "the" as in "The bourgeoisie. . . ."

✦　1. **bour geoi sie** (bōŏr′ zhwä zē′), *n.,* middle class.

      Contexts: The nobles looked down their noses at members of the bourgeoisie.

✦ 2. **con nois seur** (kon′ ə sûr′), *n., pl.* **connoisseurs,** one with fine taste and knowledge of the finer things of life, especially of the arts.

   Contexts: My friend considered himself a connoisseur of the arts; he was a patron of the opera and attended art show openings.

✦ 3. **de bris** (də brē′), *n.,* litter, discarded waste.

   Contexts: They left debris from their lunch at their picnic site without any thought for those who would come after them.

✦ 4. **de but** (dā byoo′), *n., pl.* **de buts,** first public performance by a performer; beginning event in a career.

   Related word: also a *v.* meaning to make one's first appearance as a performer.

   Contexts: When the tenor made his debut at the Metropolitan Opera, he received a standing ovation.

✦ 5. **en tre pre neur** (on′ trə prə nûr′), *n., pl.* **en tre pre neurs,** person who opens and runs a business often with some monetary risk involved; business tycoon.

   Related word: **en tre pre neu ri al,** *adj.*

   Contexts: I envied my mentor's entrepreneurial skills. He had been a successful entrepreneur for more than thirty years, and he really knew how to run a financially sound business. (Note: the word *tycoon* is from the Japanese language.)

✦ 6. **li ai son** (lē′ ā zon′), *n.,* close relationship, perhaps adulterous, as with an affair; a channel of communication between parties.

   Contexts: I often worried about the kind of liaison that seemed to exist between the two since both were married to other people.
   The governor went on to serve as liaison between the warring parties.

✦ 7. **me lee** (mā′ lā′), *n.,* generally confused fight with hand-to-hand contact, free-for-all.

   Contexts: My friend joined the melee, but I knew that things were getting out of hand. I did not want any part of it.

✦ 8. **mi lieu** (mēl yœ′), *n.,* environment, surroundings.

   Contexts: The milieu to which he was accustomed at home was far different from that which he encountered at college.

✦ 9. **pro té gé** (prō′ tə zhā′), *n., pl.* **pro té gés,** a young male whose career is advanced by someone of greater experience.

   Related word: **pro té gée,** a female whose career is advanced by someone with knowledge in the field.

Contexts: The younger man was fortunate when the noted scientist took him under his wing and made him his protégé. Under the tutelage of his mentor, the man saw his career take off.

✦ 10. **rap port** (ra pôr′), *n.,* feeling a particular closeness as a result of shared interests or qualities.

Contexts: At that time in my teaching career, I developed a rapport with the teacher in the next room. I could talk to him about my problems, and he became my mentor, helping me along by sharing his knowledge.

✦ 11. **ren dez vous** (rän′ dā vōō′), *n.,* prearranged meeting or meeting place.

Contexts: I kept my rendezvous with him against my better judgment, for I knew that he was not an honest man.

One poet wrote, "I have a rendezvous with death. . . ." Since we are mortal, that could be said of all of us.

✦ 12. **rés u mé** (rez′ oo mā′), *n.,* summary of one's background and accomplishments to date, including education and past employment.

Contexts: To get a good job, you typically must prepare a résumé that sets forth such pertinent information as your schooling and past employment.

Word Study Activities Module 4-B— Making Meaning with Nouns

4-B-1 Words in Meaningful Sentence Contexts: From the list, select the noun that best fits into the overall meaning of each sentence. Then write that word in the blank. Use each option only once.

a. bourgeoisie	d. debut	g. melee	j. protégé
b. connoisseur	e. entrepreneurs	h. rendezvous	k. rapport
c. debris	f. liaison	i. milieu	l. résumé

1. I considered the man my _____, for over the years I had done every-thing I could to further his career.

2. I felt very uncomfortable in that _____. I must admit that I am a

   member of the _____. Therefore, when I had to interact with titled lords and ladies at the English court, I did not enjoy it one bit.

3. My father considered himself a/an _____ of the arts. As a result, he would go to the Metropolitan Opera House whenever a new soprano was making her

   _____.

4. A/An _____ took place after dark in the city that was a bit rough-and-tumble, with everyone joining into the confusion. The sanitation workers had to clean up the _____ the next morning.

5. I had a/an _____ scheduled with my friend in the park that night, but she did not keep the date. We had had to keep our _____ secret since she was cohabiting with someone else at the time.

6. My brother submitted his _____ to the personnel department of the business where he hoped to get a job.

7. Bill Gates is one of the wealthiest _____ in the world. He could be called a business tycoon.

8. It was amazing how quickly we established a/an _____ that was to last for our entire lives. We were married for more than 50 years.

4-B-2 Definitional Study: Match the words on the left with those on the right. Write the correct word in each instance on the line. Do the ones you know for sure first. Cross out options as you use them.

1. **bourgeoisie**	_____	a. summary of one's background
2. **connoisseur**	_____	b. member of the middle class
3. **debris**	_____	c. feeling of closeness
4. **debut**	_____	d. free-for-all fight
5. **entrepreneur**	_____	e. business tycoon
6. **liaison**	_____	f. environment
7. **melee**	_____	g. person one helps career-wise
8. **milieu**	_____	h. prearranged meeting or meeting place
9. **rapport**	_____	i. finger snacks served before a meal
10. **rendezvous**	_____	j. close relationship, perhaps adulterous
11. **résumé**	_____	k. first public appearance by a performer
12. **protégé**	_____	l. person who has fine taste, especially in regard to the arts
13. **hors d'oeuvres**	_____	m. scattered waste

4-B-3 Sentence Writing: Select five words from the thirteen studied in this module. Write a sentence with each that clarifies the meaning of the word. Create a word study card with the five to refer to periodically.

1.

2.

3.

4.

5.

Reading with Meaning Module 4-C— Relying on Context Clues in Reading an Historical Account

Read this passage, taking care to make meaning with the boldfaced words as you go along.

The Normans Move to England: An Historical Account

In October, A.D. 1066, the Normans under the leadership of Duke William—who was to become known as William the Conqueror—crossed the English Channel and battled a large Anglo-Saxon force at Hastings in the south of England. Although the Anglo-Saxons outnumbered the Normans, the invaders **decimated** the ranks of the English, killing most of the Anglo-Saxon lords who had taken to the field on that fateful day. The few among the English nobility who escaped slaughter were **subsequently** killed as William went on to crown himself William I of England.

Actually William had some **legitimate** claim on the throne of England. Earlier in the year, Edward, who was king of England, had died childless. His mother was a Norman, which gave the duke of Normandy a **hereditary** claim to the English throne. Before his death, Edward had also acknowledged William as the future king, but the Anglo-Saxon lords had vetoed Edward's last wishes as to who would follow him upon the throne. Their **defiance** of his wishes led to the Battle of Hastings and the **rout,** or the complete defeat, of the Anglo-Saxon forces.

William I was a powerful leader. He not only made himself king but he established his own Norman lords as the new nobility, or ruling class, of England. William **solidified** his position by erecting castles across the land and placing his Norman vassals (followers) as overlords. William was also careful to maintain large tracts of land for himself and to require his vassals to swear an oath of **fealty** to him as their one and only true king. By *fealty* is meant the loyalty of a vassal to a feudal lord or, more generally today, faithfulness. Doing this, William established the monarchy of England at the top of a **hierarchy,** with all lesser lords pledging their **allegiance** to the king.

Throughout much of this period of history, **ensconced** behind the walls of their castles, the Normans spoke their native French **tongue** to one another. Meanwhile in the countryside, the lesser Anglo-Saxon vassals and serfs continued to speak an early form of English—a tongue that at this point had a very limited vocabulary compared to today.

Because some **intermingling** of the peoples occurred, however, the Anglo-Saxons began to **assimilate** French words into their language, and vice versa. Words that entered English from the French at this time included ones such as these: *reign, majestic, courage, coward, covenant, cousin, court, allow.* At the same time such Anglo-Saxon words as *knife, knave, north, clam, climb, cow, cock, coast* continued to serve as the major media of communication among the native Anglo-Saxons.

Thus the Norman invasion had two major outcomes: the **ascension** into leadership positions in England of the Normans and the introduction of French words into the Anglo-Saxon **lexicon,** or vocabulary. Additionally, the invasion gave rise to a rule of government established by William the Conqueror—that lesser lords owed allegiance to their king, who was the ultimate lord. This rule resulted in a strong central monarchy that would control most of England for many years. See Figure 4.3 for a summary of some events in English history that were to have an influence on the language.

Word Study Activities Module 4-C— Relying on Context Clues

4-C-1 Talking Points: Talk about these questions and then answer based on the selection.

1. How does an historical account differ from a legend?

2. How does an historical account differ from a myth?

3. What kinds of words tended to come into the English language from the French-speaking Normans after 1066? (Study the words given in the selection.) Why do you think these kinds of words were assimilated?

4. Why is violence against other people (as communicated in such words as *decimated* and *slaughter*) a part of so much of human history?

5. Why do some people such as William the Conqueror of the past and similar people of today seek power over others? How do you view power in your own life?

A TIME LINE OF IMPORTANT LINGUISTIC EVENTS
IN THE HISTORY OF ENGLISH

	Angles, Saxons, and Jutes wandered in northern Europe.	Ancient English borrowed words from Latin.
A.D. 449	Angles, Saxons, and Jutes moved into Britain, pushing the Celts into Wales and portions of Ireland and Scotland.	English borrowed words from Celtic.
A.D. 597	Anglo-Saxons were converted to Christianity by Latin-speaking missionaries and learned the Roman or Latin alphabet.	English borrowed words from Latin.
Old English **A.D. 866**	Anglo-Saxons opposed the invading Vikings from the North.	English borrowed words from Vikings.
1066	Normans (French) invaded, conquered, ruled Britain, and gradually became English.	English borrowed words from Old French.
Middle English	English-speaking people began to make contact with peoples speaking other languages.	English began to borrow words from a multitude of languages.
1500	English-speaking people rediscovered the classical languages, Latin and Greek.	English borrowed words from Latin and Greek.
	English-speaking people brought their language to North America (as well as to India, Australia, New Zealand, South Africa).	English borrowed heavily from other languages: American Indian, Dutch, German, French, Portuguese, Spanish, Japanese, Chinese, Hebrew, Malay, and so forth.
Modern English **1700**		

Figure 4.3 A Time Line Showing the Development of English. (*Source:* Dorothy Grant Hennings, *Communication in Action: Teaching Literature-based Language Arts,* 7th ed., © 2000. Reprinted by permission of Houghton Mifflin Publishers, Boston, MA.)

4-C-2 Context Clues: Using clues embedded in the context, predict the meanings of these words. For each, record a brief definition (simply a word or two in most cases) based on its use in this historical account.

1. decimate/decimated

2. subsequently

3. legitimate

4. hereditary

5. defiance

6. rout

7. solidify/solidified

8. fealty

9. hierarchy

10. allegiance

11. ensconce/ensconced

12. tongue

13. intermingle/intermingling

14. assimilate/assimilated

15. ascension

16. lexicon

4-C-4 Definitional Study: Pair up the words with the appropriate definitions. Write out the correct word in each case. Use the process of elimination.

1. **allegiance**	M	a.	loyalty, as that of a vassal to a lord
2. **ascension**	D	b.	faithfulness, or loyalty, in general
3. **assimilate**	A	c.	language
4. **decimate**	N	d.	rising up to a higher position
5. **defiance**	g	e.	by birth
6. **ensconced**	O	f.	total defeat
7. **fealty**	b	g.	bold resistance
8. **hereditary**	e	h.	ranked series
9. **hierarchy**	h	i.	after that
10. **intermingle**	k	j.	rightful
11. **legitimate**	j	k.	take into and be made part of
12. **lexicon**	L	l.	vocabulary, word bank or pool
13. **rout**	f	m.	come together
14. **solidify**	P	n.	completely kill off or destroy
15. **subsequently**	I	o.	settled in a secure place
16. **tongue**	C	p.	make more solid or secure

Confusing Words—*Principal* and *Principle*

Some students confuse the words *principal* and *principle*. One reason for some of the confusion is that we can trace both to the same Latin root—*prim-,* meaning "first." As a result, both words start with the identical syllables. What is the difference in meaning?

Use *principal* as either an adjective or noun. As an adjective, *principal* means "main or first in importance." You can talk about your principal reason, your principal residence, your principal concern. As a noun, *principal* means "leader of a school" or "amount of money invested and on which interest is calculated." You can talk about the principal of your local high school as well as the principal you have in your account at the local bank.

In contrast, use *principle* as a noun to mean "underlying truth or belief." You can talk about the principles in which you believe, about principles guiding your action, and about a person of high principles. You can also talk about the principle behind something—the underlying truth. As you can see, the word *principle* relates to some extent to ethical behavior. A person who is highly ethical is one who has strong principles of right and wrong.

Apply these distinctions in these contexts: Write the appropriate word in each blank.

1. John's son was the _____ recipient of the scholarship award. He got the largest amount.

2. Bruce told me to adhere to my _____ and do what I felt was right.

3. His father was the _____ in the local elementary school.

Prefixes and Other Introductory Elements That Matter

5

Word Elements—Prefixes That Tell "No," "When," "Where," or "More"

◆◆◆

Objectives: In Chapter 5, you will develop the ability to

- explain the way prefixes function by using as examples the prefixes *un-* and *dis-* on such words as *uninterested* and *disinterested;*

- interpret prefixes that tell "no": *a-, de-, dis-, in-, non-, un-, contra-*, as listed in Table 5.1;

- comprehend and use the following words featured in Module 5-A:

counteract	disqualify	inadvertent	nondescript
contradict	illegitimate	irresistible	unrelenting
disparity	impartial	noncommittal	unscrupulous
incognito (*power word*)			

- recognize and attach meaning to the base roots *cogni-* (to know) and *dict-* (to say) as featured in Module 5-A;

- recognize and interpret words that begin with prefixes that indicate "when," "where," or "more": *pre-, post-, ante-, inter-, intra-, trans-, sub-, circum-, ultra-*, as listed in Table 5.2;

- comprehend and use the following words featured in Module 5-B:

anteroom	intramural	preliminary	subterranean
circumnavigate	posthumous	premature	transformation
intervene	postscript	subservient	ultrasensitive

- recognize and attach meaning to the base root *terra-* (earth) as featured in Module 5-B;

- use context clues to figure out word meanings as you encounter unfamiliar words in context;

- explain how acronyms such as *posh* came into the English language; and

- distinguish between the words *illicit* and *elicit* and between *uninterested* and *disinterested.*

Words are, of course, the most powerful drug used by mankind.

—Rudyard Kipling, a speech, 1923

◆◆

Interesting Words to Think About—*Uninterested*, *Disinterested*, and Other Ways to Just Say "No!"

In the most recent past, an American First Lady proposed "Just say, 'No!'" as the slogan for the war against drugs. In the English language, we have numerous ways to change words to say, "No!" Think, for example, about the common adjective *uninterested,* which we all know means "without an interest in, or a positive feeling toward." The Old English prefix *un-* carries the "no" message. It means "the opposite of, not, lacking in" as seen in such adjectives as *unalterable, uncritical,* and *unmarried*—not alterable, not critical, and not married. It can also be used to mean "the reversal of some act" as in the verbs *unwind* and *unlock.* Most dictionaries list hundreds of words built with the prefix *un-.*

Another way to say "No!" is with the prefix *dis-.* It carries the meaning "no" in the sense of "being apart from" or "being in a different direction from." A disinterested person in a dispute is one who has nothing personal to lose or gain by the outcome. Sometimes we call a disinterested person "a third party" and ask him or her to **mediate,** or help to settle, a dispute. A judge should be a disinterested person in a court case; on the other hand, he or she should not be uninterested in the proceedings. If uninterested, the judge would let his or her mind wander, which would be unfair (not fair!) to the defendant.

The prefix *dis-* has two other forms—*dif-* and *di-,* as seen in *differ* and *difference, divorce* and *diversion.* Can you see the idea of "apartness" in these words? Can you also hypothesize, or predict, when we use the *dif-* and *di-* forms of the prefix instead of the *dis-* form?

Other prefixes that say "No!" in some way or form are

- *non-,* which adds a strong meaning of "not" to words, especially to nouns, adverbs, and adjectives, as in *nonconformist, nonperformer, nonentity;*
- *in-,* which adds the idea of "not" to words, especially to adjectives and adverbs, as in *insincere, indecisive,* and *inhospitable;*

- *de-*, which adds the idea of reversing an action as in *defrost* and *desensitize;* and
- *counter-* (or *contra-*), which adds the meaning "against" as in *counteract* and *counter-productive.*

Collaborative Search and Discover

- Search your dictionary for words with the prefixes *un-, dis-, dif-, de-, in-,* and *counter-.* Select two or three words that rely on each of these prefixes, and in your word study notebook record the words on prefix webs as demonstrated in Figure 5.1. Be ready to share some sample sentences using the words as part of class interaction.
- What is the meaning of the word *disassociate?* of the word *unassociated?* Check a dictionary for the distinction between the two and record your findings in your notebook.
- What is the meaning of the boldfaced word *mediate* as used in the second paragraph of the selection you just read? Circle the context clue that supplies its meaning. Record the word and your definition in your word study notebook.

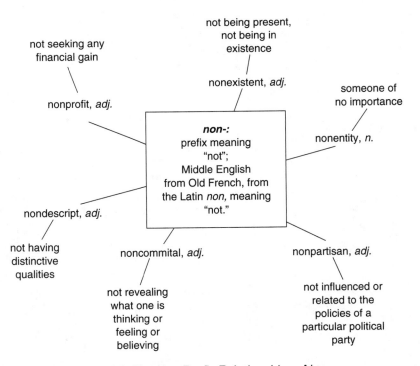

Figure 5.1 A Web Showing Prefix Relationships: *Non-*

Strategy Box 5-A—Prefix Awareness, Part I

A **prefix** is a syllable or syllables attached at the beginning of a word or a root. In contrast, a suffix is attached at the end of a word or a root. You may find it useful to think of words as having a design similar to a hamburger. The top roll represents the prefix on a word; the meat represents the root; and the suffix represents the bottom roll. On some words, one or both of the rolls may be missing. On some words, there may be more than one roll, or suffix, at the end. See the representative equations given next:

Prefix	+	Root	+	Suffix	= Word	or
Prefix	+	Root	+	Suffix + Suffix	= Word	or
Prefix	+	Root			= Word	or
		Root	+	Suffix	= Word.	

A particular prefix may have several meanings, but those meanings are relatively stable and stay the same regardless of the root to which the prefix is attached. For example, think about the word *prefix* itself. The beginning syllable (*pre-*) is a very common word starter in the English language; most dictionaries give the meanings of *pre-* as follows:

pre- (Middle English, from Old French and Latin)

1. earlier than, prior to, or before, as in *prehistoric;*

2. preparatory, as in *premedical;*

3. in advance or beforehand, as in *prepayment.*

Although most dictionaries supply the three meanings you just read, you can see that all three meanings are related to the idea of "before." As a result, if you were to see *pre-* at the beginning of an unfamiliar word, you might be able to unlock the meaning based on your ability to connect the new word to the prefix that you know, especially if you get help from context clues and from the root (if you happen to recognize it).

Keeping alert for prefixes can be a useful word-study strategy because sometimes hundreds of words incorporate a particular prefix. Here, for instance, are just a few *pre-* words: *preface, premature, prelude, prenatal, premix, premonition, preliminary.* You can find more examples in your dictionary.

The three steps in your prefix-awareness strategy are as follows:

• Step 1: Study the beginning syllable or syllables of a multisyllable word to see if you recognize a prefix you know. If you find a prefix, tell yourself the meaning of it.

- Step 2: Strip the prefix from the rest of the word and see if you recognize any part of the remaining word. If you do, review the meaning.
- Step 3: Connect the meaning of the prefix to the meaning of the rest of the word.

Let's apply the strategy. Think about the word *prenatal*. Consider the prefix *pre-* (meaning "before") at the start. Strip off the prefix and you see *natal*. You may know that *nat-* is a Latin root that has something to do with birth. Connect the two meanings: *Prenatal* means "before birth."

Table 5.1 provides a table of commonly used prefixes, the meanings of the prefixes, and sample words. Use it as a reference as you wrestle meaning from words.

Collaborative Search and Discover

- To help you become more aware of the prefixes on words, use a highlighter to mark the prefix on each of the sample words in Table 5.1.
- Search your dictionary with a friend for an additional word that relies on each of the prefixes listed in Table 5.1. Add the words to the table.

Table 5.1   Useful Prefixes That Say "No" or Reverse the Action

Prefix	Meaning	Examples of Words
a-, an-	without, not	asexual, atypical, amoral, anarchy
de-	reverse action, away	defrost, demystify, desensitize, deduct
dis-, dif-, di-	not, apart	dissatisfied, disorganized, different, divert
in-, il-, ir-, im-	not	inappropriate, invisible, illegal, irrational, immune, impossible
non-	not	nonproductive, nonessential, nonsense
un-	not	unlikely, unnoticeable, unreliable
contra-, counter-	against	contrary, contradict, counterproductive, countermand

Word Study Module 5-A—Prefixes That Say "No!"

Pronounce each featured word. Then think how you would use it in a sentence.

✦ 1. **un re lent ing** (un ri len′ ting), *adj.,* not yielding, especially to feelings of compassion; without mercy; not slacking or letting up in one's determination.

> *Related words:* **un re lent ing ly**, *adv.;* **re lent**, *v.;* **re lent less**, *adj.;* **re lent less ly**, *adv.* (Note: Interestingly, although the verb *relent* means to "become less harsh," the adjective *relentless* means "without pity, unyielding" and is a close synonym of *unrelenting.*)

> *Contexts:* The crusader was unrelenting in his determination that the people who had committed the crime had to be caught and punished. He worked unrelentingly for years in pursuit of justice. His wife also worked relentlessly in the cause of justice. Only on his deathbed did he relent and forgive his enemies.

✦ 2. **un scru pu lous** (un skrū′ pyə ləs), *adj.,* not careful about what is right or wrong action, unprincipled, without conscience or scruples.

> *Related words:* **scru pu lous**, *adj.;* **scru ples**, *n.;* **scru pu lous ly**, *adv.;* **un scru pu lous ly**, *adv.*

> *Contexts:* That contractor is unscrupulous in his business dealings. In contrast, his brother is scrupulously honest.
> A person who is without scruples is a person to stay away from. Would you pick as a friend someone who is scrupulous in her behavior or someone who is unscrupulous?

✦ 3. **dis par i ty** (dis par′ ə tē), *n.,* lack of equality or similarity between; difference; or literally, a lack of parity. (*Parity* means a close correspondence between with regard to value, state, or position.)

> *Related words:* **dis pa rate**, *adj.;* **par i ty**, *n.*

> *Contexts:* I was bothered by the disparity between his two statements; the statements differed in important respects.
> I really was seeking parity so that all parties in the case would know that they had been treated similarly.

✦ 4. **dis qual i fy** (dis kwol′ ə fī), *v.,* make unable to do something; declare as unfit to participate.

> *Related words:* **dis qual i fi ca tion**, *n.;* **qualify**, *v.*

> *Contexts:* If an athlete is on drugs, he or she is liable to be disqualified from participating in sports competitions. I was unaware of her disqualification, and so I allowed her to participate, which was really unfair to others.

✦ 5. **in ad vert ent** (in′ əd vûrt′ nt), *adj.,* not on purpose, by chance; unintentional; not attentive, careless.

Related words: **in ad vert ent ly,** *adj.;* **in ad vert ence,** *n.*

Contexts: The cook inadvertently left key components out of the cake; the result was an inedible blob that was unfit to eat. Through her inadvertent behavior, she spoiled the dinner party.

6. **im par tial** (im pär′ shəl), *adj.,* showing no greater favor to one side over another; not partial or biased in any way.

Related words: **par tial,** *adj.;* **im par tial ly,** *adv.;* **im par ti al i ty,** *n.*

Contexts: The person who makes the final decision must be impartial. What we look for in a judge or a mediator is impartiality. We don't want someone who is partial to one side, for such partiality would result in an unjust verdict.

7. **ir re sist i ble** (ir′ i zis′ tə bəl), *adj.,* too strong to be withstood or resisted; overwhelming in its power.

Related words: **ir re sist i bly,** *adv.;* **ir re sis ti ble ness,** *n.*

Contexts: The urge to eat an ice cream sundae was irresistible; I just had to do it. Ice cream has always been irresistibly delicious to me. Its irresistibleness is something that very thin people cannot understand.

8. **il le git i mate** (il′ i jit′ ə mit), *adj.,* not according to the rules or the law; not legitimate; improper; born of unwed parents.

Related words: **il le git i mate ly,** *adv.;* **il le git i ma cy,** *n.;* **le git i macy,** *n.;* **le git i mate,** *adj.*

Contexts: His claim to the throne was illegitimate. He had no legitimate rights at all. No one questioned his illegitimacy until he needed to document his claim.

◆◆◆

Power Words

in cog ni to (in kog′ ni tō′), *adj.* and *adv.,* Italian word from the Latin, meaning "having one's identity hidden or disguised."

Related word: **cog ni zant,** *adj.,* aware, fully knowledgeable about.
Contexts: He traveled incognito so that no one would recognize him.
     Barbara was cognizant of the fact that she owed money to her mother.

(**Note:** Make word cards with these two words that are derived from the Latin root *cogni-,* meaning "to know." Perhaps add other words from the same root. Check your word cards from time to time to reinforce your familiarity with these words.)

◆◆◆

9. **non de script** (non′ də skript), *adj.*, not displaying any particularly distinguishable characteristics.

> *Contexts:* He was a nondescript person who generally faded into the background; there was nothing memorable about him at all.

10. **non com mit tal** (non′ kə mit′ l), *adj.*, without saying yes or no; "on the fence."

> *Related word:* **non com mit tal ly,** *adv.*

> *Contexts:* My friend's answer was so noncommittal that I did not know whether she really wanted to go with me to the party. She replied noncommittally, keeping her options open.

11. **coun ter act** (koun′ tər akt′), *v.*, literally, act against; act to neutralize another action.

> *Related words:* **coun ter ac tion,** *n.;* **coun ter ac tive,** *adj.*

> *Contexts:* I knew I had to do something quickly to counteract what she had done. My counteractive behavior worked; no one realized she had made a faux pas. Such counteraction generally must take place quickly if it is to succeed.

12. **con tra dict** (kon′ trə dikt′), *v.*, say that the words of another person are wrong; disagree with.

> *Related words:* **con tra dic tor y,** *adj.;* **con tra dic tion,** *n.*

> *Contexts:* The man was embarrassed when his wife contradicted him in front of his boss. At that point he ignored her contradictory statement, but when they arrived home, he told his wife that he did not appreciate her contradiction of him in such a sensitive situation.

◆◆◆

Highlighted Word Elements

contra- or **counter-,** a prefix from the Latin meaning "contrary or opposite."

Words with the element: *countermand, countercharge, contrary.*

dic- or **dict-,** a root, or base, from Latin meaning "say."

Words with the element: *predict, edict, diction.*

◆◆◆

Word Study Activities Module 5-A— Making Meaning with Prefixes

5-A-1 Words in Meaningful Sentence Contexts: From the list, select the word that best fits into the overall meaning of each sentence. Then write that word in the blank. Use each option only once. Use your Know-for-sure/Process-of-elimination test-taking strategy.

a. counteract   d. disqualify   g. inadvertent   j. nondescript
b. contradict   e. illegitimate   h. irresistible   k. unrelenting
c. disparity   f. impartial   i. noncommittal   l. unscrupulous
                                                     m. incognito

1. I was fearful that the coach would _____ me in one of the early stages of the competition.

2. When I asked her where I stood, she gave me a/an _____ answer that left me uncertain as to where I stood.

3. Amazingly, the prize went to a/an _____ person who had no distinctive characteristics.

4. I worked quickly to _____ my early losses, but to no avail. I lost anyway.

5. The man's claims to the child were _____. He had forged papers to make himself appear to be the real father.

6. His _____ behavior got him nowhere. The judge perceived what the man was trying to do and turned down his request.

7. The _____ between the rich of the community and the poor became more obvious as the days went on and the depression continued.

8. The woman's mistake was _____. She did not realize what she was doing.

9. The reporters' attention to the woman's indiscretion was _____. They wrote about it day after day, month after month.

10. Because my sister and I needed a/an _____ opinion, we went to our father for his advice. My father was always scrupulously fair and never took sides.

11. "I hate to _____ you," my mother said, "but that is not the way it happened."

12. The rock star traveled _____ so that his fans would not recognize him.

13. Myra had a/an _____ desire to buy a new gown for the end-of-the-semester ball. It was something that she just had to do—perhaps to reward herself for her hard work.

5-A-2 Definitional Study: Star the word or expression that best defines each of these words.

1. **noncommittal**   a. open   b. on the fence   c. up front
                       d. related to the communist party

2. **counteract**   act to   a. neutralize another act
                     b. penalize another person   c. ignore another act
                     d. overcome an immense disadvantage

3. **impartial**   a. allowing only one part per person
                    b. dividing a whole into several parts
                    c. showing no greater favor toward one party
                    d. favoring a particular side in a dispute

4. **unrelenting**   a. unyielding   b. unreliable   c. unpleasant
                      d. undesirable

5. **disparity**   a. state of despair   b. state of disrepair
                    c. without anyone knowing   d. lack of equality

6. **illegitimate**   a. not light   b. not according to law
                       c. not connected to the human leg   d. not intimate

7. **inadvertent**   a. not an adversary   b. not in an advertisement
                      c. not on purpose   d. not verifiable

8. **disqualify**   a. declare unqualified   b. declare as unpleasant
                     c. declare a truce   d. declare an intermission

9. **unscrupulous**   a. operating without a sense of right or wrong
                       b. operating with carefulness
                       c. inconsiderate
                       d. without hope

10. **nondescript**   a. not appropriate   b. not important
                       c. not showing distinguishing characteristics
                       d. not written in clear handwriting

11. **contradict**   a. agree precisely with   b. agree to some extent with
                      c. remain neutral in regard to   d. disagree with

12. **irresistible**   a. inconclusive   b. too strong to overcome
                        c. very nice   d. indecisive

13. **incognito**   a. with hidden identity   b. with great intelligence
                     c. with high awareness   d. with negative effects

14. **cognizant**   a. unaware   b. highly aware
                     c. unidentified   d. without thought

5-A-3 Sentence Writing with Related Words: In your word study notebook, write a sentence with each of these words. It is acceptable to write a sentence using two, three, or more of the words at one time: *legitimate, scrupulous, qualify, inadvertently, contradictory, irresistibly.*

5-A-4 Prefix Review: Study the highlighted words. Put a slash between the prefix and the root of the word. Then, based on your knowledge of the prefixes studied so far, add another sentence to each that continues the thought and clarifies the meaning of the high-lighted word.

1. The boy decided to remain a **nonparticipant** in the event. He decided to

2. The dancers moved in a **counterclockwise** direction. They

3. I spent a most **unproductive** afternoon in the library. I

4. His voice was practically **inaudible.** I

5. The IRS sent me a letter saying they were **disallowing** my biggest deduction. This meant that

Strategy Box 5-B—Prefix Awareness, Part II

A prefix not only can add the meaning of "not" to a word or root but it can add the meaning of "where," "when," or "more." Study the sample words in Table 5.2 and with a colored marker, highlight the prefix in each. As you do, pronounce each word, emphasizing the prefix in each case, and think about the meaning it adds to the root or base word. In this way you will build prefix awareness.

Table 5.2   Useful Prefixes That Tell "Where," "When," or "More"

Prefix	Meaning	Examples of Words
pre-, pro-	before	pre-dinner, preliminary, previous, prologue
post-	after	postwar, postoperative, postpone
ante-	before	antecedent, antedate, antechamber
inter-	between, among	interstate, intercept, interfere
intra-	within	intramural, intrastate, intravenous
trans-	across	transcontinental, transparent, transaction
sub-	under	submarine, submerge, subjugate, subservient
circum-	around	circumnavigate, circumference, circumvent
ultra-	beyond, on the far side of, excessive	ultrasonic, ultraviolet, ultraconservative

Word Study Module 5-B—
Prefixes That Tell "Where," "When," or "Very"

Pronounce each featured word. Then think how you would use the word in a sentence.

◆ 1. **pre lim i nar y** (pri lim′ ə ner′ ē), *adj.,* coming before the main event and generally leading into something of greater importance. ~threshold~

> ***Contexts:*** During his preliminary study, the historian uncovered informa-
> tion that laid the groundwork for the steps he would take next.

◆ 2. **pre ma ture** (prē′ mə tyoor′), *adj.,* too soon, before the appropriate time.

> ***Related word:*** **pre ma ture ly,** *adv.*

> ***Contexts:*** My happiness was premature; I later learned that rather than
> being the one chosen as the main candidate, I had been disqualified.

◆ 3. **post hu mous** (pos′ chə məs), *adj.,* happening after death.

> ***Related word:*** **post hu mous ly,** *adv.*

> ***Contexts:*** The award was granted to the author posthumously; as a result, he
> never knew that his work had been honored. There is something sad about a
> posthumous award: to work so hard and never to know that one has been recog-
> nized. The Nobel Peace Prize is never awarded posthumously.

◆ 4. **post script** (pōst′ skript), *n.,* something added at the end; an after-thought added
at the end of a letter and sometimes indicated by the abbreviation P.S.

> ***Contexts:*** The posthumous award was almost like a postscript—a little
> something added at the end.

◆ 5. **an te room** (an′ ti room′), *n.,* a small room that leads into a larger room.

> ***Contexts:*** I had to wait in the anteroom before being admitted to the throne
> room for my audience with the king.

◆ 6. **in ter vene** (in′ tər vēn′), *v.,* come between, especially between people to help
settle a dispute.

> ***Related word:*** **in ter ven tion,** *n.*

> ***Contexts:*** The president attempted to intervene as tension mounted between
> the neighboring countries. However, her intervention proved unsuccessful.

◆ 7. **in tra mur al** (in′ trə myūr′ əl), *adj.,* inside; carried on within a school, as is the
case of intramural sports program.

> ***Contexts:*** Few students attended the intramural games in which different
> classes played against one another; many more came out for games in which the
> school team played intermurally.

◆ 8. **trans for ma tion** (trans′ fər mā′ shən), *n.,* change in some respect; change into a
different form.

Related words: **trans form**, *v.;* **trans form a ble**, *adj.*

Contexts: Her transformation was total; I could not recognize the nondescript person she had been in this speaker who talked so dynamically. I do not know how she had transformed herself so completely.

 9. **sub ser vi ent** (səb sûr′ vē ənt), *adj.,* obedient to the wishes and commands of another; submissive.

Related words: **sub ser vi ent ly**, *adv.;* **ser vile**, *adj.*

Contexts: As a housemaid at the turn of the twentieth century, the woman had a subservient position in the household. To have to be servile really bothered her because by nature she was a forceful person.

10. **sub ter ra ne an** (sub′ tə rā′ nē ən), *adj.,* literally, under the ground; figuratively, hidden, carried out secretly.

Related word: **sub ter ra ne ous**, *adj.*

Contexts: As a miner, he carved out subterranean passages in beds of coal day after day. He was literally a subterraneous person, one who rarely saw the light of day.

I could not follow him into the subterranean depths of his mind; his reasoning was confused.

◆◆◆

Highlighted Word Element

sub-, a prefix from Latin meaning "under, below."

Words with the element: *subhuman, subsidiary, submerge.*

terra-, a base from Latin meaning "earth."

Words or expressions with the element: *terrace, territory, terra firma.*

◆◆◆

11. **cir cum nav i gate** (sûr′ kəm nav′ ə gāt), *adj.,* sail completely around.

Related word: **cir cum nav i ga tion**, *n.*

Contexts: Magellan's ship made the first circumnavigation of the earth. It was Magellan's dream to circumnavigate the earth, but he died before completing the task.

12. **ul tra sen si tive** (ul′ trə sen′ sə tiv), *adj.,* affected by something beyond what is normal.

Related word: **sen si tive**, *adj.*

Contexts: Because the child's skin was ultrasensitive to ultraviolet light, she could not sit in the sunshine.

Word Study Activities Module 5-B— Making Meaning with Prefixes

5-B-1 Words in Meaningful Sentence Contexts: From the list, select the word that best fits into the overall meaning of each sentence. Then write that word in the blank. Use each option only once.

a. anteroom	d. intramural	g. preliminary	j. subterranean
b. circumnavigate	e. posthumous	h. premature	k. transformation
c. intervene	f. postscript	i. subservient	l. ultrasensitive

1. I spent two hours waiting in the doctor's _____ before being admitted to his office.

2. I do not consider myself to be a/an _____ person, but that truly annoyed me. My time is valuable, too.

3. I am not accustomed to having a/an _____ role, so when I took a new job where I was low-man-on-the-totem-pole, I had to be careful how I behaved.

4. The dentist's _____ examination indicated that I did not need root canal work, but x-rays suggested a different outcome.

5. The _____ I would like to see written at the end of my life is "She thought of others before she thought of herself."

6. When I retire, I hope to _____ the earth aboard a luxury cruise ship.

7. John was active in _____ sports. He enjoyed the competition between classes within his college.

8. The _____ of Mary from a girl who had no interest in learning to someone who loved to read was almost unbelievable. Going to college was what caused the change in her.

9. The _____ recognition given the man saddened his family. "If only he had had this recognition during his lifetime," they said.

10. I did not want to _____ between husband and wife, but someone had to give them some advice.

11. The young woman's hair was a/an _____ gray because of an hereditary characteristic she carried in her genes. The woman complained continuously about going gray so early in her life.

12. When I visited in Bermuda, I had a/an _____ adventure. I toured some underground caves that were glorious to behold.

5-B-2 Crossword Puzzle: Complete the crossword puzzle in Figure 5.2 with the words you have been studying in this module. If you have trouble, use the list of words in Activity 5-B-1 to guide you.

5-B-3 Word Search: In your dictionary, locate words that begin with these elements: *ante-, circum-, inter-, intra-, post-, pre-, sub-, trans-, ultra-*. Also find words that include *terra-, dict-, cogni-*. Record your words here. Include a sentence with each word as well as a brief definition. Do this collaboratively with a friend. Avoid words you have studied in this book.

1. *ante-*

2. *circum-*

3. *inter-*

4. *intra-*

5. *post-* (Note: Don't use words in which *post-* relates to sending or to the postal system.)

6. *pre-*

7. *sub-*

8. *trans-*

9. *ultra-*

10. *terra-*

11. *dict-*

12. *cogni-*

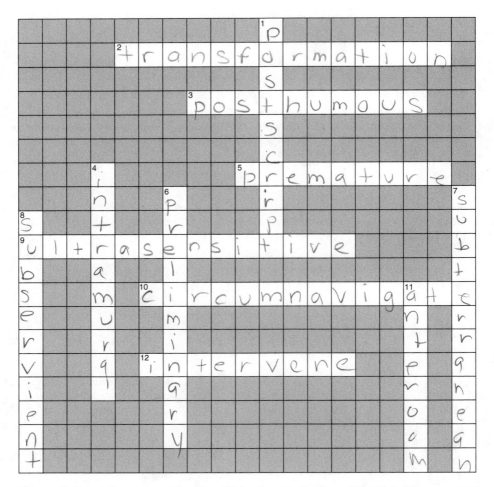

Figure 5.2   A Crossword Puzzle of Words with Prefixes That Tell When and Where

ACROSS

2 Complete change
3 After death
5 Coming before the normal time
9 Affected way beyond what is normal
10 Sail around the earth

12 Come between disputing parties to help find a solution

DOWN

1 A line or two written and added at the end
4 Within the walls of a building

6 Coming before what is really important
7 Under the earth
8 Servile
11 Small room before the main one

Reading with Meaning Module 5-C—Using Context Clues to Figure Out Unfamiliar Words; Learning about Acronyms

Read the following selection. Use the context in which the boldfaced words appear to figure out their meanings.

Posh—*An Acronym and How It Became Part of English*

In recent days, cruise lines have been bringing out larger and larger vessels with more and more **amenities.** The result is that prices for a one-week cruise have been going down and cruising has become the vacation-of-choice for many Americans. Whereas in the past the typical cruiser was a retired senior citizen, now younger people are **swarming** aboard for their week in the sun.

The new ships are **veritable** titans, with two or three swimming pools, four or five hot tubs, a fitness area, a beauty salon, three or four dining rooms—some with 24-hour dining, pizzerias, show lounges and a full theater, cabins with picture windows or sliding-glass doors that lead to **verandahs,** extravagant suites, and a medical facility. Of course, each cabin has its own private bathroom, the ships are air-conditioned throughout, and passengers control the temperature in their staterooms. To say the least, the accommodations are posh.

This is in contrast to ships of earlier days. First, the older ships were considerably smaller; even the *Titanic* was only a third the size of one of these new, large vessels, some of which exceed 100,000 tons. Second, the older ships were not air-conditioned; the cabins had portholes that could open but in high seas had to remain closed. You can imagine how unbearably hot some of those accommodations became, especially those in the **bowels** of the ship.

Because of the **oppressive** heat, English travelers heading east to India through the Mediterranean Sea, the Suez Canal, and the Red Sea reserved cabins on the port, or left side of ships. The **port** side had a northern **exposure** as a ship sailed eastward. As a result, cabins located there received fewer direct sun rays and were cooler than those on the right, or **starboard,** side.

On the trip westward from India to England, however, just the opposite was true. The most favored cabins—and for that matter the priciest ones—were on the starboard side because as the ship sailed westward, those cabins had the northern exposure. The best cabins, too, were located on the upper decks where the likelihood of getting fresh air from the outside was greatest.

And that brings us to the word *posh,* which today means "elegant or fashionable." *Posh* came into the language as the term travelers used to describe how they chose cabins aboard an India-bound ship and on the return trip. The saying was "**P**ort-side **O**ut, **S**tarboard **H**ome!" or simply POSH. The word *posh* is actually an **acronym.** An *acronym* is a word formed from the initial letter or syllables of each of the parts of the original phrase.

Word Study Activities Module 5-C—
Using Context Clues; Learning about Antonyms

5-C-1 Search and Discover: Some acronyms appear at first to be abbreviations for they are composed of the initial letters of a series of words. However, they are acronyms if you pronounce them in syllables rather than letter by letter. For example, FBI is an abbreviation. UNESCO is an acronym pronounced ū′nəs′ cō. Use a dictionary to find the origin of these acronyms: *radar, sonar, snafu.* Record your findings in your notebook.

5-C-2 Definitional Study: Write the word from the left column on the line in front of the word or phrase that best defines it.

1. **amenities** (ə men′ i tēz)   _____   a. position in relation to the sun

2. **swarming** (swôr′ ming)   _____   b. deep interior

3. **veritable** (ver′ i tə bəl)   _____   c. attractive features

4. **verandah** (və ran′ də)   _____   d. elegant, fashionable

5. **bowels** (bou′ əlz)   _____   e. word formed from initial letters of a set of words

6. **oppressive** (ə pres′ iv)   _____   f. right side of a ship

7. **port** (pôrt)   _____   g. moving in a group

8. **exposure** (ik spō zhər)   _____   h. balcony that is usually roofed

9. **starboard** (stär′ bərd)   _____   i. causing extreme discomfort

10. **posh** (posh)   _____   j. left side of a ship

11. **acronym** (ak′ rə nim′)   _____   k. true

5-C-3 Using Words in Meaningful Contexts: From this list, in each case select the word that makes the most meaning. Use each word only once.

a. acronym	d. exposure	g. posh	j. verandah
b. amenities	e. oppressive	h. starboard	k. veritable
c. bowels	f. port	i. swarming	

1. The young woman and man relaxed on their _____, enjoying the afternoon sun. Inside their room, which was not air-conditioned, however, the heat was _____.

2. The bees were _____, looking for a place to build a new hive.

3. I like things to be _____, really elegant in all respects.

4. The _____ WAC stands for Women's Army Corp.

5. I booked a cabin on the _____ side as the ship was heading east and I wanted a northern _____. Coming home in a westward direction, I booked a cabin on the _____ side.

6. Deep in the subterranean _____ of the earth, a group of miners worked to extract coal.

7. My friend is a/an _____ fount of knowledge; he seems to know something about everything.

8. The hotel offers many _____, including a pool, restaurant, and lounge. It is not exactly a posh place, but I like it nonetheless.

Confusing Words—*Illicit* and *Elicit*

In- is a prefix that adds a negative message to a root. Before roots that start with the letter *l*, *in-* becomes *il-*.

With that in mind, you can figure out the meaning of the word *illicit* (i lis′ it). *Illicit*, which generally works as an adjective, comes from the Latin *licere*—meaning "to be permitted." With the prefix *il-* up front, you can predict the meaning of *illicit* as "not permitted by law or custom." Illicit acts are ones forbidden by law or custom. To act illicitly is to do something that is unacceptable.

Confusion can enter when someone says that he or she wants to elicit a response from you. The person pronounces *elicit* exactly as he or she would pronounce *illicit*. What's up?

Elicit and *illicit* are homophones—words that are pronounced similarly but differ in spelling and meaning. *Elicit* functions as a verb and is derived from the Latin word *lacere*, meaning "entice." Up front on it is the prefix *e-* (a form of *ex-*), which means "out." *Elicit* means to "bring out, evoke, call forth," as in these sentences:

The psychologist's lecture was intended to elicit discussion on the issues.

The joke elicited laughter from members of the audience.

Context helps you know that the speaker is using the word *elicit;* spelling is a strong clue when you read.

Fill in the blanks in these sentences:

1. My friend had an _____ affair with a married man.

2. I will try to _____ a response from members of the audience as a way to keep them awake.

6

Word Elements—Prefixes That Tell "For," "Together," "Apart," . . .

◆◆

Objectives: In Chapter 6, you will develop the ability to

- explain the care you must take in applying your knowledge of prefixes to unfamiliar words by talking about such words as *invaluable, innumerable,* and *inflammable;*

- recognize and interpret words that begin with the prefixes *ab-* (off), *anti-* (against), *con-* (together), *de-* (off), *dis-* (apart), *dys-* (bad), *ex-* (out), *equi-* (equal), *extra-* (beyond), *hyper-* (excessive), *hypo-* (less than), *in-* (in), *pro-* (for), *re-* (back again), *syn-* (together), as in Table 6.1.

- comprehend and use the following words featured in Module 6-A:

abstract	antiestablishment	compatible	hypothetical
antagonist	coherent	hyperactive	proponent
antidote	compassionate	hypocrisy	rejuvenate

- recognize and attach meaning to the root *her-,* meaning "to stick," featured in Module 6-A;

- perceive words in terms of their prefixes and syllable units;

- comprehend and use the following words featured in Module 6-B:

defame	equitable	exotic	extraordinary
depersonalize	equinox	ex-president	synchronize
dysfunctional	excavate	extravagant	synthesize
exploit (*power word*)	idiosyncracy (*power word*)		

- recognize and attach meaning to the element *chron-* (time), featured in Module 6-B;

- explain how new words such as *modem, telecommunication,* and *e-mail* are being coined today and how new meanings are being attached to existing phrases, such as "going on line"; and

- distinguish between *allude* and *elude* and among *allusion, illusion,* and *elusive.*

◆◆

Interesting Words to Think About— *Invaluable, Innumerable, Inflammable,* and a Caution

How are these words similar: *indecisive, insecure, irregular, immature, illegal?* From your word studies in Chapter 5, you probably recognized the prefix *in-* (or its variations *il-, ir-,* or *im-*) at the beginning of each of the words and knew immediately that each word carried some kind of "not" message. You probably noted, too, the instances where *in-* became *il-, ir-,* or *im-.* You may have thought—*in-* generally becomes

il- before words or roots starting with the letter *l,*

ir- before words or roots starting with the letter *r,* and

im- before words or roots starting with the letter *m.*

This kind of thinking can make you a wordsmith **par excellence.** However, sometimes you must monitor your comprehension to make sure the generalization you are applying fits a particular word or situation. Think about the words *invaluable* and *innumerable.* At first glance, you might decide that *invaluable* means "not valuable" and that *innumerable* means "not numerous" or "many" based on your knowledge that *in-* often means "not." But study these sentences to see how we actually use these two words:

- His financial advice was invaluable. I followed it exactly and acquired a tidy amount to set aside for my college education.
- I made innumerable mistakes when I began my job; now, in contrast, I do my job correctly every time.

In the first sentence, *invaluable* obviously means "beyond value, of so great a value that it cannot be estimated." In the second sentence, *innumerable* means "so great a number that it cannot be counted." Here the prefix does not mean "not"; rather, it intensifies, or strengthens, the meaning of the root.

The word *inflame* is another example of an instance in which *in-* does not carry a negative meaning. *Inflame* means to "stir up," or bring into flame. An *inflammatory remark* is one that stirs up. And *inflammable pajamas* are ones that quickly go up in flames. That is the same quality possessed by a set of *flammable pajamas*. To buy PJs that will not go up in flames, you must buy flame-resistant ones! In the words *inflame, imflammatory,* and *inflammable, in-* means "in" or "into." We see this same meaning on *inject, inset, inspire,* and *institute,* to name just a few.

In summary, remember to look for prefixes you know at the beginnings of words, but do not apply your understanding **indiscriminately.** Think carefully, or you could trip up.

Developing Your Word Study Notebook and Word Study Cards

- In your word study notebook, record these words with definitions from the selection you have just read: *invaluable, innumerable, inflame, inflammable, inflammatory.* For each write a sentence that communicates the meaning.

- Predict the meaning of the word *indiscriminately,* based on the prefix and the context in which you found the word. Start a word study card with the word *indiscriminately,* and as you proceed add other words from this chapter to it. Glance at your study card from time to time to remind yourself of words to use in your writing.

- Predict the meaning of the phrase *par excellence,* based on the context in which it appears in the second paragraph of the article you just read. English has borrowed this ex-

Strategy Box 6-A—Prefix-Awareness Strategy Revisited

Recall the three steps in the prefix-awareness strategy you learned and practiced in Chapter 5:

- Step 1: Study the beginning syllable or syllables of a multisyllablic word to see if you recognize a prefix you know. If you find a prefix, tell yourself the meaning of it.
- Step 2: Strip the prefix from the rest of the word and see if you recognize any part of the remaining word. If you do, review the meaning.
- Step 3: Connect the meaning of the prefix to the meaning of the rest of the word.

To make this strategy work for you, you must know some more prefixes. Table 6.1 presents some additional prefixes. With a colored marker, highlight the prefix on each sample word. As you do this, pronounce each word, thinking about the meaning that the prefix adds to it. Then try to add at least one more example to the table for each prefix.

Table 6.1   Useful Prefixes That Indicate Various Relationships

Prefix	Meaning	Examples of Words
ab-, a-, abs-	off, from, away from	abduct, absent, abstract
anti-	against	antiwar, antiunion, antiAmerican
con-, com-, col-	together	conspire, congregation, collect
de-	make the opposite of, off, remove from, apart	deduct, deduce, decrease, dehumanize
dis-, di-, dif-	apart	dispute, divorce, divert, differ
dys-	bad	dysfunctional
ex-, ec-	out, from	expel, execute, exploit, exude, ecstasy
equi-	equal	equidistant, equitable
extra-, extro-	beyond, outside	extravagant, extravaganza, extramarital, extraordinary
hyper-	excessive, over	hypertension, hyperacid, hypercritical, hyperbole
hypo-	under, below, less than normal	hypodermic, hypothesize, hypothetical
in-, im-, en-, em-	in, into, against	intrude, invasive, injection, emigrate
pro-	for, in favor of	proponent, pro-American, promote
re-, red-	back again, again	return, reunite, redeem
syn-, sym-, syl-, sy-, sys-	with, together	synonym, sympathy, system

pression from the French language. Check a dictionary to validate your prediction. Record the phrase on a word study card.

Word Study Module 6-A—Prefixes That Indicate a Variety of Relationships

Pronounce each featured word or phrase. Then, based on the definition, create a sentence in which you use it following the pattern offered in the sample sentence. Using the context of the sample sentences, decide on the meanings of any related words or phrases.

✦ 1. **ab stract** (ab strakt′), *adj.,* opposite of concrete, not practical, hard to understand.

> *Related word:* **ab strac tion,** *n.*

> *Contexts:* I am not a strong abstract thinker; for that reason I knew I could not succeed as a scientist. In contrast, my friend can handle abstractions with ease.

✦ 2. **an tag o nist** (an tag′ ə nist′), *n.,* person who opposes or works against something or someone; the character in a novel who opposes the hero, or protagonist.

> *Related words:* **an tag o nism,** *n.;* **an tag o nize,** *v.;* **an ta go nis tic,** *adj.*

> *Contexts:* My brother had been my antagonist for many years. His antagonism toward me seemed to increase each day. I had never done anything to antagonize him, but he continued to interact with me in an antagonistic manner.

✦ 3. **an ti dote** (an′ tē dōt), *n.,* remedy that counteracts the effects of poison; remedy that counteracts the effects of any bad thing or action.

> *Contexts:* I recommended that she take a long vacation as an antidote to her depression.
> The doctor gave the child an antidote after she had been stung by a swarm of bees.

✦ 4. **an ti es tab lish ment** (an′ tē i stab′ lish mənt), *adj.,* opposed to traditional political, social, and economic values; generally against anything associated with government; literally, against the establishment.

> *Contexts:* My friend's antiestablishment attitudes were the exact opposite of my way of thinking. In this respect, we were incompatible.

✦ 5. **co her ent** (kō hîr′ ənt), *adj.,* sticking together (when used in a literal sense); logically ordered or interconnected.

> *Related words:* **co he sive ness,** *n.;* **in co her ent,** *adj.*

> *Contexts:* The lawyer presented a coherent argument, but the defendant was incoherent when she testified.
> I sensed a cohesiveness within our class that I had not felt earlier in the semester.

✦✦

Highlighted Word Element

her- or **hes-,** a Latin root meaning "to stick."

Words with the element: *adhere, adhesive, cohesive.*

✦✦

✦ 6. **com pas sion ate** (kəm pash′ ə nit), *adj.,* sympathetic, showing concern to the extent of suffering along with another.

Related words: **com pas sion,** *n.;* **com pas sion ate ly,** *adv.*

Contexts: My nurse was a warm, compassionate human being who felt deeply about her patients. Ms. Brogan's compassion was evident to anyone with whom she came into contact. She acted compassionately no matter where she was.

✦ 7. **com pat i ble** (kəm pat′ ə bəl), *adj.,* capable of living in harmony with others, able to get along with others.

Related words: **in com pat i ble,** *adj.;* **com pat i bil i ty,** *n.;* **in com pat i-bil i ty,** *n.;* **com pat i bly,** *adv.*

Contexts: Compatibility is important in a marriage. Where husband and wife are incompatible, life can be far from peaceful. So in seeking a mate, seek someone with whom you are compatible—someone with whom you can live compatibly.

✦ 8. **hy per ac tive** (hī pər ak′ tiv), *adj.,* excessively active, often to the point of being abnormally active.

Related word: **hy per ac tiv i ty,** *n.*

Contexts: The kindergartner was a hyperactive child who could never sit still. His hyperactivity annoyed the other children in his class.

✦ 9. **hy poc ri sy** (hi pok′ ri sē), *n.,* act of expressing opinions in which one does not believe and leaving the impression that one truly believes that way; dissemblance.

Related words: **hyp o crite,** *n.;* **hy po crit i cal,** *adj.*

Contexts: I was struck by the sheer hypocrisy of that politician's words. I knew that what he believed was far different from what he was saying. He was a true hypocrite, one whom I could never trust. Finally his hypocritical behavior caught up with him, and he lost his position in the House of Representatives.

✦ 10. **hy po thet i cal** (hī′ pə thet′ i kəl), *adj.,* considered true for the purposes of argument.

Related words: **hy poth e sis,** *n.;* **hy poth e size,** *v.;* **hy po thet i cal ly,** *adv.*

Contexts: Even though we were discussing a hypothetical situation, I got very angry. I disagreed violently with my opponent's basic hypothesis.
Try to hypothesize what would happen if the dam were to break. Although we are speaking hypothetically, such a situation could come to pass.

✦ 11. **pro pon ent** (prə pō nənt), *n.,* supporter, generally one who speaks out on a particular issue.

Related words: **pro pose,** *v.;* **pro po si tion,** *n.;* **pro po sal,** *n.*

Contexts: The governor was a proponent of equal pay for equal work.

✦ 12. **re ju ve nate** (ri jōō′ və nāt′), *v.,* restore one to a younger appearance or state of mind.

Related word: **re ju ve na tion,** *n.*

Contexts: A trip to a warm climate will rejuvenate a person; he or she will return feeling like a younger person. I went to Florida in search of rejuvenation.

Word Study Activities Module 6-A— Making Meaning with Words

6-A-1 Words in Meaningful Sentence Contexts: From the list, select the word that best fits the overall meaning of each sentence. Write that word in the blank. Use each option only once. Apply your Know-for-sure/Process-of-elimination test-taking strategy.

a. abstract	d. antiestablishment	g. compatible	j. hypothetical
b. antagonist	e. coherent	h. hyperactive	k. proponent
c. antidote	f. compassionate	i. hypocrisy	l. rejuvenate

1. My friend is not a/an _____ thinker. He is a practical person, more concerned with actual things than with complex relationships.

2. Some people are _____; they are always on the go, rarely taking time to sit down and think.

3. From the moment we met, I knew we were _____; we liked to do the same things and we had the same values.

4. A/An _____ for boredom is a good book!

5. I posed a/an _____ question to my professor as a way of problem solving; in this way, we were able to consider all the options.

6. A tall glass of iced tea can _____ me on a hot day; I feel years younger and ready to take on the world.

7. I began to hate the _____ in the novel, for he was perpetually stirring up trouble; I very quickly learned to like the protagonist, who became my hero in the story.

8. We came up with a/an _____ plan that was logical; each step we would take would build on the steps that had preceded them.

9. The young man was a/an _____ of affirmative action. He spoke actively for this cause in which he believed.

10. Critical about how the government was being run, the candidate maintained a/an _____ position on most issues.

11. My technician did not have a/an _____ nature; she was cold and matter-of-fact in all that she did.

12. I was overwhelmed by the _____ that I saw around me. The people with whom I worked would take a position not based on what they believed or thought to be right but based on what they thought their supervisor wanted to hear.

6-A-2 Antonym Study: Match the word on the left with the appropriate antonym on the right. Write the word from the list on the left on the blank next to its antonym. Use each option only once.

1. **abstract**	_____	a. age
2. **antagonist**	_____	b. opponent
3. **antidote**	_____	c. actual
4. **antiestablishment**	_____	d. honesty
5. **coherent**	_____	e. calm
6. **compassionate**	_____	f. incompatible
7. **compatible**	_____	g. cruel
8. **hyperactive**	_____	h. incoherent
9. **hypocrisy**	_____	i. proestablishment
10. **hypothetical**	_____	j. poison
11. **proponent**	_____	k. concrete
12. **rejuvenate**	_____	l. protagonist

6-A-3 Definitions of Related Words: Write a few words on the line that clarify the meaning of the derivative at the left. Try not to use a form of the word that you are defining as part of your clarification.

1. **compassionately**   functioning with _____

2. **abstraction**   something that is _____

3. **incompatibility**   inability to _____

4. **hyperactivity**   activity that is characterized by _____

_____

5. **hypocrite**   one who _____

6. **hypothesis**   an idea that _____

7. **propose**   make _____

8. **protagonist**   one who _____

9. **incoherent**   not _____

10. **to disestablish**   is to _____

6-A-4 Applying Our Understanding of Prefixes to New Words: Star the option that best defines or explains the highlighted word. Use your knowledge of prefixes and context clues to guide you.

1. The judge ruled that my brother's acceptance of responsibility **absolved** me of any responsibility in the case. I would be a hypocrite if I did not admit that I was relieved to hear the judgment.
   a. solved a puzzle for me
   b. declared free of blame
   c. sucked up as a liquid
   d. declared as being to blame

2. Oddly enough, my friend who tends to be antiestablishment, maintains a **proabortion** position.
   a. for abortion   b. against abortion   c. neutral

3. In contrast, my other friend is **antiabortion.**
   a. for abortion   b. against abortion   c. neutral

4. I studied the **pros and cons** relative to the case and hypothesized that the judge would rule in favor of the defense.
   a. arguments for   b. arguments against
   c. arguments for and against

5. The judge eventually ruled that the evidence was **inconclusive** and ruled in favor of the defense. In that respect, my hypothesis proved to be accurate.
   a. not convincing   b. not compatible
   c. not clear   d. not complete

6. The youngster **resumed** the hyperactive behavior that had got him into trouble originally; as a result he ended up in more trouble.
   a. gave back   b. continued
   c. started up again   d. stopped

7. My friend's mother was **hypercritical.** She was a noncompassionate person who was always reminding my friend of where he had gone wrong.
   a. incompatible with him   b. overly faultfinding with him
   c. insincere toward him   d. unloving

8. **Hypodermic** needles need to be disinfected between uses.
   a. for injecting under the skin   b. for making overactive
   c. for rejuvenating   d. for proposing a solution

9. My uncle would travel into the country to **commune** with nature.
   a. make a comparison to   b. have a sentence lessened
   c. travel to work   d. get close to and talk

10. The principal decided to **rescind** her order that no one leave the school during lunch break.
    a. cut away   b. think about
    c. repeat   d. take back

Strategy Box 6-B—Prefixes and Syllable/ Sound Awareness

When you see a word, do you see it simply as a random string of letters or do you see it as a series of syllable units chained together with perhaps a prefix at the beginning? Do you pronounce words by pronouncing the syllable units, each in turn, starting with the syllable or syllables that comprise the prefix?

A strategy that can help you pronounce longer words is to break down words into syllables and pronounce the syllables one by one. In doing this, you may discover that you actually know a word that on paper at first seemed unfamiliar. For example, can you pronounce this word?

deice

On first try, did you pronounce the word as one syllable? Try pronouncing *deice* as two syllables, remembering that in English each syllable contains one vowel sound:

de ice

As soon as you divided the word into two syllable units, you probably got the meaning and may have related the word to what is done to airplanes when the temperature drops below freezing. Before taking off, airplanes must be deiced. You may have recognized the prefix at the beginning—*de-*.

In reading a new word, therefore, think in terms of syllable units that make up the word. Don't think in terms of one continuous string of letters. You just might happen to recognize a prefix within the word or the word itself if you pronounce it correctly.

Here are some guidelines for recognizing syllable breaks in words:

1. Each syllable must contain a vowel sound. Pronounce and beat out the syllables in these words: *continuous* (con tin u ous), *contemplate* (con tem plate), *decisive* (de ci sive). Can you hear the long and short sounds of the vowels: *a, e, i, o, u?* Sometimes, too, the letter *y* is used to represent a vowel sound as in the word *fury,* which is a two-syllable word.

2. Some words contain within them a vowel followed by two consonants as in *furry* (fur ry) and *syllable* (syl la ble). Typically the syllable break occurs be-

tween the two consonants, as you can see from those examples. Pronounce and beat the syllables in these words: *possibility, opposition, seldom, hassle, difference*. In the margin, write the words to show the syllable breaks between the two consonants.

3. Some consonants generally stick together and are pronounced as one blended or combined sound; *br, gr, tr, st, str, pl, cr, dr, ph, ch, th,* and *sh* are examples, but there are others as well. Pronounce these words, and listen for the syllable breaks: *telephonic, trapeze, implication.*

4. When words end in a consonant plus *le*, pronounce this combination as one unaccented syllable. Here are some examples: *example* (ex am ple), *invaluable* (in val u a ble), *indistinguishable* (in dis tin guish a ble). List two or three other possibilities in the margin.

In sum, as you encounter unfamiliar words, see and hear them as units of sounds rather than strings of individual letters.

Word Study Module 6-B— More Prefixes That Indicate Other Relationships

Pronounce each featured word. Then based on the definition and the sample sentences, create a sentence in which you use the word. Using the context of the sample sentences, decide on the meanings of any related words or phrases.

◆ 1. **de fame** (di fām′), *v.*, attack by libeling, or telling untruths about, and in so doing destroy someone's good name.

   Related words: **de fam a tory,** *adj.;* **de fam a tion,** *n.*

   Contexts: The malicious man tried to defame his opponent. He made defamatory remarks about his opponent to everyone he met. As a result, he was sued for defamation of character.

◆ 2. **de per son al ize** (dē pûr′ sə nə līz′), *v.*, take away personal or individual character; make impersonal.

   Related words: **de hu man ize,** *v.;* **de po lit i cize,** *v.*

   Contexts: When we depersonalize a situation, we strip it of all caring and compassion.
   When we dehumanize, we strip away human qualities; the result is coldness.
   When we depoliticize an issue, we remove it from the political arena.

◆ 3. **dys func tion al** (dis fungk′ shən əl), *adj.*, impaired, disordered, not functioning normally.

   Related word: **dys func tion,** *n.*

Contexts: The child had grown up in a dysfunctional family that had left him scared. His dysfunction was obvious to any observer; he never paid attention.

✦   4. **e qui ta ble** (ek′ wi tə bəl), *adj.,* fair and just.

> *Related word:* **e qui ta bly,** *adj.*

> *Contexts:* The governor sought equitable funding for the schools in her state. She dealt equitably with each person with whom she came in contact.

✦   5. **e qui nox** (ē′ kwə noks′), *n.,* time (which happens twice a year) when the sun crosses the equator and day and night are equal in length. (Note: In Latin, *nox* means "night.")

> *Contexts:* In the northern hemisphere, the spring equinox occurs in March; the fall equinox occurs in September.

✦   6. **ex ca vate** (ek′ skə vāt′), *v.,* dig out a hole, remove by scooping out. (Note: In this case *ex-* means "out.")

> *Related words:* **ex ca va tor,** *n.;* **ex ca va tion,** *n.*

> *Contexts:* To construct the building, we first had to excavate for the basement. A major excavation proved necessary, for the zoning board had strict requirements. We had to employ a qualified excavator.

✦✦✦

Power Words

ex ploit′, as a verb—to make unfair use of, to take advantage of, as in the sentence, "The explorer exploited the local people, making use of them without taking into consideration their needs." The word first appeared in Middle English and was derived from Old French. Through the French, it can be traced back to the Latin word *explicare,* meaning "to explicate."

ex′ ploits, as a noun—usual and oftentimes heroic deeds or activities as in the sentence, "The TV documentary chronicled the exploits of the astronauts who walked on the moon."

(Special note: Notice that when the word functions as a verb, the accent is on the second syllable. In contrast, when the word serves as a noun, the accent is on the first syllable. Similarly, other words such as *present, conduct, subject,* and *rebel* shift the position of the accent when they shift their role in a sentence. The accent is on the second syllable of the verb, whereas the accent is on the first syllable of the noun.)

✦✦✦

✦   7. **ex-ot ic** (ig zot′ ik), *adj.,* strikingly different.

> *Related word:* **ex ot i cal ly,** *adv.*

> *Contexts:* While she was in college, she worked as an exotic dancer.

✦ 8. **ex-pres i dent** (eks′ prez′ i dənt), *n.*, one who has been president but is out of office. (Note: Here, *ex-* means "former.")

> *Related word:* **ex-gov er nor,** *n.* (Think of other "ex-people.")

> *Contexts:* I met the ex-president at a rally for the new president. The ex-governor was also there.

✦ 9. **ex trav a gant** (ik′ strav′ ə gənt), *adj.*, given to lavish spending, especially beyond what is reasonable; extreme in cost.

> *Related words:* **ex trav a gant ly,** *adv.;* **ex trav a gance,** *n.*

> *Contexts:* My friend's extravagant spending left her with large credit card debts. Such extravagances were beyond my comprehension for I had always been frugal in my spending. Very often, she was extravagantly dressed, which made her debts even greater.

✦ 10. **ex traor di nar y** (ik′ strôr′ dn er′ ē), *adj.*, beyond that which is common; exceedingly exceptional.

> *Related word:* **ex traor di nar i ly,** *adv.*

> *Contexts:* Her mother was an extraordinary woman; she was an entrepreneur who had made a fortune in her own business. She was an extraordinarily gifted person; she must have had an exceptionally high IQ.

✦ 11. **syn chro nize** (sing′ krə nīz), *v.*, make happen at the same time.

> *Related word:* **syn chro nous,** *v.*

> *Contexts:* Synchronize your watches so that we will arrive at the same time. The synchronous movements of the two birds were part of their mating ritual.

✦✦

Highlighted Word Element

chron-, a Greek root meaning "time."

Words with the element: *chronology, chronic, chronicles.*

✦✦

✦ 12. **syn the size** (sin′ thi sīz), *v.*, put together to form something new.

> *Related words:* **syn the sis,** *n.;* **syn thet ic,** *adj.*

> *Contexts:* My job was to come up with a synthesis that represented the ideas found in both reports. My synthesis of the ideas was rather original; I saw something that no one else had recognized.
> A synthetic ruby is not genuine.

◆◆

Power Word

id i o syn cra sy (id′ ē ō sing′ krə sē), *n.; pl.* **sies,** characteristic or quality unique to one individual or group, a personality peculiarity; from the Greek *idios* meaning "own" and *sunkrasis* meaning "mixture."

Related word: **id i o syn crat ic,** *adj.*

Contexts: Roy had more idiosyncrasies than any other person I knew. As he grew older, he became more idiosyncratic.

◆◆

Word Study Activities Module 6-B— Making Meaning with Words

6-B-1 Words in Meaningful Sentence Contexts: From the list, select the word that best fits the overall meaning of each sentence. Write that word in the blank. Use each option only once.

a. defame	d. equitable	g. exotic	j. extraordinary
b. depersonalize	e. equinox	h. ex-president	k. synchronize
c. dysfunctional	f. excavate	i. extravagant	l. synthesize
			m. idiosyncrasies

1. Her command of calculus was _____; as a result the help she gave me proved invaluable.

2. My job was to organize and _____ the material into a report to share with my colleagues.

3. His job as the executor of the estate is to see that all assets are distributed in a/an _____ manner.

4. In society today, we often _____ relationships so that at times we do not even know who our neighbors are.

5. I was concerned when a colleague attempted to _____ me in front of my employer. My reputation could have been harmed.

6. The archaeologist decided to _____ in large areas of the region in her search for clues about people who had lived thousands of years before.

7. My university sociology professor believes that much of society has become _____, with the parts not operating as they should.

8. Because she was accustomed to great wealth, she tended to be _____ in her spending; she never asked the price before purchasing items she desired.

9. As _____, Roxanne held a seat on the executive council and so continued to be an influence in the association.

10. At the spring _____, the sun is directly over the equator and the day is equal to the night across the world.

11. Greg had many _____ that made him an unlikely choice for president of our club.

12. I stumbled on this _____ bird as I walked through the rain forest. It was a magnificent creature, so rare that few others had ever seen it.

13. We tried to _____ our activity to ensure a successful outcome.

Same   Opp.

6-B-2 Synonyms or Antonyms: Each set of words in the following list is either a pair of synonyms or a pair of antonyms. On the line at the right of each set, write Synonym or Antonym depending on the category to which the set belongs.

1. defame/glorify   _____

2. depersonalize/personalize   _____

3. dysfunctional/operational   _____

4. equitable/fair   _____

5. equinox/long day—short night   _____

6. excavate/dig up   _____

7. exotic/plain   _____

8. ex-president/past president   _____

9. extravagant/frugal   _____

10. extraordinary/common   _____

11. synchronize/act together   _____

12. synthesize/put together   _____

13. idiosyncrasies/personality pecularities   _____

14. exploit/use fairly   _____

6-B-3 Crossword Puzzle: Complete the puzzle in Figure 6.1.

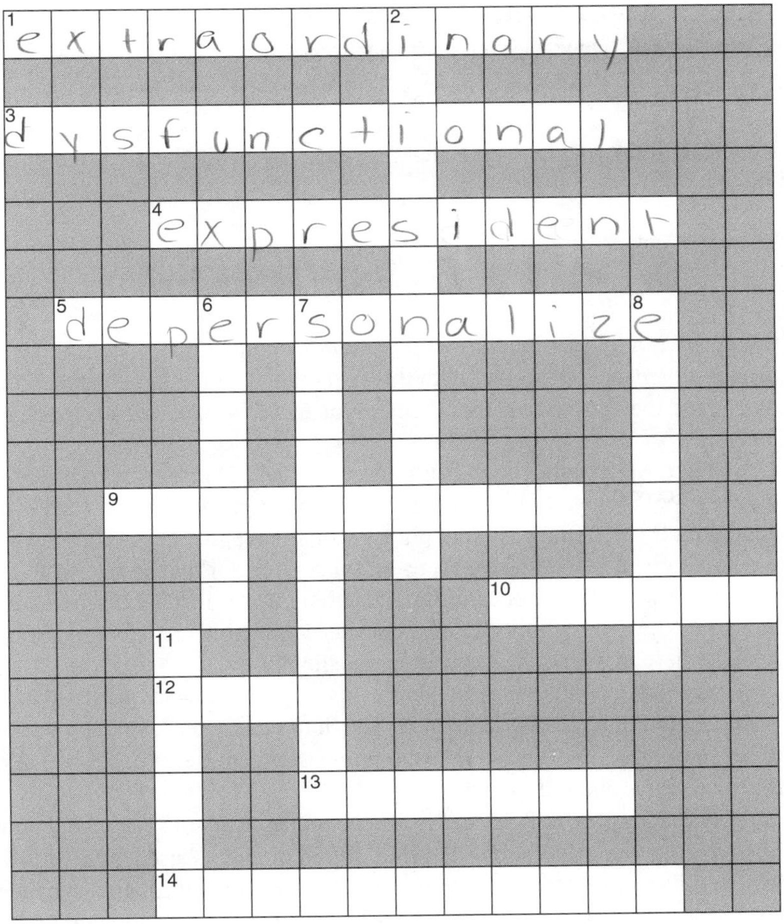

Figure 6.1   Crossword Puzzle of Words with Prefixes That Indicate Key Relationships

ACROSS
1 Exceedingly exceptional
3 Impaired, not operating normally
4 Former leader of government
5 Take away the individual character of
9 Put together to form something new
10 Strikingly different
12 Fair and just
13 Make unfair use of
14 Given to lavish spending

DOWN
2 Personality peculiarity
6 Time when day and night are the same length
7 Make happen at the same time
8 Dig out a hole
11 Attack by telling untruths about

Reading with Meaning Module 6-C— Using Context Clues; Understanding How Words Are Coined

Read the following passage, making meaning with the highlighted words as you go along.

The Coinage of New Words

Language is a vibrant medium of communication that is in a continuous state of change. Even as you interact with this paragraph, something is happening to transform words and the way we use them. Let's look at a few **innovations** that have occurred recently.

First, we have begun to use some words and phrases for purposes different from the way we employed them previously. For example, today everyone is talking about "going on line." In the past, that phrase would have meant **queuing** up as we do when we stand on a line with people waiting for service. Or that phrase would have been used when we talked about starting something up, as in "We brought a new machine on line." Now "going on line" often means connecting one's computer to the Internet with the help of a modem and a telephone hookup.

Second, technological developments are emerging so quickly that we have no words within our existing **lexicon** by which to call them. Just a few years ago, the Internet, modem, and even e-mail were nonexistent entities. People had to coin words so they could talk about these innovations.

For example, the **Internet** is a **telecommunication** system that connects millions of computers and allows the sharing of computer-based data, or information. Where did the word Internet come from? It was coined through a **synthesis** of the prefix *inter-,* meaning "between," and the word *net,* meaning "something that is woven together." Similarly, someone coined the term **modem** for the device that converts information from telephone form to a form a computer can interpret, and vice versa. **Modem** was coined by taking parts of two words mo(dulator) and dem(odulator) and joining those parts together. As for **e-mail,** that's easy to explain: electronic mail. Some **wits** have even begun to call ordinary, postal service mail "snail mail."

Here are a few other recent **coinages:** *cyberspace, cell phone, videoconference.* You may see these in a dictionary published recently, but if your dictionary is five years old or older, you will probably not find any of them. Your search will be fruitless. You will have to define these based on their common usage today:

- Regardless of where she was, she walked around with her cell phone at her ear.
- During our **videoconference,** we were able to talk to specialists in our profession even as we saw them on a television screen.
- Cyberspace is that vast "space" filled with computers and their contents that connects us to one another in new and original ways. It is "out there" on the Net.

Word Study Activities Module 6-C—
Using Context Clues and Word Elements
to Make Meaning with Words

6-C-1 Figuring Out Meanings: Answer these questions in the space provided.

1. What do we do when we **coin** new words? What is meant by the phrase "recent word coinage"?

2. What kinds of things would we categorize as **innovations?**

3. What do you do when you **queue up?** What is a **queue?** What is a **cue?**

4. What is the **Internet?**

5. What is the meaning of **telecommunication?**

6. What is a **modem?** How did it receive its name?

7. What is **e-mail?**

8. What kind of a person is a **wit?**

9. What is **snail mail?**

10. What do you do when you have a **videoconference?** How does a videoconference differ from a teleconference?

Confusing Words—*Allude, Elude, Allusion, Illusion*

These words can confuse you:

allude, elude;
allusion, illusion.

Allude (ə lōōd′) generally works as a verb in sentences. It means "to refer only in-directly to something, to mention in passing." It is made up of two parts: the prefix *ad-*, meaning "to," and the root *lude* from the Latin *ludere,* meaning "play a game." I suppose you are playing a game when you only allude to something rather than stating it outright: You are keeping your audience guessing as in a game. Here is an example: My friend alluded to the fact that I had stayed out overnight.

The noun form is *allusion,* meaning "an indirect or slight reference." In talk-ing, you can make an allusion to something. You might also make a literary allusion as when you refer to something from literature. If you say, "He is a Huck-Finn type of person," you are using a literary allusion—a reference to a story character—to make a point about the person.

Elude is pronounced much the same as *allude.* However, it means "to escape through a clever act, to stay undiscovered." It is formed from the prefix *ex-* or *e-,* meaning "out or away," and the Latin root *ludere*—"to play." You could say, "The bombing suspect eluded the police by hiding out in the mountains." Or "The point he was trying to make eluded me." Someone who is hard to capture is *elusive.* A point can also be elusive. One character from a story was particularly elusive. He was called the elusive Scarlet Pimpernel.

Now for the word *illusion.* Formed from the same Latin root as the other two but with the prefix *il-* up front, meaning "against," *illusion* means an "appearance that is deceiving or misleading." You might have heard of an optical illusion—an image that deceives you. You may say, "I thought there was water in the road, but it was only an illusion caused by the reflection of the light." You might also remark, "I was under the illusion that he loved me, but afterward I realized that he had been putting on a good show."

Note that what makes a difference among these words are the prefixes they bear "up front." Fill in the blanks of these sentences with the appropriate forms:

1. I listened carefully, but the point that he was trying to make _____ me.

2. My friend only _____ to the illicit relationship I had with his sister; he was too embarrassed to come right out and say something about it.

    However, I understood his _____, and I was embarrassed, too.

3. I thought I saw a patch of green on the desert, but unfortunately it was only an _____.

Word Elements—Introductory Bases That Tell "How Many" or "How Big"

Objectives: In Chapter 7, you will develop the ability to

- explain the way English uses elements to tell "how many" and "how big" by referring to such words as *millennium, millimeters,* and *millipedes;*

- recognize and interpret words that begin with elements that say, "how many" and "how big," such as *mono-, prime-,* and *uni-* (one), *bi-* and *di-* (two), *tri-* (three), *quad-* (four), *cent-* (one hundred), *omni-* and *pan-* (all), *multi-* (many), *mini-* and *micro-* (small), *maxi-* (large), as in Table 7.1;

- comprehend and use the following words featured in Module 7-A:

bilateral	dilemma	minimal	multiple	quadruple
centennial	maximize	monopoly	omnipotent	unanimous
century	microscopic	monotonous	prime	unilateral

  pandemonium and panacea (*power words*);

- recognize and attach meaning to the element *pot-,* meaning "power," when you encounter it in such words as *potent* and *impotent;*

- make connections among words as a way to figure out unfamiliar words;

- comprehend and use the following words featured in Module 7-B:

abraded	deduce	ecstasy	introspection
atypical	dichotomy	evolve	prehistoric
composite	diverge	intercept	replenish

- recognize and attach meaning to the element *volv-* or *volut-,* meaning "to roll";

- use context clues and word elements to crack the meaning of unfamiliar words and explain how names of the months evolved; and

- distinguish between the words *accept* and *except* and between *acceptance* and *exception.*

Everyone has experienced how learning an appropriate name for
what was dim and vague cleared up
and crystallized the whole matter.

—John Dewey, *How We Think,* 1933

◆◆

Interesting (and Contradictory) Number-Stating Words— *Millennium, Millionaire,* and *Multimillionaire*

In English we have numerous ways to communicate "how many" and "how big." Of course, on paper we can rely on the Arabic numerals, such as 1, 23, and 201, or the Roman numerals, such as I, V, and L. Mathematicians prefer that we call these characters numerals rather than numbers.

A second way to tell "how many" is with number-indicating words, such as *one, thirteen, twenty-two, one hundred and ninety-nine.* Notice how we add the hyphen to the numbers from twenty-one to ninety-nine, but not between the one and hundred in the phrase *one hundred.*

A third way is through number-indicating words of a different **ilk:** *first, fourth, twenty-ninth, fortieth, eighty-eighth, one hundredth.* Mathematicians like to call these the ordinal numbers to contrast them with the cardinal numbers such as one, four, twenty-nine, forty, eighty-eight, and one hundred.

But in writing and speaking, we rely on a host of elements that are integrated into words to communicate "how many" and "how big." For example, the element *mill-* is from the Latin and means "thousand." We use *mill-* in a variety of word contexts. We talk about *millimeters, milliseconds,* and even *millipedes.* A millimeter is a thousandth of a meter, a millisecond is a thousandth of a second, and a millipede is a creepy-crawly with lots of legs. The Roman numeral M stands for 1,000.

But the *mill-* word that really excites us is *millennium*—a thousand-year span. We began a new millennium at midnight on December 31, 1999, when we entered the year 2000. Some people disagree with the idea that the new millennium began then; they contend that the change occurred at midnight on December 31, 2000, when we began the year 2001. Be that as it may, the millennium engendered lots of excitement, much partying, and much computer activity as computer programmers prepared computers to roll from 1999 to 2000.

Unfortunately, in English we sometimes do things with language that result in a bit of confusion. We all know that although we use *mill-* in words to say "one thousand," we also talk about millionaires who have a million dollars or more in the bank, not a mere thousand. And we all know that we would prefer to have that million rather than only a thousand. As a matter of fact, wouldn't it be lovely to be a multimillionaire—one who has many millions of dollars to play with?

The reason for the confusion is that the word *million* came into our language through the French, whereas the element *mill-* came more directly from the Latin. What can we do about it? Simply be aware that there are two possible and conflicting meanings and use the context in which a word is used to get things straight in our minds.

Collaborative Search and Discover

- Hypothesize the meanings of these words: *milliliter, milligram, billionaire, multibillionaire.* Record your hypotheses in your word study notebook to share later.
- Hypothesize the meaning of the element *multi-.* What other words do you know that rely on this element? List at least two in your notebook.
- In your notebook, write the following numerals as number-stating words: 72, 87, 234.
- Use context clues to figure out the meaning of the word *ilk* found in paragraph three of the passage. Write its meaning in the margin. Check your hypothesis in your dictionary.

Strategy Box 7-A—Element Awareness: Introductory Bases That Tell "How Many" or "How Much"

Recall your prefix-awareness strategy. Here it is in brief:

- Step 1: Look for a prefix at the start of a word. If you find one, tell yourself its meaning, strip the prefix from the rest of the word, and see if you recognize any part of what remains. If you do, review the meaning.
- Step 2: Connect the meaning of the prefix to the meaning of the rest of the word.

In Table 7.1 are some common elements derived primarily from Latin that are among the most easily recognizable introductory bases and will help you to figure out meanings that relate to number and size. Using a colored marker, highlight the number-indicating bases on the sample words.

Word Study Module 7-A— Introductory Bases That Tell "How Many" or "How Big"

Pronounce each featured word, listening for the element and syllable breaks; then with a marker, highlight the number-telling element and think about the meaning it adds to the root or base word.

Table 7.1   Introductory Bases That Tell "How Many" or "How Much"

Bases	Meanings	Examples of Words
un-; mono-; prim-	one, first, single	unit, unanimous; monologue, monogram; primary, prime
bi- and bin- (before vowels); di-, du-	two, twice	bicycles, binary, binoculars; dilemma, duplicate
tri-	three	triangular, triplets, trio
quadr (u)-; or quart-	four, fourth	quadrangle, quadrant, quadruplicate; quarter
quint-	five	quintet, quintessence, quintuplet
sext-; sex-; hex-	six	sextet, sexagenarian, sexennial; hexagon
sept-	seven	September, septet
oct-; octav-	eight, eighth	octet, October, octave, octagonal
novem-; non-	nine, ninth	November
deci-; decim-	ten, tenth	December, decimal, decade
cent-	hundred	centennial, century, cent (Reminder: C is the Roman numeral for 100.)
mill-	thousand	millimeter, millennial, mill (Reminder: M is the Roman numeral for 1,000.)
multi-	many	multimedia, multicultural, multilingual, multisyllabic
poly-	many, much, excessive	polygon, polyglot, polygyny
pan-	all	pandemic, Pan-American, panacea
omni-	all	omnipotent, omniscent, omnibus
semi-	partly	semitransparent, semisweet
micro-; mini-	small, very small	microbe, microcosm, microscope; miniature, minor, minimal
magni-; maxi-; macro-	large, great in size	magnify, magnificent; maximize; macrocosm, macromanage

Bases That Indicate "One" or "First"

✦   1. **mo nop o ly** (mə nop′ ə lē), *n.,* exclusive control by one group or person, often (but not always) of the means of production or distribution of goods and services.

> *Related words:* **mo nop o lize,** *v.;* **mo nop o lis tic,** *adj.*

> *Contexts:* Janet told her friend, "Don't think you have a monopoly over my time. Under no conditions will I let you monopolize me. I am averse to monopolistic behavior in any form."

✦   2. **mo not o nous** (mə not′ n əs), *adj.,* repetitiously dull and colorless.

> *Related words:* **mo not o ny,** *n.;* **mo not o nous ly,** *adv.*

> *Contexts:* He lived a monotonous existence, going from home to work and work to home with no variation in his daily pattern. The monotony of it all finally got to him; he no longer could endure living so monotonously.

✦   3. **prime** (prīm), *adj.,* first in excellence or value; *n.,* position of excellence.

> *Related phrases and words:* **prime meridian,** *n.* (the zero meridian that passes through Greenwich in England and from which all east-west directions are measured); **prime minister,** *n.* (the main leader of some countries); **prime mover,** *n.* (the one who gets things started); **pri ma ry,** *adj.* (first in importance).

> *Contexts:* The television stations air some of their best programs during prime time.
> I buy only prime cuts of meat.
> The man felt that he was in his prime—the time of his life when he could make his greatest achievements. His primary consideration was that his children be taken care of if something should happen to him.

✦   4. **u nan i mous** (yo͞o nan′ ə məs), *adj.,* being fully in agreement; by vote, 100%.

> *Related words:* **u nan i mous ly,** *adv.;* **u na nim i ty,** *n.*

> *Contexts:* We voted during the meeting; the results were unanimous, with everyone favoring the action. I was amazed to find such unanimity among my contemporaries. We had never voted unanimously before.

✦   5. **u ni lat er al** (yo͞o′ nə lat′ ər əl), *adj.,* involving only one party or entity.

> *Related words:* **un i lat er al ly,** *adv.;* **un i lat er al ism,** *n.*

> *Contexts:* The United States took unilateral action without assistance from its allies. The country had to act unilaterally for none of its allies would help. Unfortunately, afterward the other countries criticized the United States for its unilateralism.

Bases That Indicate "Two" or "Twice"

✦ 6. **bi lat er al** (bī lat′ ər əl), *adj.,* affecting two parties; having two sides.

> *Related words:* **bi lat er al ly,** *adv.;* **bi lat er al ism,** *n.*

> *Contexts:* The United States entered into a bilateral trade agreement with Japan; both countries agreed to the terms. Previously, rather than acting bilaterally, the countries had acted unilaterally. In this case bilateralism achieved a better solution than unilateralism would have.

✦ 7. **di lem ma** (di lem′ ə), *n.,* a predicament that requires a choice between two evenly balanced options.

> *Contexts:* I faced a dilemma: Should I attend my best friend's wedding where I had agreed to serve as best man, or should I attend my beloved aunt's funeral, which was to take place at the same hour?

Bases That Indicate "Four"

✦ 8. **quad ru ple** (kwo dr$\overline{oo}$′ pəl), *v.,* multiply by four; *adj.,* having four parts.

> *Related words:* **quad ran gle,** *n.;* **quad ru pli cate,** *adj.*

> *Contexts:* "If you buy this stock," the agent said, "you will quadruple your money in six months." I did not believe him.
>
> My father had to have quadruple bypass surgery in which his surgeons bypassed four major arteries in his heart.
>
> The quadrangle on our campus is the heart of university life. At the university, every document has to be submitted with quadruplicate copies.

Bases That Indicate "One Hundred"

✦ 9. **cen ten ni al** (sen ten′ ē əl), *adj.,* related to a hundred-year period; *n.,* a 100th anniversary of an event or its celebration.

> *Related words:* **bi cen ten ni al,** *adj.* and *n.;* **tri cen ten ni al,** *adj.* and *n.*

> *Contexts:* In 1776, the United States became an independent nation. In 1876, the country celebrated its centennial. In 1976, the country celebrated its bicentennial. In 2076, the country will celebrate its tricentennial.

✦ 10. **cen tu ry** (sen′ chər rē), *n.,* a hundred-year period.

> *Contexts:* During the century that began in 1800, the United States experienced a great wave of immigration.

Bases That Indicate "All," "Many," "Small," or "Great"

✦ 11. **om nip o tent** (om nip′ ə tənt), *adj.,* all-powerful, having absolute power.

> *Related words:* **om nip o ten cy,** *n.;* **om nip o tence,** *n.*

> *Contexts:* In the days of William the Conqueror, the king was omnipotent. To question his omnipotency was often to court death. The king believed in his own omnipotence.

◆◆◆

Highlighted Word Element

pot-, a Latin root meaning "to have power."

Words with the element: *potent, impotent, potential.*

◆◆◆

✦ 12. **mul ti ple** (mul′ tə pəl), *adj.,* having to do with more than one.

> *Related word:* **mul ti ply,** *v.*

> *Contexts:* We had to make multiple copies of our reports so we could share them with our classmates. Multiply your concern by ten, and you will know how concerned I am.

✦ 13. **min i mal** (min′ ə məl), *adj.,* very small in amount.

> *Related words:* **min i mum,** *n.* or *adj.;* **min i mize,** *v.*

> *Contexts:* The man's influence was minimal even though he thought he was having a great impact. I do not intend to minimize your contribution, but others have done more. At a minimum, you should put in three hours of study for each hour of class attendance.

✦ 14. **mi cro scop ic** (mī′ krə skop′ ik), *adj.,* very, very small; too small to be seen un- aided with the naked eye.

> *Contexts:* The surgeon made an incision that was microscopic. It was so small that she had to use a microscope to view the region of the eye on which she was working.

✦ 15. **max i mize** (mak′ sə mīz′), *v.,* make as great as possible; assign the greatest value to.

> *Related words:* **max i mum,** *n.;* **max i mal,** *adj.*

> *Contexts:* Maximize your chances of doing well in a college course by sit- ting in the front row. This will give you the maximal opportunity to participate in the class discussion. Work to your maximum.

◆◆

Power Words

pan de mo ni um, as a noun—great noise and disorder, or a place having this characteristic, as in the sentence, "In the city there was great pandemonium after the earthquake." Note: John Milton was the first to use *pandemonium*. He used it to name the capital of hell in his book *Paradise Lost,* a volume he wrote in the seventeenth century. Remember that *pan-* is an element meaning "all." Can you see the demon in the base part of the word?)

pan a ce a, as a noun—a remedy, or cure-all, for all ills or troubles (from the Greek).

Contexts: Pandemonium broke out when the people discovered that what they believed was a panacea was only a trick.

◆◆

Word Study Activities Module 7-A—
Making Meaning with Number-Indicating Bases

7-A-1 Words in Meaningful Sentence Contexts: From the list, select the word that best fits the overall meaning of each sentence. Write that word in the blank. Use each option only once.

a. bilateral	d. dilemma	g. minimal	j. multiple	m. quadruple
b. centennial	e. maximize	h. monopoly	k. omnipotent	n. unanimous
c. century	f. microscopic	i. monotonous	l. prime	o. unilateral

1. The young man gave only _____ attention to his studies; as a result, his grade point average was very low.

2. The two foreign ministers attempted to hammer out a/an _____ economic agreement between their countries.

3. You can _____ your income by investing in the right kinds of properties. A fourfold return on your money is certainly something you would enjoy.

4. The vote was _____. Everyone wanted to see a new approach to the problem.

5. A/An _____ consideration in the company's downsizing the number of people employed by the firm was to increase earnings.

6. I lived a/an _____ existence; each day seemed exactly like the previous one. I was certainly in a rut.

7. During the twenty-first _____, I know that we will see drastic innovations in the way we attack our problems.

8. The Holy Roman Emperor was _____; he controlled the life and activity of all his subjects.

9. I sustained _____ injuries during the accident; as a result, I had to be hospitalized for more than a week.

10. What was required was a/an _____ examination of each and every element of our plan.

11. That entrepreneur held a/an _____ over the collection of garbage in a wide area. No one else could collect garbage there.

12. A/An _____ change made without consultation with one's allies may not endure.

13. I understood the _____ that my friend faced; however, I could not help her to make the difficult choice she had to make.

14. The town in which I lived celebrated its _____ in 1999. The town had been incorporated in 1899.

15. We all want to _____ our strengths and minimize our weaknesses.

7-A-2 Definitional Study: Match the word on the left with the most appropriate definition on the right. Write the word in the blank. Remember to use each option only once.

1. **bilateral**	_____	a. noisy, wild uproar
2. **centennial**	_____	b. with 100 percent agreement of all parties
3. **century**	_____	c. first in excellence
4. **dilemma**	_____	d. in a rut
5. **maximize**	_____	e. exclusive rights to manage
6. **microscopic**	_____	f. multiply by four
7. **minimal**	_____	g. so small that it is invisible to the naked eye
8. **monopoly**	_____	h. having to do with more than one
9. **monotonous**	_____	i. involving two parties
10. **multiple**	_____	j. 100-year period
11. **omnipotent**	_____	k. 100-year celebration
12. **prime**	_____	l. make as great as possible
13. **quadruple**	_____	m. cure-all

14. unanimous   _____   n. predicament requiring a tough choice

15. unilateral   _____   o. very small in amount

16. panacea   _____   p. all-powerful

17. pandemonium   _____   q. involving only one party

7-A-3 Sentence Completion: Complete each sentence, being sure to use at least one of the featured or related words from this section. If possible, use two or even three of your words in one sentence.

1. The vote

2. I knew that I had to have surgery, but

3. The two countries

4. The girl was faced with

5. I live

6. I believe that

7. The business tycoon tried to

Same   Opp

7-A-4 Synonyms or Antonyms: Indicate whether the members of each word pair are synonyms or antonyms. Write Synonym or Antonym on the line following a pair.

1. monopoly/exclusive control _____

2. monotonous/boring _____

3. bilateral/unilateral _____

4. minimize/maximize _____

5. microscopic/tiny _____

6. omnipotent/weak _____

7. dilemma/predicament _____

    8. multiple/many _____

    9. prime/first _____

  10. monotonous/exciting _____

  11. panacea/cure-all _____

  12. pandemonium/quiet peacefulness _____

7-A-5 Word Search: Use your dictionary to locate other words that start with the number-indicating bases listed in Table 7.1. Add at least ten words to the table. Try not to select words most of which start with the same base. Be ready to tell the meanings of the words you have added.

7-A-6 Hypothesizing Meanings: Use your knowledge of number-stating bases to propose the following:

1. How many sides would you expect to find on each on the following geometric shapes? (Note: *-gon* is a suffix from the Greek indicating that you are dealing with a geometric figure having a specified number of angles.)
   a. octagon
   b. hexagon
   c. pentagon
   d. quadrangle
   e. polygon
   f. triangle

2. How many years are being celebrated in each instance? (Note: *-annus* is from the Latin word for year; in these words, you see it as *-ennial*. If you remember that, you will have no trouble with the double-*n* spelling.)
   a. septennial
   b. centennial
   c. bicentennial
   d. tercentennial
   e. millennium

3. How many full notes are there in a musical octave?

Word Study Module 7-B—
Words with Prefixes That You Have
Already Met: A Review

Pronounce each word, listening for the prefix and syllable breaks; then highlight the prefix and think about the meaning it adds to the root or base word.

Strategy Box 7-B—Word Connections

Most words are related to other words in some way. Because of the interconnected-
ness of words, when you find an unfamiliar one, you should ask yourself, "Is this
word related to a word or part of a word that I already know?" You might just get
lucky. Take, for example, the five-syllable word *indisputable*. This word is a relative, or kin, of the word *dispute*. You may recognize it, for at sometime you may
have had a dispute, or disagreement, with someone and come away angry. You may
also recognize the prefix *in-*, meaning "not," and the suffix *-able*, meaning "able to
be." Making these three connections, you can predict that *indisputable* means "not
able to be disputed or questioned." So don't think of words as separate, discrete
items, or entities. Try to make word connections. Meeting an unfamiliar word,
apply this one-step question strategy:

Ask, "Is there some part of this word that is similar in some way to another
word that I already know? Is there a part of this word that I recognize?"

Let's apply the strategy to the word *enamored* that we considered in an earlier
Strategy Box. At that point, we used a phrase of opposite meaning to help us unlock
that word. You also could have used the Word Connections strategy if you already
were familiar with such related words as *amorous*—loving, *amorously*—in a loving
way, *amorousness*—condition of feeling loving and made the connection between
those words and *enamored*. *Amorous* means "loving." Hence, to be enamored of is
to feel lovingly toward.

1. **a brade** (ə brād′), *v.*, wear away as by friction, erode. (Reminder: *Ab-* means "off.")

    Related words: **ab ra sion,** *n.;* **ab ra sive,** *adj.*

    Contexts: I was afraid that the rubbing of my shoe against my heel would
abrade the skin.

    When an abrasion does occur, repair the damage with an antibiotic cream.
My uncle had a very abrasive personality. He irritated everyone with whom
he interacted.

2. **a typ i cal** (ā tip′ i kəl), *adj.,* not conforming, unusual. (Reminder: *A-* means
"without" or "not.")

    Related word: **a typ i cal ly,** *adv.*

    Contexts: My friend was not your usual kind of guy. He was atypical in
many respects. He acted atypically in most situations.

3. **com po nent** (kəm pō′ nənt), *n.,* element that makes up a larger system. (Reminder: *Com-* means "together.")

Related word: **com pose,** *v.*

Contexts: The one component of his plan that I disliked was its reliance on the factor of chance. "Try to compose an alternative that does not rely on chance," I suggested.

✦ 4. **de duce** (di do͞os′), *v.,* reach a conclusion, generally through rational thought; reason from a general principle to a specific example or instance. (Reminder: *De-* can mean "away.")

Related words: **de duc tive,** *adj.;* **in duc tive,** *adj.*

Contexts: You cannot deduce that from the generalization. Deductive thinking is difficult; it requires the application of a general idea to a particular situation. Inductive thinking is also difficult; it requires the synthesis of ideas and the development of something original out of them.

✦ 5. **di chot o my** (dī kot′ ə mē), *n.,* division into two seemingly opposite parts. (Reminder: *Di-* means "two.")

Related word: **di chot o mize,** *v.*

Contexts: I sensed a growing dichotomy within the group that I knew had to be addressed if we were to succeed in our task. "Try not to dichotomize the group; we need unity," I urged.

✦ 6. **di verge** (di vûrj′), *v.,* move or lie in different directions from a common point, branch off, differ. (Reminder: *Di-* means "apart.")

Related words: **di ver gence,** *n.;* **di ver gent,** *adj.*

Contexts: Where a path diverges, a person must stop to consider which branch to follow. When a group goes in divergent directions, chaos can result. Such divergence can cause unpleasantness.

✦ 7. **ec sta sy** (ek′ stə sē), *n.,* intense delight; a state of mind where one is simply carried away. (Reminder: *Ex-* means "out.")

Related words: **ec stat ic,** *adj.;* **ec stat i cal ly,** *adv.*

Contexts: When the young woman became engaged to be married, she was ecstatic. She smiled ecstatically. Her ecstasy was short lived, however, for the next day her husband-to-be was killed in a car accident.

✦ 8. **e volve** (i volv′), *v.,* achieve or develop gradually over time. (Reminder: *Ex-* means "out.")

Related word: **ev o lu tion ary,** *adj.*

Contexts: Her concern evolved out of her interest in helping those who were more disadvantaged than she was. His thinking was evolutionary in that it developed very slowly.

◆◆◆

Highlighted Word Element

volv- or **volut-,** a Latin root meaning "to roll."

Words with the element: *revolve, involve, revolution.*

◆◆◆

◆ 9. **in ter cept** (in′ tər sept′), *v.,* take or seize on the way from one place to another, or cut off; stop the progress of. (Reminder: *Inter-* means "between.")

> *Related word:* **in ter cep tion,** *n.*

> *Contexts:* My friend tried to intercept the letter before it reached its destination, but to no avail. His interception failed because he did not act quickly enough.

◆ 10. **in tro spec tion** (in′ trə spek′ shən), *n.,* contemplation of one's own feelings and thoughts. (Reminder: *Intro-* means "within.")

> *Related word:* **in tro spec tive,** *adj.*

> *Contexts:* The man was given to introspection; he spent considerable time thinking about what he was doing and why he was doing it. His introspective behavior became extreme, and he lost contact with what was going on around him.

◆ 11. **pre his tor ic** (prē′ hi stôr′ ik), *adj.,* of a time before written records. (Reminder: *Pre-* means "before.")

> *Related word:* **pre his tory,** *n.*

> *Contexts:* In prehistoric times, dinosaurs roamed the land. My friend was a student of prehistory, the history of humankind before there were written records.

◆ 12. **re plen ish** (ri plen′ ish), *v.,* fill again, add to the supply. (Reminder: *Re-* means "again.")

> *Related word:* **re plen ish ment,** *n.*

> *Contexts:* After the party, the hostess had to replenish her supply of dips and chips. For that matter, her entire pantry was in need of replenishment.

Word Study Activities Module 7-B— Making Meaning with Prefixes

7-B-1 Words in Meaningful Sentence Contexts: From the list, select the featured word that best fits the overall meaning of each sentence. Write that word in the blank. Use each option only once.

a. abraded   d. deduce   g. ecstasy   j. introspection
b. atypical   e. dichotomy   h. evolve   k. prehistoric
c. composite   f. diverge   i. intercept   l. replenish

1. Our paths in life were to _____; he was to go his way and I mine.

2. Before we set off for our hike across the ridge, we had to _____ our supplies.

3. The final plan was a/an _____ of the two sets of plans we had developed earlier.

4. You could really say that our plans had started to _____ from an initial beginning many years before.

5. I have always been intrigued by events that occurred in _____ times, and I have wondered how humans came to be the kinds of beings we are.

6. My husband tried to _____ me as I left work to come home, but he failed to catch me.

7. She was in perfect _____ when she learned she had won the scholarship; she emitted a loud scream and smiled so broadly that I thought her face would split in two.

8. On that day her behavior was _____; generally she does not get excited and can control her emotions.

9. The continued rubbing of the rake handle against the palm of my hand _____ the skin.

10. My friend spent much time in _____, considering the propriety of his prior acts.

11. I was able to _____ from your obvious limp that your accident was a serious one.

12. I sensed a/an _____ in the way the two senators viewed the issue. One was very conservative; the other was very liberal.

7-B-2 Writing with Verbs: Use each word as a verb in a sentence; you may prefer a past tense form such as *abraded*.

1. abrade

2. deduce

3. diverge

4. evolve

5. intercept

6. replenish

7-B-3 Writing with Adjectives: Use each as an adjective in a sentence.

1. abrasive

2. atypical

3. ecstatic

4. introspective

5. deductive

6. divergent

7-B-4 Definitional Study: Match each word on the left with its definition at the right. Write the word from the left on the line in each case. Use each word only once.

1. **abrade**   _____   a. before written records

2. **atypical**   _____   b. act of looking inward

3. **composite**   _____   c. change over time

4. **deduce**   _____   d. unusual

5. **dichotomy**   _____   e. refill, fill up again

6. **diverge**   _____   f. think logically from a point

7. **ecstasy**   _____   g. combination made up of other items

8. **evolve**   _____   h. separate into two paths

9. **intercept**   _____   i. rub off

10. **introspection** _____   j. great delight

11. **prehistoric**   _____   k. division between two parties or points

12. **replenish**   _____   l. stop on the way

Reading with Meaning Module 7-C—
Learning How the Months Were Named;
Using Context Clues and Word Elements

Read the following passage, especially making meaning with the boldfaced words.

A Bit of a Contradiction: Things Are Not as They Seem

In this chapter, as you studied the bases that tell "how many," you probably wondered about the four calendar words that carry some of these elements: *September, October, November,* and *December.* "Wait a minute," you might have said, "September isn't the seventh month; October isn't the eighth month; November isn't the ninth month; and December isn't the tenth month. What is wrong here?"

The answer is simple from a historical **perspective.** The old Roman calendar from which we derive the English names for the months was composed of only ten months. On that calendar, September was the seventh month, October the eighth month, November the ninth month, and December the tenth month. The year actually started with the month of March. This ten-month calendar was not synchronized with the time the earth took to **revolve** around the sun once. As a result, the calendar months did not match the seasonal changes in a **consistent** manner, and the people **periodically** had to add some days and even months to **realign** the calendar with the seasonal changes. To **counteract** this problem, at some point along the way, two months (January and February) were added to the calendar—initially at the end of the year but eventually at the beginning.

About 46 B.C. Julius Caesar did some more **tinkering** with the Roman calendar. He added a few days here and there and changed some month names. Although September, October, November, and December ended up as the ninth, tenth, eleventh, and twelfth months **respectively,** they kept their original names. That is why you see an apparent **contradiction** in the calendar that we use today.

Here is a summary of how all twelve months received their names:

- January for Janus, the Roman god of gates, who is generally **depicted** with two faces looking in opposite directions;

- February from the Latin festival of **purification,** or personal cleansing;

- March for Mars, the Roman god of war (this was originally the first month on the Roman calendar);

- April, origin uncertain, perhaps from the Latin *apero,* meaning "second" (April was the second month on the Roman calendar); or perhaps from *Aphro,* a pet name for Aphrodite, the Greek goddess of love (spring is the time of love);
- May from an Italic goddess;
- June after Juno, the queen of the gods and goddesses;
- July for Julius Caesar—a new name given at the time that J. C. was emperor of Rome;
- August for Augustus Caesar;
- September for its seventh position in the original month **sequence;**
- October for its eighth position;
- November for its ninth position;
- December for its tenth position.

Interestingly, the words for *day, night, month,* and *year* are all derived from the Anglo-Saxons, the early settlers of Britain who carried their language with them as they migrated from the European mainland onto the British Isles. Most of the names of the days of the week have a similar origin.

Word Study Activities Module 7-C— Using Context Clues and Word Elements to Figure Out Meanings

7-C-1 Talking Points: Hypothesize: Why are the words for *day, night, month,* and *year* as well as most of the names of the days of the week derived from the early Anglo-Saxon tongues? Why are the names for the months derived from the Romans? Write your hypotheses in your word study notebook.

7-C-2 Context Clues and Word Elements: Hypothesize the meanings of these words based on how they function in the passage. Just jot down next to each a few words that come to your mind. The words are listed in the order in which they appear in the selection.

1. perspective

2. revolve

3. consistent

4. periodically

  5. realign

  6. counteract

  7. tinker

  8. respectively

  9. contradiction

  10. depicted

  11. purification

  12. sequence

7-C-3 Definitional Study: Based on the hypotheses you made in 7-C-2, match each word with its corresponding definition by writing the word from the left column on the line by its definition.

1. **consistent**	_____	a. symbolic cleansing
2. **contradiction**	_____	b. point of view
3. **counteract**	_____	c. order of events
4. **depicted**	_____	d. from time to time
5. **periodically**	_____	e. put back in the correct lineup
6. **perspective**	_____	f. singly in the order indicated
7. **purification**	_____	g. act so as to overcome another act
8. **realign**	_____	h. compatible with
9. **respectively**	_____	i. act of saying something that is opposite
10. **revolve**	_____	j. go around
11. **sequence**	_____	k. toy with so as to change a little
12. **tinker**	_____	l. represented, as in a picture

Confusing Words—*Accept* and *Except*

Two words that many people confuse are *accept* and *except*. *Accept* generally functions in sentences as a verb; it means "to take or receive what is offered." People accept invitations, proposals of marriage, excuses, plans, ideas—among other things. Derivatives include *acceptance, acceptable,* and *unacceptable*. People send in their acceptances to invitations. Most things are either acceptable—OK—or unacceptable—far from OK.

Accept is made up of two parts. The prefix *ad-* (changed to *ac-* because the base starts with the letter *c*) is at the beginning and means "to." The root is *cept* from the Latin and means "take." Literally to accept is "to take to."

Except comes from the same Latin root, but the prefix it bears is *ex-*, which means "out." Its literal meaning is "to take out." Today *except* generally is used to mean the following:

- "other than," as in the sentence "Everyone came except for my friend."
- "only but" as in the sentence "She would have come except that she was sick."

In both instances, as you can see, *except* is functioning as an adverb. A derivative is the noun *exception*. People talk about things being "exceptions to the rule."

Fill in the blanks with *accept/except* or their derivatives:

1. She had to _____ her father's help in meeting her tuition payments.

2. She would have worked at night _____ that she had no means of transportation.

3. When she received her _____ letter from her college of choice, she was ecstatic.

4. The professor made no _____; if your paper was not turned in on time, she lowered your grade one full mark.

PART IV

SUFFIXES AND OTHER FINAL ELEMENTS TO LOOK OUT FOR

8

Adjective-Forming Suffixes— Describing People and Things

◆◆

Objectives: In Chapter 8, you will develop the ability to

- explain the relationship between the part of speech of a word and the spelling of a suffix it carries by talking about such words as *ridiculous, rhinoceros,* and *hippopotamus;*
- recognize and interpret adjective-forming suffixes (see Table 8.1 for a list);
- comprehend and use the following adjectives featured in Module 8-A:

belligerent	deceitful	impulsive	remorseful
boisterous	docile	incredulous	tenacious
complacent	eccentric	intrepid	vulnerable
culpable	feisty	loquacious	

- recognize and make meaning with the element *credi-,* meaning "to believe";
- comprehend and use the following adjectives and power words featured in Module 8-B:

ambiguous	compulsory	feasible	precarious
amicable	crucial	fraudulent	resistant
collaborative	deficient	mundane	turbulent

caucus and seminar (*power words*);

- recognize and make meaning with the element *turb-,* meaning "to disturb";
- decide when to drop the final *e* on a word when adding a suffix to it; and
- distinguish between the words *affect* and *effect* and between *affective* and *effective.*

The story of language is the story of human civilization.
Nowhere is civilization so perfectly mirrored as in speech.

—Mario Pei, *The Story of Language,* 1949

◆◆◆

Interesting Words to Think About— *Ridiculous, Rhinoceros,* and *Hippopotamus*

The children's writer Bernard Waber has given us a delightful story titled *"You Look Ridiculous," Said the Rhinoceros to the Hippopotamus*. In creating his tongue-tickling title, Waber selected three words all of which have almost the same final rhyming sounds. Look, however, at the letters that compose, or make up, those sounds. The final sounds of *ridiculous* are spelled *-ous,* the final sounds of *rhinoceros* are spelled *-os,* whereas the final sounds of *hippopotamus* are spelled *-us*.

Some of us **bemoan** the problems associated with English spellings and wonder if there is any rhyme or reason to explain how we encode such English words. In this case, reason does rule. The ending on *ridiculous* is an adjective-forming suffix that generally means "full of" and is spelled *-ous*. If you think for a moment, you can name numerous words that end with this suffix—commonly heard adjectives such as *glorious, marvelous,* and *generous* and less commonly heard ones such as *treacherous, invidious,* and *lecherous*.

In English we have at our disposal other suffixes that also say "full of": *-ful* as on *graceful; -ose* as on *verbose;* and *-olent* as on *violent*. In each case, a word ending with the suffix functions in sentences as an adjective.

But let's get back to *rhinoceros* and *hippopotamus*. Obviously these words work as nouns, not as adjectives. You can trace *rhinoceros* back through the Latin to the Greek word *rhinokerōs* (which in turn comes from two Greek words—one for nose and one for horn). The *-os* is a common ending in the Greek language; you already have encountered it on *chaos* and *cosmos;* another example is *pathos*.

In contrast, although *hippopotamus* also came to us through the Latin from the Greek, in so doing it picked up the Latin noun ending *-us*. Other nouns with this Latin ending include *circus, walrus, prospectus, status, nucleus, eucalyptus*.

What implications does this have for you? In spelling adjectives like *ridiculous,* remember that you are working with a suffix that means "full of" and spell the ending *-ous*. Where the meaning is different and the word is functioning as a noun, choose either *-os* or

-*us*. Actually if you are uncertain and you cannot check a dictionary, go with -*us*, which is found more often in English than -*os*. Of course, in such instances, you would be wise to trust your dictionary.

Collaborative Search and Discover

- In your word study notebook, make a chart on which you list -*ous*, -*ful*, -*ose*, -*olent* each at the head of a column. Beneath each, write down as many words as you can that end with the suffix.

- Hypothesize the meaning of the verb *bemoan* as it is used in the second paragraph of the passage. Then look it up in your dictionary. In your notebook write down its etymology and meaning. Can you locate other verbs that start with the prefix *be-?* Here is one to get you started: *bedevil*.

Strategy Box 8-A—Suffix Awareness

A **suffix** is a series of letters attached to the base or central part of a word at the end of it. Etymologically, *suffix* means "to fasten underneath"—which really is what happens when a suffix is added to a base.

A first step in your suffix-awareness strategy is to recognize the ending syllable or syllables of a multisyllabic word as a suffix you know and tell yourself the meaning of it. To do this, of course, you must have knowledge of suffixes. The second step is to strip the suffix from the base part of the word and see if you recognize anything about the part that is left. The third step is to connect or relate the meaning of the suffix to the base part of the word. This strategy is essentially the same as your prefix-awareness strategy except that here you are working with final syllables of words.

Let's see how this three-step strategy works in interpreting a word such as *transmittal* in this sentence:

> Complete and attach a transmittal slip before sending the package to the agent in charge.

What does *transmittal* mean here? What is a *transmittal slip?*

Applying the first step of your strategy, you see the suffix -*al* at the end of the three-syllable word *transmittal*. You may recognize it as an adjective-building suffix that means "being involved with, related to, pertaining to." Second, you strip off the suffix and see the verb *transmit*, which you know means "send." Third, you relate the two parts and conclude that *transmittal* merely means "being involved in the sending of something." The transmittal slip is the form that you must complete before sending something forward.

Because the meanings of suffixes are often not too helpful in cracking the meanings of longer words, you will probably learn more about an unfamiliar word from the prefix you find at the beginning rather than from a suffix you find at the end. However, knowledge of suffixes can help you to pronounce and spell words. If you recognize a suffix, you can use your knowledge of it to decide how to pronounce it, for you rarely if ever put the accent on the suffix within a word. Similarly, once you know you are handling a suffix, spelling it may become a bit easier as you saw in the case of adjectives that end with -ous.

Obviously, to make suffixes work for you, you must have knowledge of suffixes and their meanings. Table 8.1 offers some common adjective-forming suffixes with meanings and examples. You will be working with some of these later in this chapter, but for now highlight with your marking pen the suffix on each of the exemplar words in Table 8.1. Notice, too, that most of these suffixes say "pertaining to," or "having the characteristic of," or something rather close to that.

Table 8.1   Adjective-Forming Suffixes

Suffix	Meaning	Examples
-ful	full of, having the characteristic of	remorseful, delightful
-ous	full of, having the characteristic of	glorious, religious, luminous
-ose	full of, having the characteristic of	grandiose, verbose, bellicose
-olent or -ulent	full of, having the characteristic of	violent; turbulent
-some	full of, having the characteristic of	awesome, handsome, wholesome
-ish	full of, having the characteristic of	boyish, girlish
-ary	having the characteristic of, pertaining to	temporary, sedentary, contemporary
-ile	pertaining to	docile, hostile, agile
-al	pertaining to	ethical, moral, critical, temporal, pivotal
-ic	pertaining to	epidemic, dynamic, aquatic
-ant	pertaining to	malignant, militant
-ent	pertaining to	complacent, resilient, confident

Table 8.1   Adjective-Forming Suffixes *(cont.)*

Suffix	Meaning	Examples
-ine	pertaining to	masculine, feminine, porcine
-ate	pertaining to	insubordinate
-able or -ible	able to be, inclined to	equitable, memorable, culpable, viable, navigable
-acious	inclined to, tending to	tenacious, audacious, mendacious
-ive	inclined to, tending to	impulsive, compulsive, invasive
-id	inclined to, tending to	humid, florid
-itious or -icious	inclined to, tending to	fictitious; delicious
-ory	inclined to, tending to	compulsory, cursory
-uous	inclined to, tending to	continuous
-y	inclined to, tending to	pesky, feisty
-less	without	worthless, groundless

Word Study Module 8-A—
Adjectives You Use to Describe People

As you have just discovered, you can identify some words as adjectives from the suffixes they carry. When you see one of these endings, apply the meaning of "full of," "having the characteristic of," "inclined to," or "pertaining to" and decide whether that helps you make any greater sense with the word.

You can change adjectives to add the meaning of "more" or "most." You can say that someone is happy, happier (the comparative form), or happiest (the superlative form). Or you can say that someone is energetic, more energetic, or most energetic. Use *-er* and *-est* to form the comparative and superlative forms of short adjectives. Use *more* and *most* to form the comparative and superlative forms of long adjectives. Mentally form the comparatives and superlatives of the adjectives in Table 8.1

In this module are words you can use to describe people. Pronounce each of them, with a marker highlight any suffixes and prefixes they carry, and then devise sentences using them. Also look for other words in the model sentences that carry an adjective-forming suffix, circle the suffix, and be ready to hypothesize its meaning.

✦ 1. **bel lig er ent** (be lij′ ər ənt), *adj.,* eager, or "itching" for a fight, warlike.

   Related words: **bel lig er ence,** *n.;* **bel lig er ent ly,** *adv.*

   Contexts: The president's belligerent attitude frightened us for we worried that it would lead us into war. His belligerence was unreasonable, given the current state of affairs.

✦ 2. **com pla cent** (kəm plā′ sənt), *adj.,* overly content with what is.

   Related words: **com pla cen cy,** *n.;* **com pla cent ly,** *adv.*

   Contexts: Even as I was becoming more uneasy about what was going on, my mother became more complacent. Her complacency finally got to me. "How can anyone sit back so complacently," I asked her, "when the world is in turmoil around us?"

✦ 3. **bois ter ous** (boi′ stər əs), *adj.,* loud in behavior, sometimes to the point of being undisciplined.

   Related words: **bois ter ous ness,** *n.;* **bois ter ous ly,** *adv.*

   Contexts: Having been at the bar for over an hour, Joe became so boisterous that the bartender asked him to leave. I had never seen Joe act so boisterously; usually he exerted good control over himself. "I cannot condone such boisterousness," Joe's mother told him.

✦ 4. **in cred u lous** (in krej′ ə ləs), *adj.,* disbelieving to the point of being very skeptical.

   Related word: **in cred u lous ly,** adv.

   Contexts: I could tell by the look on the professor's face that she was incredulous. I stood nearby and watched incredulously as the belligerent student tried to make excuses for his behavior.

✦✦

Highlighted Word Element

cred- or **credit-,** a Latin root meaning "to believe, to trust."

Words with the element: *incredible, credit, discredit.*

✦✦

✦ 5. **lo qua cious** (lō kwā′ shəs), *adj.,* extremely talkative to the point of overdoing it.

   Related word: **lo qua cious ness,** *n.*

   Contexts: My grandfather became loquacious in his elder years; he told stories of his early exploits over and over. People would walk the other way when they saw him to avoid being subjected to his loquaciousness.

✦ 6. **te na cious** (ti nā′ shəs), *adj.,* persistent, holding stubbornly to an activity and not easily pulled away from it.

   Related word: **te nac i ty,** *n.*

   Contexts: My father was a tenacious man; once he got started on a task, nothing could divert him from it. His tenacity was an asset at times, but sometimes it became a handicap.

✦ 7. **cul pa ble** (kul′ pə bəl), *adj.,* responsible for something bad or evil; blameworthy.

   Related words: **cul pa bil i ty,** *n.;* **cul prit,** *n.;* **in cul pa ble,** *adj.*

   Contexts: I knew that my friend was culpable for I saw her take the money. She was the culprit! I was absolutely certain of her culpability. However, I could not claim to be totally inculpable for I did not alert the authorities.

✦ 8. **vul ner a ble** (vul′ nər ə bəl), *adj.,* open to attack, liable to be wounded.

   Related word: **vul ner a bil i ty,** *n.*

   Contexts: The soldier at the front of the column of troops is the most vulnerable. His vulnerability is especially great when the column first emerges from the trees and he can be picked off by the opposing forces.

✦ 9. **de ceit ful** (du sēt′ fəl), *adj.,* inclined to be untruthful or deliberately misleading.

   Related words: **de ceit ful ness,** *n.;* **de ceit,** *n.*

   Contexts: My cousin is the most deceitful person I have ever met; there is always a lie on his lips. Can you comprehend such deceit?

✦ 10. **re morse ful** (ri môrs′ fəl), *adj.,* experiencing or expressing regret for having done a wrong.

   Related words: **re morse,** *n.;* **re morse less,** *adj.*

   Contexts: Although one of the criminals was remorseful, the other was remorseless and would not extend an apology to those whom he had harmed. My remorse was heightened when I saw the outcome of my evil deed.

✦ 11. **doc ile** (dos′ əl), *adj.,* submissive, easily controlled.

   Related words: **do cil i ty,** *n.;* **doc ile ly,** *adj.*

   Contexts: The little girl was very docile for a two-year-old. She docilely did what she was told to do. Such docility is abnormal in a two-year-old; most toddlers want to do it their way.

✦ 12. **ec cen tric** (ik sən′ trik), *adj.,* strange, departing from what is normal.

   Related word: **eccentricity,** *n.*

   Contexts: His eccentric behavior drew everyone's eyes to him. "What is he doing?" people asked as they wondered about his eccentricity.

✦ 13. **feist y** (fī′ stē), *adj.,* full of spirit. (Note: *Feisty* is an Americanism used in some regions of the country, especially as part of informal speech.)

   Contexts: My aunt is a feisty gal. She is not at all mild-mannered.

✦ 14. **im pul sive** (im pul′ siv), *adj.,* tending to act without thinking.

   Related words: **im pul sive ness,** *n.;* **im pul sive ly,** *adv.*

   Contexts: My sister was an impulsive child, given to action rather than thought. Her impulsiveness got her into trouble on numerous occasions. When she acted impulsively, she often found herself "in over her head."

✦ 15. **in trep id** (in trep′ id), *adj.,* fearless.

   Contexts: John Glenn is the epitome of an intrepid adventurer. At the age of seventy-six he went into space for the second time in his life.

Word Study Activities Module 8-A— Making Meaning with Adjectives

8-A-1 Words in Meaningful Sentence Contexts: From the list, select the word that best fits the overall meaning of each sentence. Write that word in the blank. Use each option only once. Rely on your Know-for-sure/Process-of-elimination test-taking strategy.

a. belligerent	e. deceitful	i. impulsive	m. remorseful
b. boisterous	f. docile	j. incredulous	n. tenacious
c. complacent	g. eccentric	k. intrepid	o. vulnerable
d. culpable	h. feisty	l. loquacious	

1. Because the man was so _____ about the trouble he had caused me, instead of being hostile toward him, I was cordial.

2. The _____ child told several lies to avoid punishment.

3. In that situation, I felt _____ because I knew I was alone and totally responsible for myself.

4. That morning the mare was _____ to the point where I had trouble controlling her. In contrast, the stallion was more _____, responding quickly to my commands.

5. Throughout my ordeal, I behaved like a/an _____ warrior. Only afterward did I collapse in shock.

6. I was amazed at how _____ she seemed to be about her living conditions, given the level of poverty at which she had to exist.

7. My former secretary is a naturally _____ person who spent more of her time talking on the phone than attending to her work.

8. I was _____ when my secretary told me that her former employer accepted such unprofessional behavior from her.

9. The children at my son's birthday party became so _____ that the neighbors complained about the loud noise and commotion.

10. It was his _____ attitude that bothered me; he took offense even at the most innocent suggestions that I offered.

11. My cousin is _____ in his manner of dress; he enjoys wearing the wildest forms of attire.

12. Wendy is a/an _____ sort of person; she typically acts on her whims rather than on a rational analysis of a situation.

13. Gail was _____ in her search for answers to her health problem; she did not rest until she got to a doctor who could help her.

14. _____, I knew that sooner or later my misstep would catch up with me.

8-A-2 Synonym Study: Match the word or word element on the left with the appropriate word or phrase on the right. Write the word on the blank. Use each option only once. Use the process of elimination to help you.

1. **belligerent**   _____   a. untruthful

2. **boisterous**   _____   b. disbelieving

3. **complacent**   _____   c. submissive

4. **culpable**   _____   d. nonthinking

5. **deceitful**   _____   e. loud and undisciplined

6. **docile**   _____   f. open to attack

7. **eccentric**   _____   g. talkative

8. **feisty**   _____   h. strange

9. **impulsive**   _____   i. regretful

10. **incredulous**   _____   j. fearless

11. **intrepid**   _____   k. warlike

12. **loquacious**   _____   l. believe

13. **remorseful**   _____   m. persistent

14. **tenacious**   _____   n. content with

15. **vulnerable** _____   o. guilty of

16. **cred-** _____   p. spirited

8-A-3 Antonym Study: Star the option that is the opposite of the word at the left.

1. **intrepid**	a. feisty	b. fitful	c. fearful	d. friendly
2. **loquacious**	a. silly	b. sensible	c. silent	d. strange
3. **vulnerable**	a. safe	b. sane	c. satisfied	d. scared
4. **tenacious**	a. still	b. sharp	c. swayable	d. significant
5. **docile**	a. feisty	b. fabulous	c. fake	d. fearful
6. **eccentric**	a. normal	b. negligent	c. native	d. naive
7. **impulsive**	a. temporary	b. tense	c. thorough	d. thoughtful
8. **remorseful**	a. unrepentant	b. untruthful	c. unselfish	d. unreliable
9. **culpable**	a. innocent	b. ideal	c. ignorant	d. indecisive
10. **belligerent**	a. parallel	b. peace-loving	c. pale	d. popular
11. **boisterous**	a. quiet	b. quick	c. questionable	d. quirky
12. **complacent**	a. doubtful	b. discontented	c. dedicated	d. desirable
13. **feisty**	a. colossal	b. calm	c. complaining	d. clean
14. **incredulous**	a. boiling	b. bookish	c. bordering	d. believing
15. **deceitful**	a. hopeful	b. heavenly	c. hurtful	d. honest

8-A-4 Sort and Search: Sort the adjectives in this module into categories based on their suffixes. In other words, group together all the adjectives that end with *–ful,* as in *deceitful;* do the same with the other adjectives and their suffixes. Then brainstorm a few more adjectives that bear each of the suffixes. Develop your sorted lists here.

8-A-5 Related Words in Meaningful Sentence Contexts: From the list below, select the word that best fits the overall meaning of each sentence. Write that word in the blank. Use each option only once.

a. belligerence	e. deceit	i. impulsiveness	l. remorse
b. boisterously	f. docilely	j. incredulously	m. tenacity
c. complacency	g. eccentricity	k. loquaciousness	n. vulnerability
d. culpability	h. impulsively		

1. Faced with such _____, I gave in just to keep the peace.

2. My mother acted too _____ when, without thinking about the consequences, she invited to her house someone whom she had never met.

3. Because of the man's _____, he was able to conquer what at first had seemed an impossible task.

4. I like a bit of peace and quiet, so the woman's _____ quickly got on my nerves.

5. _____ the children jumped around and hollered out as they played.

6. In contrast, the well-behaved child followed behind her mother and father and _____ did what she was told.

7. "Do you mean to say that you were offered a million dollars to do that?" I asked _____.

8. After the serious accident that she had caused, the drunken driver expressed no _____.

9. The lawyer was a master of _____; he knew exactly how to bend the law to meet his own malevolent ends.

10. I had never seen him exhibit such _____ before; his outfit was too bizarre for me to try to describe to you, and his behavior was absolutely weird.

11. The teacher regretted her _____ as soon as she agreed to delay the due date on the assignment. "Why did I not think through the situation?" she asked herself.

12. Because of his _____, he had to accept any job that was offered him. He realized that since he was unemployed and desperate for money, he had no choice.

13. His _____ was obvious to the judge. The evidence of his guilt was undeniable.

14. As she grew older, my friend's _____ also grew. She wanted nothing about her life to change, although she could have enjoyed a much more eventful life.

Word Study Module 8-B—
Adjectives You Use to Describe Things
and Events in the World around You

Pronounce each word; with a marker, highlight the suffix in each case. Then read the definition and sample contexts and propose a sentence using each word.

✦   1. **am big u ous** (am big′ yü əs), *adj.,* unclear in meaning, having more than one possible meaning.

   Related words: **am bi gu i ty,** *n.;* **am big u ous ly,** *adv.;* **un am big u-ous ly,** *adv.*

Contexts: Because the doctor gave me ambiguous directions, I did not take my medication on schedule; this delayed my recovery. From that experience, I learned the importance of speaking unambiguously. I learned also that ambiguity can have disastrous results.

✦ 2. **pre car i ous** (pri ker′ ē əs), *adj.,* not secure, shaky, dangerous.

Related words: **pre car i ous ness,** *n.;* **pre car i ous ly,** adv.

Contexts: The expensive vase sat in a precarious position high on the mantel. I wondered who had arranged it so precariously close to the edge.

I recognized the precariousness of my position; I was the last hired and most likely to be the first fired.

✦ 3. **am i ca ble** (am′ ə kə bəl), *adj.,* peaceable, friendly, and without anger.

Related words: **am i ca bil i ty,** *n.;* **am i ca bly,** adv.

Contexts: The previously belligerent nations came to an amicable settlement of their differences. They resolved their disagreements amicably without resorting to warfare. They set a fine precedent for amicability among nations.

✦ 4. **fea si ble** (fē′ zə bəl), *adj.,* capable of being done or accomplished, possible.

Related words: **fea si bil i ty,** *n.;* **fea si bly,** *adv.;* **in fea si ble,** *adj.*

Contexts: Although others believed that it was a feasible plan, I disagreed. We had not investigated the feasibility of it. "Could we feasibly achieve our purposes in this way?" I asked. Down deep, I knew that the procedure would prove to be infeasible.

✦ 5. **col lab o ra tive** (kə lab′ ə ra tiv), *adj.,* jointly working with others on a project.

Related words: **col lab o rate,** *v.;* **col lab o ra tion,** *n.;* **col lab o ra tive ly,** *adv.* (See also Power Words on p. 159.)

Contexts: Students generally enjoy collaborative activities in their classes. Working together on a task, they learn the advantages of collaboration. This is vital if they must collaborate on projects when they enter the workforce. So work collaboratively with your friends to get important tasks done.

✦ 6. **com pul sor y** (kəm pul′ sər ē), *adj.,* required.

Related words: **com pel,** *v.;* **com pul sion,** *n.;* **com pul sive,** *adj.*

Contexts: Attendance at the preregistration meeting was compulsory for freshmen, but noncompulsory for upperclassmen. I was compelled to speak out at the meeting.

Betsy was driven by some inner compulsion to be the best in everything she attempted. At some point her behavior became compulsive; she actually had little control over what she did.

◆◆◆

Power Words—Ways to Work Together

sem i nar, a noun meaning "a meeting for the exchange of ideas, especially a meeting of advanced students organized under the guidance of a professor" (from the Greek via Latin).

cau cus, a noun meaning "a closed meeting of members of a political party, especially a meeting to decide on important policy positions"; a verb meaning "to hold such a meeting" (from the American Algonquin language).

Contexts: Collaborative activity is important within a seminar because students must share their research findings.

The representative could not attend the Democratic caucus because he was a Republican.

◆◆◆

◆   7. **cru cial** (krū′ shəl), *adj.,* very important, decisive to the point that it makes a difference to the outcome, critical.

    Contexts: I knew that I was at a crucial point in my career; decisions I made then would have a radical effect on my future.

◆   8. **de fi cient** (di fish′ ənt), *adj.,* not enough in amount, lacking in, incomplete.

    Related words: **di fi cien cy,** *n.;* **de fi cit,** *n.* or *adj.*

    Contexts: If you are deficient in credits, you will not graduate with your class. You can make up your deficiency by going to summer school.

    Some families believe in deficit spending. They spend more each year than they earn.

◆   9. **fraud u lent** (frô′ jə lənt), *adj.,* dishonest often to the point of being illegal, gotten by illicit means.

    Related words: **fraud,** *n.;* **fraud u lent ly,** *adv.*

    Contexts: Bruce amassed his wealth through fraudulent wheeling and dealing, which eventually brought him to the attention of the FBI. Bruce knew how to manipulate money fraudulently by moving it electronically from one bank to another. Eventually he was convicted of fraud.

◆   10. **tur bu lent** (tèr′ byə lənt), *adj.,* rough, causing disorder or commotion, stormy.

    Related words: **tur bu lence,** *n.;* **tur bu lent ly,** *adv.*

    Contexts: The sea was turbulent with huge waves that struck the land with horrific force. When the airplane encountered extreme turbulence, items that were not secured flew helter-skelter in the cabin. (Note: we also talk of "turbulent times."

◆◆◆

Highlighted Word Element

turb-, a Latin root meaning "to disturb."

Words with the element: *disturbance, turbine, perturb.*

◆◆◆

◆ 11. **mun dane** (mun′ dān), *adj.,* concerned with the ordinary, of the earth in contrast to the heavenly.

> *Contexts:* My sister spends her time preoccupied with mundane matters; she never focuses on what is really crucial in her life.

◆ 12. **re sis tant** (ri zis′ tənt), *adj.,* opposed to change.

> *Related words:* **re sist,** *v.;* **re sis tance,** *n.*

> *Contexts:* The scientist struggled to discover an antibiotic that would destroy that resistant strain of bacteria, but to no avail.

> My friend resisted all my attempts to resolve our disagreement amicably. I could not overcome his violent resistance.

Word Study Activities Module 8-B— Making Meaning with Adjectives

8-B-1 Words in Meaningful Sentence Contexts: From the list below, select the featured word that best fits the overall meaning of each sentence. Write that word in the blank. Use each option only once.

a. ambiguous	d. compulsory	g. feasible	j. precarious
b. amicable	e. crucial	h. fraudulent	k. resistant
c. collaborative	f. deficient	i. mundane	l. turbulent

1. As an educator, my mother believes wholeheartedly that school attendance should be _____ until one reaches the age of eighteen.

2. I had lived through the _____ period during which the United States was involved in the Vietnam War, and I realized the effect that unsettled conditions can have on everyday activities.

3. The man's position in the company became _____ when the management changed and there were cutbacks in the number of employees.

4. I had to make a/an _____ decision: Should I accept my friend's proposal or should I reject it?

5. I did not understand what my brother was implying because his statement was too

_____.

6. "Some _____ activity is necessary to get the job done," my boss said. "Let's work together on this project."

7. The stain on Mark's coat was a particularly _____ one. No matter how he worked on it, he could not get it out.

8. After many hours of negotiation, we finally arrived at a/an _____ resolution of our differences.

9. Sometimes I get frustrated because I seem to spend most of my time tending to

_____ matters rather than handling more crucial concerns.

10. Because her body was _____ in calcium, my grandmother broke her hip when she fell.

11. The chief executive officer, or the CEO, was charged with the _____ manipulation of the stocks of the company that he ran. He was indicted for his illegal activity.

12. The CEO established a committee to determine whether the plan was

_____. When the committee reported that the plan seemed sound, the

chief executive officer went ahead with it.

Same   Opp.

8-B-2 Synonym or Antonym: Next to each pair, write either Synonym or Antonym, based on the relationship between the words.

1. ambiguous/clear   _____

2. amicable/belligerent   _____

3. collaborative/together   _____

4. compulsory/required   _____

5. crucial/unimportant   _____

6. deficient/enough   _____

7. feasible/impracticable   _____

8. fraudulent/dishonest   _____

9. mundane/crucial   _____

10. precarious/unsafe   _____

11. resistant/changeable   _____

12. turbulent/wild   _____

8-B-3 Crossword Puzzle: Complete the crossword puzzle in Figure 8.1 based on your knowledge of the words in this module. Use the list of words from the prior activity to help you.

Figure 8.1   A Crossword Puzzle of Words Describing Things Around You

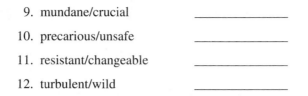

ACROSS

1 Dishonest to the point of being illegal
3 Required
4 Closed meeting of members of a political party
6 Concerned with the ordinary
10 Unclear in meaning
11 Meeting for the exchange of ideas, especially a meeting of advanced students of a subject
12 Jointly working with others
13 Capable of being done, possible
15 Opposed to change

DOWN

2 Rough, stormy
5 Critical, very important
7 Peaceable, friendly
8 Lacking in, not enough in amount
9 Not secure, shaky
14 Word element meaning "to disturb"

8-B-4 Related Words in Meaningful Sentence Contexts: From the list, select the word that best fits the overall meaning of each sentence. Write that word in the blank. Use each option only once. Use the process of elimination.

a. ambiguity   d. compelled   g. feasibility   j. precariously

b. amicably   e. deficiency   h. fraudulently   k. resist

c. collaborate   f. deficit   i. precariousness   l. tenacity

1. I admired my friend for his _____ in the face of so many losses. Regardless of them all, he persisted.

2. The man did not realize the _____ of his own position in the hierarchy. He held his position only because of his wife's influence.

3. By the end of the year, as a result of spending beyond my income, I had run up a large _____ for the year.

4. His friend wanted to _____ with him on the project, but he wanted to work alone.

5. Regardless of that, the two students got along _____ without having major disagreements.

6. I must admit that any _____ bothers me; I function best in situations where directions are clear and I know exactly what is required of me.

7. Her innate honesty _____ her to tell the truth.

8. Before proceeding with the project, the president authorized a study of the _____ of it.

9. The rock was perched _____ on the ledge, from which it could have fallen as a result of a sudden jolt.

10. The boss had to _____ her natural inclination to help since this was a training session for her employees. They had to learn by doing the task by themselves.

11. There was absolutely no way that Arif could make up his _____ in college credits in time to graduate with his friends.

12. Because everyone knew that Amos had dealt _____ with his friends, after that no one would have anything to do with him.

8-B-5 Word Sort: Add the highlighted words from module 8-B to the adjective word sort that you began in activity 8-A-4.

Reading with Meaning Module 8-C—
Learning to Add Suffixes to Roots and Words

Read the following passage to learn how to handle the spelling of words when adding a suffix at the end.

Retain or Drop: The Problem of the Final e

Study these words, noting what happens to the final *e* on a word when you add a suffix or ending:

arrange + ment	arrangement
pale + ness	paleness
premature + ly	prematurely
whole + some	wholesome
nine + teen	nineteen
hope + ful	hopeful

What do you notice? In each case, when you add the ending, you retain the final *e* on the original word as you spell the new word.

Next consider these words. Note that the original word also ends with an *e*.

migrate + ed	migrated
hope + ing	hoping
love + able	lovable
collapse + ible	collapsible
guide + ance	guidance
stone + y	stony
white + ish	whitish

"Hey, there! What's happening?" you may have thought. "In each of these cases, to spell the word correctly, I've got to drop the final *e* on the word before adding a suffix. This is confusing. How do I know when to retain that final *e* and when to drop it?"

There is a generalization that can help you. Look at the letter at the beginning of the suffix. In the first list, in each case that first letter is a consonant. In the second list, that letter is a vowel. When a suffix begins with a consonant, generally you retain the final *e* on a word before adding the suffix. When a suffix begins with a vowel or the letter *y* (which here makes the sound of the long *e*), you generally drop the final *e*. That's neat, isn't it?

Apply the generalization by spelling the word that results from the addition of the suffix to each base word given. You should be able to explain the reasoning that supports your spelling.

free + dom   _____

misplace + ment   _____

mature + ly   _____

grace + ful   _____

remorse + ful   _____

blue + ish   _____

desire + able   _____

offense + ive   _____

smoke + y   _____

Unfortunately, in the English language exceptions to spelling rules are **rife.** Here are two to remember: true + ly = truly, acknowledge + ment = acknowledgment.

Also English has another characteristic that requires you to think twice when you add such an ending as -able to a word. The letters g and c have both soft and hard sounds. The soft sounds are the sounds you hear at the starts of these words:

giant, gem, and *generous;*

cease, cite, and *city.*

The hard sounds are the sounds you hear at the starts of these words:

gate, gale, and *game;*

cat, cake, and *came.*

Pronounce these simple words slowly. Listen to the sounds you make and become aware of the way you form the sounds with your mouth.

Now let us talk about spelling. The g and c never have the soft sound when these letters come before an a. As a result, when you add the suffix -able to words that end with a ce or a ge, you've got to **retain** the e. If you didn't, your spelling would not reflect the correct pronunciation with the soft sound.

Here are some examples. You fill in the blanks

manage + able   manageable

change + able   _____

marriage + able   _____

notice + able   noticeable

peace + able   _____

service + able   _____

Word Study Activities Module 8-C— Adding Suffixes to Roots and Words That End with the Letter *e*.

8-C-1 Review: Summarize in your word study notebook the spelling generalization that guides you when you add a suffix to a word ending with *e*. Then record two words that **adhere** (or stick) to the generalization.

8-C-2 Review: Summarize in your notebook the spelling generalization that guides you when adding the suffix *-able* to words ending with *ge* or *ce*. Then record two words that adhere to, or follow, the generalization.

8-C-3 Context Clues: Based on the way these words are used in the passage and the activities (as well as your knowledge of the root *her-*), hypothesize their meanings and star the definition that makes the most sense:

1. **rife**   a. rare   b. ripe   c. widespread   d. related to a gun
2. **adhere**   a. stick to   b. criticize   c. contradict   d. deceive
3. **retain**   a. reach for   b. realize   c. keep   d. reap

Confusing Words—*Affect* and *Effect*

Two words that many people confuse are *affect* and *effect*. *Affect* generally works as a verb and very often means "to have an influence on" or "to stir the feelings of." Here are some sample sentences:

• Her poor vision affected her driving ability.

• My professor's decision not to give a second test affected me directly because my grade on the first test had been low.

• The movie about slavery affected me more than I can tell you.

   Affect has a second kind of meaning, one less commonly used. *Affect* can mean "pretend to have," as in this sentence:

• That pompous woman affected a British accent, although she had never been to England.

A related adjective is *affective,* formed by the addition of the suffix *-ive*. *Affective* relates to feelings and emotions. An affective response is one that involves your feelings in contrast to a cognitive response that taps into your intellect. You can remember that by relating *affective* to the noun *affection,* as in the sentence "I felt great affection toward him." *Affection,* as you know, means "a warm and caring feeling toward."

In contrast, *effect* generally serves as a noun and means "result." An effect is an outcome of a cause. People talk about causes and effects, and the two do go together. Here are some sample sentences:

- The effect of her decision was that I failed the course.
- The medicine had a delayed effect.

When *effect* does serve as a verb—and this happens more rarely than its use as a noun, *effect* means "to bring about." Here is a sample sentence:

- My father effected a change in the way his firm handled accounting procedures.

A derivative is the adjective *effective* that ends with the suffix *-ive*. Something that is effective produces a desired effect or gets results. You can talk about effective plans, effective techniques, effective strategies, effective rules, and effective medication.

Test yourself by filling in the blanks in these sentences with *affect, affective, effect,* or *effective*:

1. What will be the _____ of adding more sugar to the cake batter?

2. More sugar will _____ the taste.

3. The boy _____ an "I-don't-care" attitude when he really did care very much.

4. My response to the character in the novel *The Color Purple* was more _____ than it was cognitive.

5. Through our collaborative efforts we were able to devise an _____ plan for distributing the food in the flooded areas.

9

Noun and Verb-Forming Suffixes— Making Words Name and Act

◆◆◆

Objectives: In Chapter 9, you will develop the ability to

- explain how through the addition of suffixes such as *-or* and *-tion,* you form related words and change the way words function in sentences;

- perceive noun-forming suffixes on words (See Table 9.1);

- comprehend and use the following nouns featured in Module 9-A:

contrition	instigator	optimist	persecutor	sagacity
deception	integrity	paganism	pessimist	skepticism
eloquence	multitude	paucity	platitude	vehemency

- recognize the elements *ex-* (out), *loqui-* (speak), and *optimus-* (best) featured in Module 9-A;

- perceive verb-forming suffixes on words (See Table 9.2);

- comprehend and use the following verbs and power word featured in Module 9-B:

annihilate	mediate	ostracize	modify
elucidate	antagonize	scrutinize	signify
illuminate	demoralize	dignify	testify

  indignation (*power word*)

- recognize the elements *medi-* (middle), *digni-* (worthy), *modi-* (measure), and *sign-* (sign) featured in Module 9-B;

- explain the generalization governing the doubling of a single, final consonant before adding an ending or suffix; and

- distinguish between *council* and *counsel.*

> **R**emember what it means to have a broad vocabulary.
> Knowing a lot of words means knowing a lot of things.
> Words refer to things.
>
> —E.D. Hersch, Jr., *The Dictionary of Cultural Literacy,* 1988

✦✦✦

Interesting Words to Think About—
Procrastinate, Procrastinator, and *Procrastination*

Have you ever procrastinated? Have you put off till tomorrow what you could have, and perhaps should have, done today? Undoubtedly, you answered, "Yes," for we all have procrastinated from time to time.

Most dictionaries define *procrastinate* as meaning "to put things off until later; to delay, especially repeatedly." Dictionaries indicate that we use this word as a verb to show action and that linguists have traced it back to the Latin word *procrastinatum,* meaning "to postpone." Linguists have traced it ultimately to two Latin elements: the prefix *pro-,* meaning "forth", and the root *cras-,* meaning "tomorrow."

Some of us seem to be born procrastinators. We always seem to be delaying until tomorrow what we should be doing now. We seem to be addicted to procrastination.

How are the words *procrastinate, procrastinator,* and *procrastination* related? *Procrastinate* functions as a verb and bears an ending, or suffix, that is typical of words that function in sentences as verbs—the suffix *-ate. Procrastinator* is derived from *procrastinate* by dropping the final *e* and adding the suffix *-or.* The suffix *-or* generally means "one who" and is found on words that work as nouns in sentences. When we see that ending on *procrastinator,* we know that the word means "one who procrastinates or delays, especially on a repeated basis." In contrast, *procrastination* is derived from *procrastinate* by dropping the final *e* and adding the suffix *-ion.* The ending *-ion* generally means "the process or act of" and is found on words that function as nouns in sentences. Therefore, when we see that suffix on *procrastination,* we know that we are dealing with a noun that means "the process or act of putting off work that we should be doing right now." In your own life, you know what the implications of doing that are.

The connections among *procrastinate, procrastinator,* and *procrastination* highlight the importance of suffixes in the English language. In English, through the addition of suffixes, we build related words. The result is a set of words that share a common root and a related meaning. However, in adding a suffix, we sometimes change the way a word functions in sentences—in other words, its part of speech. In this case, adding *-or* or *-ion* to a verb ending in -ate allows the word to function in sentences as a noun. This is really a neat aspect of English words and the way they are interrelated.

Collaborative Search and Discover

- Let us apply the principle about which you just read to a series of English verbs all of which end in the suffixes -ate or -gate: legislate (to make into law); *investigate* (to look into and find out about); *accumulate* (to amass); *interrogate* (to question). Based on the information given about the meaning of the verb form of these words and your knowledge of -or and -ion, fill in the meanings of the words in the table.

The Verb -ate or -gate	The Word with -or	The Word with -ion
legislate, which means "to make as a law"	*legislator,* which means	*legislation,* which means
investigate, which means "to look into and find out about"	*investigator,* which means	*investigation,* which means
accumulate, which means "to amass or pile up"	*accumulator,* which means	*accumulation,* which means
interrogate, which means "to question"	*interrogator,* which means	*interrogation,* which means

- Form another derivative of each of the verbs in the table by affixing the adjective-forming suffix -ive. Place the words in the margin at the right.

Strategy Box 9-A—Developing Awareness of Noun- and Verb-Forming Suffixes

As you learned in Chapter 8, it pays to look for suffixes you know in words. This helps you with pronunciation, spelling, and to some extent meaning. A simple strategy for working with suffixes is to keep in mind the structure of many English words derived from Latin or Greek:

> Prefix + root + suffix = word.

Here is an example: e   lucid   ate

Be aware, too, that some words double up the suffixes at the end. They have a structure like this:

> Prefix + root + suffix + suffix = word.

Here is an example: im   medi   ate   ly

In Table 9.1 is a list of suffixes that you find on nouns. With a marker, highlight the suffixes you see on the ends of the example words to heighten your awareness of them.

Table 9.1   Noun-Forming Suffixes

Noun Suffixes	Meaning	Examples
-ness	full of	heaviness, thoughtfulness
-dom	full of	freedom, martyrdom, wisdom
-ary -arium	place for	library, aviary, aquarium, terrarium
-ician	one who works at	magician, musician, physician
-ist	one who works in or believes in	geologist, communist, optimist
-ism	belief in	communism, socialism, pessimism
-er, -or	one who works in	practitioner, gardener, instigator
-ment	state, or condition of; agent of; means of action for	government, parliament, indictment
-(t)ion, -(s)ion	state, or condition of; act of	communication, decision, addition, deletion
-ity	quality or state of	society, priority, gravity
-(i)tude	quality or state of	multitude, platitude

(continued)

Table 9.1 Noun-Forming Suffixes (*cont.*)

Noun Suffixes	Meaning	Examples
-acy	quality or state of being	democracy, accuracy
-ence, -ency, -ance, -ancy	state of being full of	influence, confluence, penitence, fluency, vigilance, extravagance, infancy

Word Study Module 9-A— Nouns That Bear Suffixes

Nouns are words that have a plural form and can be changed to indicate "more than one." You can talk about "an indicator" of future unrest. You can talk about "many indicators." In these contexts, the word *indicator* or *indicators* is a noun that changes to show plurality. You probably remember that you form the plural of most words simply by adding -*s*. When words end with *s, x, ch,* or *sh,* however, you form their plurals by adding –*es*, as in these words: *dresses, boxes, benches,* and *brushes.*

In this module, you will study words that generally function as nouns and bear some noun-forming suffixes. Pronounce the featured words and mark with a highlighter the suffix you see on each.

◆ 1. **con tri tion** (kən trish′ ən), *n.,* regret or sorrow for having committed a misdeed, especially a deed considered sinful.

> *Related words:* **con trite,** *adj.;* **con trite ly,** *adv.*

> *Contexts:* Her contrition was reflected in her face and her body; she surely was sorry for her actions. Contritely, she stood before us and tendered her apology. I was touched because I knew that she was truly contrite.

◆ 2. **de cep tion** (di sep′ shən), *n.,* misleading action, trick or fraud done to fool another person.

> *Related words:* **de ceive,** *v.;* **de cep tive,** *adj.*

> *Contexts:* I was completely taken in by my financial consultant's deception. The man intentionally deceived me; he led me to believe that the investment was sound. I will not be misled again by such deceptive behavior.

◆ 3. **in sti ga tor** (in′ sti gāt′ ər), *n.,* one who stirs things up and gets things going, often for a bad reason.

> *Related words:* **in sti gate,** *v.;* **in sti ga tion,** *n.*

> *Contexts:* My friend Kevin was the instigator of the plot; he dreamed it up and got it going. At his instigation, we went to the professor's office to demand a retest. I wondered what trouble he would instigate next.

✦ 4. **per se cu tor** (pėr′ sə kyū′ tər), *n.,* one who does harm to another or who treats a person badly because of his or her beliefs.

> *Related words:* **per se cute,** *v.;* **per se cu tion,** *n.*

> *Contexts:* Hitler was a persecutor of the Jewish people who lived in Europe. His persecution of those whom he hated was unconscionable. He persecuted his enemies until others finally rose up and took action.

✦ 5. **el o quence** (el′ ə kwəns), *n.,* exquisitely fluent or easy manner of speech; ability to persuade through speaking in a fine and melodious way.

> *Related words:* **el o quent,** *adj.;* **el o quent ly,** *adv.*

> *Contexts:* The president was known for his eloquence; words rolled smoothly off his tongue as water flows powerfully over a falls. During his inaugural speech, the president spoke eloquently of the need to give to one's country rather than to expect to get something from it. No one could deny that he was an eloquent speaker.

◆◆◆

Highlighted Word Elements

loqui-, a Latin root meaning "speak."

Words with the element: *elocution, circumlocution, eloquent.*

ex-, a prefix meaning "out."

Words with the element: *emission, excavate, exhume.*

◆◆◆

✦ 6. **ve he men cy** (vē′ ə mən cē), *n.,* full of strong expression or passion.

> *Related words:* **ve he ment,** *adj.;* **ve he ment ly,** *adv.*

> *Contexts:* The minister spoke with such vehemency that her parishioners knew that she believed strongly in what she was saying. She was a vehement supporter of pacifism. She spoke out vehemently for the cause in which she believed.

✦ 7. **in teg ri ty** (in teg′ ri tē), *n.,* great honesty, uprightness.

> *Contexts:* No one ever questioned my mother's integrity. She was the epitome of truthfulness and honesty.

✦ 8. **pau ci ty** (pô′ sə tē), *n.,* small amount to the point generally of being insufficient; lack of.

> *Contexts:* As a result of the war, there was a paucity of supplies, particularly of food to feed the people. We must avoid such paucity at all costs.

✦ 9. **sa gac i ty** (sə gas′ i tē), *n.,* wisdom, state of having great perceptivity.

Related words: **sa ga cious,** *adj.;* **sage,** *n.*

Contexts: The older woman was respected for her sagacity; people came from all over to speak to her for she was truly a sage—one whose opinion was sound and could be relied on. The country needs a sagacious leader who is keen of mind and makes wise decisions.

✦ 10. **pa gan ism** (pā′ gə niz′ əm), *n.,* belief of those who are not adherents of Islam, Judaism, or Christianity; sometimes, belief of those who have no religion.

Related word: **pa gan,** *n.* or *adj.*

Contexts: One form of paganism is the belief in many gods as was the norm in ancient Greece.

Because he was a pagan, he felt uncomfortable when he saw others worshipping in the synagogue.

✦ 11. **skep ti cism** (skep′ ti siz′ əm), *n.,* doubting and questioning attitude or approach to life.

Related words: **skep tic,** *n.;* **skep ti cal,** *adj.*

Contexts: After a time my father's skepticism began to bother me, for he seemed to question everything that was important to me. His skeptical attitude got me down.

My father was a skeptic, one who questioned the very meaning of existence.

✦ 12. **op ti mist** (op′ tə mist), *n.,* one who always thinks on the bright side and expects a positive outcome.

Related words: **op ti mism,** *n.;* **op ti mis ti cal ly,** *adv.*

Contexts: Jane is an optimist, who always thinks that tomorrow will be better than today; in contrast, Harold is a perpetual pessimist who thinks that doomsday is around the corner. I envy Jane her optimism. I sometimes have trouble thinking optimistically and tend to be more pessimistic.

◆◆

Highlighted Word Element

optimus-, a Latin root meaning "best."

Words with the element: *optimum, optimal, optimize.*

◆◆

✦ 13. **pes si mist** (pes′ sə mist), *n.,* one who expects a negative outcome or who is always anticipating the "worst-case scenario."

Related words: **pes si mism,** *n.;* **pes si mis ti cal ly,** *adv.*

Contexts: I would find it difficult to live with a pessimist who can view things only from a negative perspective. Eventually his or her pessimism would affect me. At some point, I think I too would view the world pessimistically.

✦ 14. **mul ti tude** (mul′ ti tōōd′), *n.,* condition or state of being many in number.

       Contexts: My young puppy came with a multitude of problems, but I loved him nonetheless.

✦ 15. **plat i tude** (plat′ i tōōd′), *n.,* expression that is bland and almost meaningless.

       Context: That politician was prone to deliver one platitude after another. As a result, no one bothered to listen to him.

Word Study Activities Module 9-A— Making Meaning with Suffixes

9-A-1 Words in Meaningful Sentence Contexts: From the list, select the word that best fits the overall meaning of each sentence. Write that word in the blank. Use each option only once. Use your Know-for-sure/Process-of-elimination test-taking strategy to eliminate options as you use them.

a. contrition	d. eloquence	g. optimist	j. paucity	m. sagacity
b. deception	e. instigator	h. pessimist	k. persecutor	n. skepticism
c. multitude	f. integrity	i. paganism	l. platitudes	o. vehemency

1. I did not know who my _____ was; all I know was that he or she was relentless in his or her efforts to make me <u>suffer</u> cruelly.

2. My mother discovered my sister's _____ and punished her for her dishonesty.

3. When my mother confronted her, my sister's _____ was obvious; she <u>hung her head</u> as she apologized for what she had done.

4. In contrast, no one ever questioned my brother's _____; he always told the truth.

5. The _____ of her denial was unexpected. She stood up and shouted that she was innocent.

6. I have to admit to my _____; I was a true Doubting Thomas in this instance.

7. When the speaker left the podium, the members of the audience rose to their feet to applaud her _____. She had spoken as with a silver tongue.

8. As we were growing up, my brother was always the _____, whereas I was the follower.

9. The sermon was filled with _____ that rang hollow because I had heard the words so often.

10. In ancient Egypt the people were believers in _____. They worshipped many different gods.

11. I never viewed myself as a/an _____, but then again I never viewed myself as a/an _____. I guess the way I view the world depends on the situation and how good or bad it is.

12. By the time we completed our analysis, we knew we had a/an _____ of problems with which we had to deal over the coming months.

13. Because conditions in the world are so perilous, we need leaders who are known for their _____ and have the mental agility to solve difficult problems.

14. Instead, our leaders have a/an _____ of ideas; they have very few creative thoughts with which to lead us into the future.

9-A-2 Synonyms and Definitions: Write the word you see on the left on the line in front of the synonym or phrase on the right that is closest in meaning.

1. **contrition**   _____   a. honesty

2. **deception**   _____   b. wisdom

3. **multitude**   _____   c. one who anticipates the worst

4. **eloquence**   _____   d. one who stirs up

5. **instigator**   _____   e. one who anticipates the best

6. **integrity**   _____   f. one who harms another

7. **optimist**   _____   g. large quantity

8. **pessimist**   _____   h. remorse

9. **paganism**   _____   i. lack of

10. **paucity**   _____   j. meaningless words

11. **persecutor**   _____   k. strong expression

12. **platitudes**   _____   l. doubting attitude

13. **sagacity**   _____   m. flowing speech

14. **skepticism**   _____   n. belief in no religion

15. **vehemency**   _____   o. misleading action

9-A-3 Related Words: Place each word in the sentence where it fits most meaning-fully. Use each word only once and cross it out as you use it. You will not need to use one of the words. Create a sentence using that word when you have finished the exercise.

adj   a. contrite *adj*   d. eloquent *adj*   g. optimal   *verb* j. persecute *adj* m. skeptical

verb   b. deceive *adverb* e. eloquently *adverb* h. pessimistically *n* k. persecution *adj* n. vehement

adj   c. deceptive *n* f. instigation *adj* i. pessimistic   *n* l. sage

1. A/An _____*noun*_____ one time told me that the most important thing in life is what you do for others. I have to admit that I was ___*adj*___ about his ad-vice, and I was ___*adj*___ in my response to him, letting him know in no uncertain way that I disagreed.

2. I spoke ___*adverb*___ for my cause. I even had to endure ___*noun*___ from those who believed differently.

3. I tried to appear ___*adj*___ as I tendered my apology. Unfortunately for me I did not ___*verb*___ anyone as to my true feelings. Everyone quickly picked up on my ___*adj*___ behavior and figured out that I was only pre-tending.

4. Bruce was a/an ___*adj*___ speaker who could arouse an audience in sup-port of a cause. At his ___*noun*___, many people went to complain about what had happened.

5. Too often in the history of the world, people have tried to ___*verb*___ others who differ from them in some way. As I say that, you may be thinking that I view the world ___*adverb*___. But that is generally untrue, for I tend to be an optimist.

6. Alex was always looking for the ___*adj*___ advantages for himself. His point of view, in short, was "I deserve nothing but the best."

9-A-4 Sentences: Complete each of the following sentences, using a word or related word that is featured in this module. You may try to include more than one featured word in a sentence.

1. I recognized immediately that she was

2. He spoke

3. It is wrong to

4. What I appreciated about her

5. By the end of the day, I felt

Strategy Box 9-B—Developing Awareness of Verb-Forming Suffixes

Keep thinking of words in terms of this word-building sequence:

Prefix   Root   Suffix

Remember that the suffixes on words help you decide on the meaning of a word because the suffix a word bears generally indicates how it is functioning in a sentence. In Table 9.2 are verb-forming suffixes that are among the most common endings you will encounter on English words. Mark the suffixes on the sample words with a highlighting pen to help you see words in terms of their component elements.

Table 9.2   Verb-Forming Suffixes

Verb Suffixes	Meaning	Examples
-ate	make	gravitate, initiate, delineate
-ify	make	qualify, quantify, simplify, clarify
-igate	make, drive	navigate, irrigate, investigate
-ize	make	generalize, sanitize, reorganize

Word Study Module 9-B—Verbs That Bear Suffixes

Verbs are words that can be changed to indicate time. You can talk about what you did yesterday, what you are doing today, and what you will do tomorrow. As you know, *did, are doing,* and *will do* are functioning as verbs in the sentence. Some words also carry suffixes that let you know that they are operating as verbs. In this module, you will study some of these words. Pronounce each featured word, and with a marker highlight the suffixes you see on each.

✦ 1. **an ni hi late** (ə nī′ ə lāt′), *v.,* wipe out so that no traces exist at all; make void; overcome totally.

   Related word: **an ni hi la tion,** *n.*

   Contexts: What the dictator wanted was to annihilate all those who opposed him. Nothing short of their complete annihilation was acceptable to him.

✦ 2. **e lu ci date** (i lōō′ si dāt′), *v.,* make clear, clarify.

   Related word: **e lu ci da tion,** *n.*

   Contexts: When I asked my professor to elucidate, she presented an extensive explanation that clarified the point for me. I needed that kind of elucidation because the concepts were very abstract.

✦ 3. **il lu mi nate** (i lōō′ mə nāt′), *v.,* brighten up with light, fill with light.

   Related word: **il lu mi na tion,** *n.*

   Contexts: Don't illuminate this area so brightly. Illumination that is too strong detracts from the warm effect we are trying to achieve.

✦ 4. **med i ate** (mē′ dē āt), *v.,* serve between parties to help settle a dispute.

   Related words: **med i a tor,** *n.;* **med i a tion,** *n.*

   Contexts: The two sides in the dispute called in a neutral party to mediate their disagreement. The mediator was trained in conflict resolution. As a result, his mediation was effective, and the disagreement was resolved in an equitable way.

✦✦✦

Highlighted Word Element

medi-, a Latin root meaning "middle."

Words with the element: *median, medial, middle, intermediate.*

✦✦✦

✦ 5. **an tag o nize** (an tag′ ə nīz′), *v.*, make an enemy of; arouse an intense dislike toward.

> *Related words:* **an tag o nist ic,** *adj.;* **an tag o nism,** *n.*

> *Contexts:* He antagonized us to the point where we could no longer take his mistreatment of us. Even before that, however, he was antagonistic toward us, verbally abusing us without cause. I had never experienced such severe antagonism before, and I was overwhelmed by it.

✦ 6. **de mo ral ize** (di môr′ ə līz), *v.*, weaken the spirit, confidence, or courage of.

> *Related word:* **de mo ral i za tion,** *n.*

> *Contexts:* Our enemy tried to demoralize our soldiers by broadcasting lies to them about the annihilation of our other troops in the field. This attempt at demoralization was unsuccessful for the soldiers knew the truth.

✦ 7. **os tra cize** (os′ trə cīz′), *v.*, banish from society, not allow to participate in social activities.

> *Related word:* **os tra cism,** *n.*

> *Contexts:* The group of men ostracized those who disagreed with them in any way. It is not pleasant to be ostracized. None of us reacts well to ostracism.

✦ 8. **scru ti nize** (skrōōt′ n īz), *v.*, examine very carefully, especially for any defects.

> *Related word:* **scru ti ny,** *n.*

> *Contexts:* Before buying my Oriental carpet, I scrutinized it to be sure that it was flawless.

> Because of his careful scrutiny, the girl blushed.

✦ 9. **dig ni fy** (dig′ nə fī), *v.*, make worthwhile or valid, add honor to.

> *Related words:* **dig ni ty,** *n.;* **dig ni fied,** *adj.;* **dig ni fied ly,** *adv.*

> *Contexts:* I would not dignify his insulting question with an answer. Instead I acted in a dignified manner and refrained from answering in a nasty way. I have found through experience that it pays to act dignifiedly in the face of unpleasantness. It pays to maintain one's own dignity.

✦✦

Highlighted Word Element

digni-, a Latin root meaning "worthy."

Words with the element: *dignity, indignity, dignified.*

✦✦

✦✦

Power Word

in dig na tion, a noun meaning "anger aroused by unjust, mean, or unworthy treatment"; from the Latin via Middle English.

Related words: **in dig nant,** *adj.;* **in dig ni ty,** *n.*

Contexts: The young woman expressed indignation when the award went to someone less qualified. To say that she was indignant would be an understatement; she was absolutely furious.

At some point, we all have had to suffer indignities—degrading treatment by others.

✦✦

✦   10. **mod i fy** (mod′ ə fī), *v.,* change or alter in form or character.

Related words: **mod i fi a ble,** *adj.;* **mod i fi ca tion,** *n.*

Contexts: We had to modify the design of our house to meet the zoning requirements. Actually the modification we had to make resulted in a more attractive dwelling. I guess this indicates that most of our ideas are modifiable to some extent.

✦✦

Highlighted Word Element

modi-, a Latin root meaning "measure."

Words with the element: *modifier, module, modulate.*

✦✦

✦   11. **sig ni fy** (sig′ nə fī), *v.,* mean, indicate, be a sign of, have importance as.

Related words: **sig nif i cant,** *adj.;* **sig nif i cance,** *n.*

Contexts: "What does that signify?" the student asked as she tried to figure out the importance of the event the professor was discussing. The significance of an event can often be judged only years after the event has occurred. At that point, historians can judge whether what happened then made a significant impact on events to come.

✦✦

Highlighted Word Element

signi-, a Latin root meaning "sign" or "seal."

Words with the element: *signature, sign, signet.*

✦✦

✦ 12. **tes ti fy** (tes′ tə fī), *v.*, give evidence, often under oath in a court of law.

>   ***Related word:*** **tes ti mo ny,** *n.*

>   ***Contexts:*** The witness was called to testify in the court case. Her testimony made a difference in the final judgment of the jury.

Word Study Activities Module 9-B— Making Meaning with Verbs

9-B-1 Words in Meaningful Sentence Contexts: From the list, select the verb that best fits the overall meaning of each sentence. Write that word in the blank. Use each option only once.

a. annihilate	d. mediate	g. ostracize	j. modify
b. elucidate	e. anatagonize	h. scrutinize	k. signify
c. illuminate	f. demoralize	i. dignify	l. testify

1. Unless you _____ your behavior, you will not be accepted by the "in-crowd." The members of that group will _____ you.

2. The large stadium lights will _____ the field during the night games.

3. If you keep making those pessimistic statements, you will _____ the players.

4. The religious leader tried to _____ the dispute but to no avail.

5. As a result the combatants went on to _____ one another on the field of battle.

6. The host tried to _____ the event by inviting a nationally known rabbi to offer the benediction.

7. During the court case, the witness had to _____ about what happened the night of the robbery.

8. Before letting me enter the country, the immigration agents will _____ my documents to verify that I hold a green card.

9. Every statement he made tended to _____ me even more until I knew that he and I could no longer be friends.

10. "Put your initials on this line to _____ that you have read the document," the nurse told me before giving me a flu shot.

11. My teacher asked me to _____ the point that I had made on the examination. She wanted to be certain that I understood it fully before giving me a grade.

9-B-2 Crossword Puzzle: Complete the crossword puzzle in Figure 9.1, using the words highlighted in Module 9-B.

Figure 9.1   A Crossword Puzzle of Some Enlightening Verbs

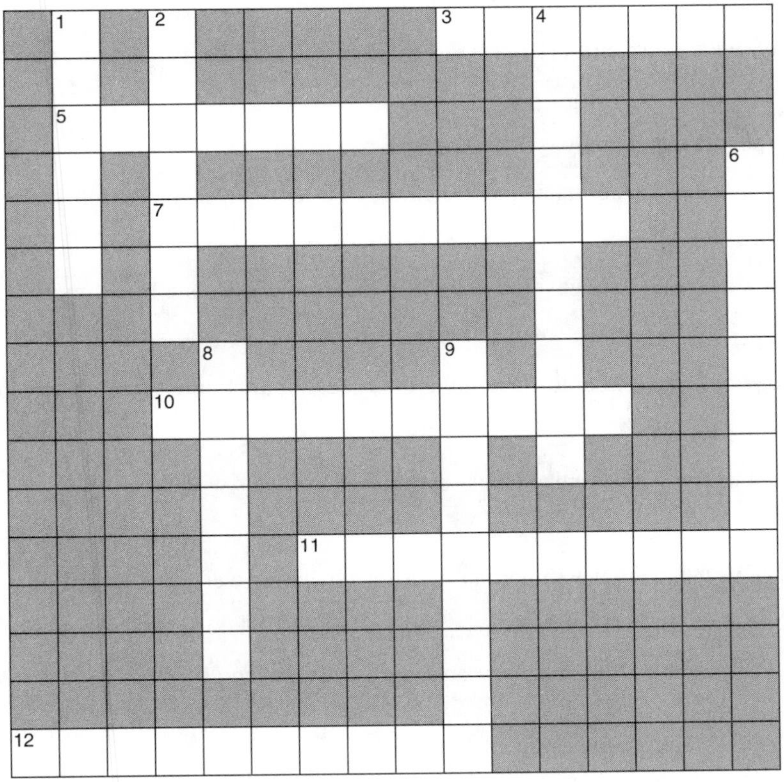

ACROSS
3 Give evidence about
5 Make worthwhile or add honor to
7 Light up
10 Weaken the spirit of
11 Wipe out
12 Arouse intense dislike

DOWN
1 Alter
2 Indicate or mean
4 Examine, especially for defects
6 Banish from society
8 Help to settle a dispute
9 Clarify, make clear

9-B-3 Truth or Falsity: Decide whether each of these statements is more likely to be true or false. Write True or False on the line.

1. Most people look forward with pleasure to being annihilated. _____

2. If a person is called to testify in a court case, he or she is probably going to be nervous. _____

3. Most good coaches do not demoralize their team members before an important game. _____

4. Everyone appreciates being ostracized. _____

5. To be an effective mediator takes considerable skill. _____

6. Today, with electricity priced as it is, you can illuminate a large area at night for a very low cost. _____

7. Most people enjoy being scrutinized from top to toe. _____

8. When asked to make major modifications to a term paper, most students react with pleasure. _____

9. A smile on one's face generally signifies pleasure, whereas a frown means displeasure. _____

10. Some people have trouble elucidating their ideas so that others can understand them. _____

11. Most of us try to antagonize others in our daily contacts with them. _____

12. Most of us try to dignify important occasions by being well dressed, arriving on time, and being on our best behavior. _____

13. When people are indignant, they are angry because they know they have been mistreated. _____

9-B-4 Sentence Writing: Use each phrase in a sentence that shows its meaning.

1. antagonistic manner

2. complete annihilation

3. great significance

4. effective mediator

5. major modification

6. dignified manner

7. righteous indignation

9-B-5 Basic Word Elements: Select the meaning of the boldfaced element in each word from those offered. Star it.

1. **digni**ty	a. sign	b. worthy	c. best	d. speak
2. **signi**ficant	a. sign	b. worthy	c. best	d. speak
3. **optim**al	a. sign	b. worthy	c. best	d. speak
4. **loqu**acious	a. sign	b. worthy	c. best	d. speak
5. **ex**ternal	a. out	b. above	c. toward	d. in
6. inter**medi**ate	a. measure	b. middle	c. many	
7. **mod**erate	a. measure	b. middle	c. many	

Reading with Meaning Module 9-C—
Learning How to Add Endings to Words

Read this passage to develop an understanding of how to add some endings to words.

To Double or Not to Double—That Is the Question

Have you ever had problems deciding whether to double the single final consonant on a word when adding a suffix that begins with a vowel? Have you generally just operated on **instinct** rather than on reason in making a spelling decision such as this one? Sometimes, as in the case of doubling or not doubling a single final consonant, there actually is a generalization you can apply to help you as you spell. And that generalization is really very easy to handle.

To figure out the generalization that explains this **problematic** situation, write the new word that results when the ending element is added to each of these words that ends with a final single consonant:

word + ending	=	new word
prefer + ed	=	_____
omit + ing	=	_____
occur + ence	=	_____
red + er	=	_____
step + ed	=	_____

How did you spell the five resulting words? The correct spellings are *preferred, omitting, occurrence, redder, stepped.* Correct any misspellings by writing the resulting word next to your attempt.

Here are some words that also end with a consonant. Decide how to spell the word that results when the ending is added to it. Be very careful here.

word + ending	=	new word
benefit + ed	=	_____
profit + ing	=	_____
differ + ence	=	_____
pagan + ize	=	_____
travel + er	=	_____

How did you spell the five resulting words? The correct spellings are *benefited, profiting, difference, paganize, traveler.* Correct any misspellings by writing the resulting word next to your attempt.

Obviously, with the first group of words, you had to double the final consonant before affixing the ending. With the second set, you did not double. Can you see or hear anything in the words in each list to account for this difference?

Let me elucidate. Notice that the accent in the words in the first set is on the last syllable. When a word has only one syllable as in *red* and *step,* that syllable is the last syllable. Notice that the accent in the words in the second set is on the first syllable. Pronounce all the listed words and listen for the accent.

Here is the explanation: When the accent is on the last syllable, you double the final consonant. When the accent is not on the last syllable, you do not double.

Now that sounds simple enough. But in English, you know that you generally are faced with numerous exceptions to spelling rules. Exceptions exist in this case as well. For example, if you check a dictionary, you will find that you are actually allowed to spell *traveller* with two *l*s. The single *l* spelling is preferred, but the double *l* spelling is acceptable.

The point is, however, that the generalization works more often than it does not. When you are unsure and can't check a dictionary, applying the generalization is your safest bet.

By now you may be wondering who is responsible for this **frustrating** spelling mess. There is indeed a **culprit.** His name is Noah Webster, the man who wrote one of the first American dictionaries. Wanting to make American English distinctive from British English, Webster decided that he would modify the spellings of some words in his dictionary. The British dictionaries listed *benefited* with two *t*s, so in his American dictionary, he listed it with one. He did that with most words where we do not place the accent on the final syllable. If you go to England today, you will discover that the Brits still double that final consonant in those cases where we are stuck trying to figure out whether to double or not.

Word Study Activities Module 9-C—
Spelling, Context Clues, and Word Elements

9-C-1 Spelling Applications: With spelling, of course, we generally end with a test, so here we go. Based on the generalization you have just read about, spell the resulting word in each case.

word	+ ending	
submit	+ ed	_____
admit	+ ance	_____
abut	+ ing	_____
orbit	+ ing	_____
conquer	+ ed	_____
modern	+ ize	_____

9-C-2 Context Clues: Hypothesize the meanings of these words based on the context in which you find them in the passage. Then write the word on the line in front of the definition that best matches it.

1. **instinct**   _____ guilty one

2. **problematic**   _____ natural feeling

3. **frustrating**   _____ difficult to decide or solve

4. **culprit**   _____ causing a discouraging feeling, or bafflement

9-C-3 Sentence Writing: Use these words in sentences: *instinct, problematic, frustrating, culprit.* You may be able to write one sentence in which you use all four words.

9-C-4 Review of Highlighted Elements: Match each element with its meaning by writing the element on the appropriate line.

1. **digni-**   _____ a. measure

2. **ex-**   _____ b. middle

3. **loqui-**   _____ c. worthy

4. **medi-**   _____ d. sign/seal

5. **modi-**   _____ e. out

6. **optim-**   _____ f. speak

7. **signi-**   _____ g. best

In each case list one word that contains the element:

1. **digni-**   _____

2. **ex-**   _____

3. **loqui-**   _____

4. **medi-**   _____

5. **modi-**   _____

6. **optim-**   _____

7. **signi-**   _____

Confusing Words—*Council* and *Counsel*

Some students confuse the words *council* and *counsel*. Can you explain the differences in meaning?

Council functions as a noun and means "a group of people that meets together as a board to discuss issues and resolve problems." Some councils have members who are elected to their positions. You can talk about a meeting of a council or a council meeting. The members of a council are councilors, councilmen, or councilwomen.

In contrast, *counsel* serves either as a noun or verb. As a noun, it means "advice." You can talk about supplying someone with wise counsel, about seeking counsel from a lawyer or religious leader. As a verb, *counsel* means "to give advice." You can say that someone counseled you to spend more time studying. A person who gives the advice is a counselor; lawyers are sometimes known as counselors-at-law. Some commonly used phrases in which this term appears are *to keep one's own counsel,* which means "to keep quiet about one's own affairs" and *to keep counsel together,* which means "to consult together."

Apply these distinctions in these contexts: Write the appropriate word in each blank.

1. Janet decided to run for a seat on the city _____. She won the seat and really enjoyed her position as _____.

2. I sought _____ from the guidance director at my university.

3. The guidance _____ recommended that I move out of the dormitory and find a place where I could concentrate on my studies.

In your notebook compose one sentence with the word *council,* one with *counsel* used as a noun, one with *counsel* used as a verb.

Word Elements—Ruling, Schooling, Measuring, Writing, and Viewing

◆◆

Objectives: In Chapter 10, you will develop the ability to

- explain the meaning-based relationship among words that bear common elements, such as *-cracy* and *-archy*—*democracy* and *theocracy, monarchy* and *hierarchy*—and interpret the roots *demo-* and *theo-* when you see them in words;

- perceive word elements derived from Greek roots that tell about ruling and schooling as listed in Table 10.1;

- comprehend and use the following words featured in Module 10-A:

anarchy	autonomy	democrat	matriarch
aristocracy	biology	economy	patriarch
autocrat	bureaucracy	geology	terminology
hierarchy (*power word*)			

- attach meaning to the word elements *auto-, matri-, patri-, bio-* (featured in Module 10-A) when you see them in words;

- perceive word elements derived from Greek roots that tell about measuring, writing, and viewing as listed in Table 10.2;

- comprehend and use the following words featured in Module 10-B:

autobiographical	grammatical	monograph	scope
barometer	graphic	optometry	symmetrical
bibliography	monogram	perimeter	telescope

- attach meaning to the elements *peri-* and *opti-* from Module 10-B when you see them in words;

- interpret the negative or positive connotation of a word and recognize euphemisms and doublespeak; and

- distinguish between the words *imply* and *infer*.

Every vital development of language
is a development of feeling as well.

—T. S. Eliot, *Philip Massinger, 1920*

◆◆◆

Interesting Words to Think About—
Democracy, Monarchy, and *Theocracy*

"We, the people of the United States, . . . do ordain and establish this Constitution for the United States of America." So begins the **Preamble** to the **Constitution** that describes the source of power upon which the American democracy is founded—**the people!** Similarly, Abraham Lincoln in his oft-quoted Gettysburg Address ends with the words "that government of the people, by the people, for the people shall not perish from the earth"—words that Martin Luther King quoted in his "I have a dream" speech.

In these statements, the writers clarify the essential meaning of the word *democracy*. The Greek root *-cracy,* which we generally use in the manner of a suffix, means "rule by." *Demo-,* another Greek root, means "people." Put the two together, and we have *democracy* —"rule or government by the people." Actually, the founders of the American republic established a representative democracy as opposed to direct democracy. In a representative democracy, the people elect men and women to carry out the functions of government for them, but the bottom line is that the people have the ultimate power.

Why did the founders of the American form of government stress "rule by the people"? We have only to look back into the **annals** of history for an answer. Many of the early settlers of the North American continent came from Europe where absolute or constitutional monarchies were the norm, not the exception. In France, an absolute monarch sat upon the throne—a monarch in whom all power was vested. In England, a constitutional monarch reigned, his or her powers limited a bit by a document, the Magna Carta, which the members of the nobility forced King John to sign in 1215. The word *monarchy* says it all. The Greek root *-archy* means "rule by" just as *-cracy* does. *Mono-* is a prefix that means "one." A monarchy is a government in which one person rules—the monarch, who is all-powerful. No wonder the leaders of the American Revolution stressed the importance of government by the people. They had had enough of government by one man or one woman!

Even after 1776 when the founding leaders wrote the Constitution and designed a representative democracy, government by one person continued to exist in countries around the world. In some places, as we have seen in recent years, the government was really a theocracy—rule by religious officials or priests claiming that their authority was derived from God. We saw a theocracy develop in Iran when the Shah, who was an absolute monarch, lost power and was replaced by an **ayatollah,** a religious leader who claimed that he represented God and his acts were sanctioned by God. The parts of the word *theocracy* again communicate its meaning: *Theo-* is a Greek root that means "god," and *-cracy* means "rule by."

Given the fact that rule "of the people, by the people, for the people" was uncommon in 1776, we can understand why that concept was truly a revolutionary one. Even today democracy is not something that we can take for granted. **We are "the people."** When we go to the polls to vote in local, state, and national elections, we are accepting our responsibility as members of a representative democracy.

Collaborative Search and Discover

- Brainstorm and list one other word for each of these elements:

    1. -archy

    2. demo-

    3. mono-

    4. theo-

From your knowledge of the elements, hypothesize the meaning of the words you identify.

- Working with a friend, look up in your dictionary the etymology and meanings of these terms as they relate to their boldfaced use in the article you just read:

1. preamble

2. constitution

3. annals

4. ayatollah

Strategy Box 10-A—Recognizing Word Elements That Communicate Ideas about Ruling and Schooling

The English language relies on some endings that communicate considerable meaning about ways of ruling and kinds of studies. These endings are really Greek roots, but because in English we tend to use them at the ends of words, we sometimes think of them as suffixes. Your strategy for handling them is relatively simple:

Step 1: Look for an ending element that you recognize and attach the meaning to it that you know. The meanings of some of these ending elements that relate to ruling and schooling are summarized in Table 10.1.

Step 2: Connect the meaning of the ending to the meaning of the base root and its prefix.

In Table 10.1, with a marker highlight the element on each example that communicates ideas about ruling or schooling.

Table 10.1   Special Endings That Come from Greek Roots—Ruling and Schooling

Ending	Meaning	Examples
-cracy	rule by	democracy, bureaucracy, aristocracy, theocracy
-crat	one who advocates rule by	democrat, bureaucrat, aristocrat, plutocrat
-archy	rule by	monarchy, anarchy
-arch	one who rules	monarch, matriarch, patriarch
-nomy	science or system governing	autonomy, economy
-ology	study of or science of	biology, geology, theology, terminology, psychology

Word Study Module 10-A—Endings That Communicate Ideas about Ruling and Schooling

Pronounce the featured words, highlight with a marker the meaningful ending on each, study the definitions and examples, and then in your mind make up a sentence using each word.

✦ 1. **ar is toc ra cy** (ar′ i stok′ rə cē), *n.,* privileged, hereditary ruling class, the nobility; rule by people who are of a privileged class into which members are born.

> *Related words:* **a ris to crat,** *n.;* **a ris to crat ic,** *adj.*

> *Contexts:* During the French Revolution, members of the aristocracy were often put to the guillotine. Because he was an aristocrat, the baron had to flee France during the Reign of Terror.
> He affected aristocratic mannerisms that made him unpopular with his associates.

✦ 2. **bu reauc ra cy** (byōō rok′ rə cē), *n.,* administration of government by nonelected officials who run offices; also administration characterized by red tape that gets in the way of progress.

> *Related words:* **bu reau crat,** *n.;* **bu reau crat ic,** *adj.*

> *Contexts:* I am fed up with a bureaucracy that requires me to waste my time filling in so many useless forms and to meet so many impossible deadlines.
> My friend is a typical bureaucrat; he loves to produce time-wasting procedures for others to follow. I got bogged down in bureaucratic red tape.

✦ 3. **au to crat** (ô′ tə crat′), *n.,* ruler with unlimited powers.

> *Related words:* **au to crat ic,** *adj.;* **au toc ra cy,** *n.*

> *Contexts:* My boss really was an autocrat in the office. If you did not do exactly as he said, you were "out of there." His autocratic ways made everyone jump to his command.
> In an autocracy, government is by a person having unlimited authority. Such a state is not one where I could be happy.

✦✦✦

Highlighted Word Element

auto-, a Greek root meaning "self."

Words with the element: *autopilot, autograph, automatic.*

✦✦✦

✦ 4. **dem o crat** (dem′ ə crat′), *n.,* one who believes in government by the people. (Note: when the first letter is capitalized, as in *Democrat,* we are talking about a member of a particular political party.)

> *Related words:* **dem o crat ic,** *adj.;* **de moc ra cy,** *n.*

> *Contexts:* Although Abraham Lincoln was the first Republican president, he was a true democrat for he believed in government by and for the people. His democratic beliefs led him to free the slaves through his Emancipation Proclamation.

Because the peoples of Russia lived under communism so long, when democracy came, they were unprepared for it.

◆ 5. **an ar chy** (an′ ər kē), *n.,* absence of any form of government, political chaos. (Note the prefix *an-,* which means without.)

>   *Related words:* **an ar chism,** *n.;* **an ar chist,** *n.*

>   *Contexts:* After the revolution, people feared that there would be anarchy; instead, democracy ruled and a responsible government emerged.
>   At heart, my friend was an anarchist who believed that active resistance against the state was justified. No matter how I reasoned with him, I could not shake his belief in anarchism.

◆◆◆

Power Word with the Same Root

hierarchy, a word that means "graded ranking of people or things" from the Greek *hieros* meaning "sacred" and *arkhos* meaning "leader"; see also Module C of Chapter 4.

Related words: hierarchical, hierarch.

Contexts: In universities, you find a rather definitive hierarchy within the professorial ranks. An instructor holds a low position in the ranking, and a full professor holds a high position. Where does the student fit in this hierarchical system?

◆◆◆

◆ 6. **ma tri arch** (mā′ trē ärk′), *n.,* woman who rules or dominates a society, state, or family.

>   *Related words:* **ma tri ar chy,** *n.;* **ma tri ar chal,** *adj.;* **ma tri ar chate,** *n.*

>   *Contexts:* After my mother died, my aunt viewed herself as the matriarch of the family. She began to act in a matriarchal manner, keeping the family together through annual gatherings of the clan.
>   In a matriarchy, descent is traced through the female side of the family rather than through the male side as is currently the norm in American society. In some societies, a matriarchate is the norm, with a woman holding dominant power.

◆◆◆

Highlighted Word Element

matri-, matro-, matr-, a Latin element meaning "mother."

Words with the element: *maternal, maternity, matrimony.*

◆◆◆

✦   7. **pa tri arch** (pā′ trē ärk′), *n.,* man who rules or dominates a society, state, church, or family.

> ***Related words:*** **pa tri ar chy,** *n.;* **pa tri ar chal,** *adj.;* **pa tri ar chate,** *n.*

> ***Contexts:*** My uncle thought himself the chief patriarch of the family. He assumed a patriarchal manner in all that he did.

> The head of the Greek Orthodox Church is called the patriarch of that church.

> In a patriarchy, descent is traced through the male side of the family. In some societies, a patriarchate is the norm, with a man holding dominant power.

✦✦

Highlighted Word Element

patri-, patr-, a Latin element meaning "father."

Words with the element: *patron, paternal, patriot.*

✦✦

✦   8. **au ton o my** (ô ton′ ə mē), *n.,* condition of being self-governing.

> ***Related word:*** **au ton o mous,** *adj.*

> ***Contexts:*** That province has been seeking autonomy for many years. The people living there want to become an autonomous state rather than being under the control of a government that is far away.

✦   9. **e co no my** (i kon′ ə mē), *n.,* careful management of financial matters; the system relative to the resources, income, labor, and business dealings of a country or area.

> ***Related words:*** **e con o mist,** *n.;* **e con o mize,** *v.;* **ec o nom i cal,** *adj.*

> ***Contexts:*** In his State of the Union address, the president announced that the economy was in fine shape. In response, a respected economist criticized the president for misinterpreting conditions in the nation. Instead, the economist suggested that times were bad and that everyone should economize. I did try to be more economical, but I always seemed to be in debt by the time my next paycheck arrived.

✦   10. **bi ol o gy** (bī ol′ ə jē), *n.,* science or study of living things.

> ***Related words:*** **bi o log i cal,** *adj.;* **bi o lo gist,** *n.*

> ***Contexts:*** My brother decided to major in biology because he was a naturalist at heart and enjoyed studying living organisms. He quickly got involved in biological investigations, and he made some exciting discoveries. He never regretted his decision to become a biologist.

✦✦✦

Highlighted Word Element

bio-, a Latin prefix meaning "life."

Words with the element: *biography, autobiography, biosphere, biochemistry.*

✦✦✦

✦   11. **ge ol o gy** (jē ol′ ə jē), *n.,* science or study of the origin, history, and structures of the earth (Note: *Geo-* is a prefix that comes from the Greek myth about Gaia, the earth goddess. See Chapter 2.)

           ***Related words:* ge o log ic,** *adj.;* **ge ol o gist,** *n.*

           Contexts: As part of my studies in geology, I investigated the layers, or rock strata, found locally. I learned that in our geologic past, conditions were far different than today. My instructor was a well-known geologist who had written extensively on stratigraphy.

✦   12. **ter mi nol o gy** (tûr′ mə nol′ ə jē), *n.,* technical vocabulary, especially the terms associated with a particular area of study.

           Contexts: One of the most difficult parts of the study of psychology and sociology for me was the terminology that I had to learn.

Word Study Activities Module 10-A— Making Meaning with Words

10-A-1 Words in Meaningful Sentence Contexts: From the list, select the word that best fits the overall meaning of each sentence. Write that word in the blank. Use each option only once. Apply your Know-for-sure/Process-of-elimination test-taking strategy.

a. anarchy	d. autonomy	g. democrat	j. matriarch
b. aristocracy	e. biology	h. economy	k. patriarch
c. autocrat	f. bureaucracy	i. geology	l. terminology

1. Frank had a great interest in rocks and minerals; when he went to college, therefore, he decided to major in _____.

2. The entire family looked to their _____ for advice because his knowledge of people and finances was so extensive.

3. The group gave full _____ to the trusted committee members to make decisions on their own as to how the money was to be spent.

4. When the government collapsed and rule of law completely broke down, the country was thrown into _____.

5. Her vocabulary was very limited, which meant that she had difficulty with the _____ in her technical courses.

6. Because she was the oldest member of the family, the grandmother considered herself to be the _____.

7. Ecology, the study of the interrelationships of living things and their environment, is a branch of _____.

8. The mayor constantly ignored the suggestions of the council and acted as a/an _____ when he ruled every motion out of order.

9. The Federal Reserve chairman looked over the country's _____ and found that the jobless rate was down and that new businesses were flourishing.

10. The nobles' complete disregard for the welfare and basic needs of the ordinary people led to the overthrow of the _____.

11. He went from office to office within the administrative _____ trying to get approval of the plans he needed.

12. A true _____ believes that the opinions and beliefs of others are as worthy of consideration as are his own.

10-A-2 Synonyms and Definitions: Write the word on the left on the line in front of the synonym or phrase at the right that is closest in meaning.

1. **anarchy**   _____ a. male head

2. **aristocracy**   _____ b. study of earth

3. **autocrat**   _____ c. social chaos

4. **autonomy**   _____ d. female head

5. **biology**   _____ e. believer in self-government

6. **bureaucracy**   _____ f. believer in government by the people

7. **democrat**   _____ g. study of living organisms

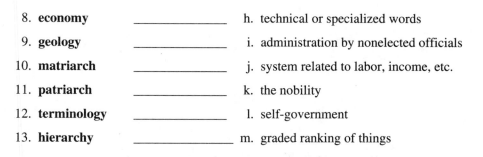

8. **economy**   _____   h. technical or specialized words

9. **geology**   _____   i. administration by nonelected officials

10. **matriarch**   _____   j. system related to labor, income, etc.

11. **patriarch**   _____   k. the nobility

12. **terminology**   _____   l. self-government

13. **hierarchy**   _____   m. graded ranking of things

10-A-3 Review of Word Elements:

1. There are numbers of elements that say "one who. . . ." Here are some of those elements: *-er* and *-or; -ist; -crat; -arch;* and *-ician.* On the web in Figure 10.1, branching out from each of these elements, write down several different words that contain each element. For example, branching from *-or,* you could write the word *doctor.* Branching from *-er,* you could write the word *founder.*

Figure 10.1   A Web of Related Endings

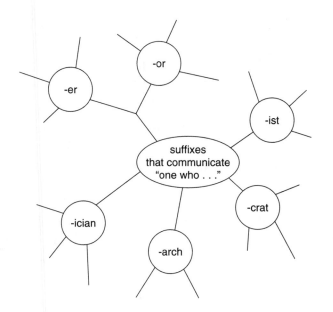

2. You have been studying two elements that mean "the science governing" or "the study of": *-nomy* and *-ology.* Brainstorm some other words that incorporate these elements. Try to list at least two for each element.

- -nomy

- -ology

3. Use the word *hierarchy* in a sentence that suggests its meaning.

10-A-4 Related Words in Meaningful Sentence Contexts: From the list, select the word that best fits the overall meaning of each sentence. Write that word in the blank. Use each option only once.

a. anarchists	d. autonomous	g. democratic	j. geologic
b. aristocrat	e. biologist	h. economically	k. matriarchy
c. autocratic	f. bureaucratic	i. economize	l. patriarchal

1. The _____ showed the children how to identify the leaves by their shapes and kinds of edges they have.

2. The husband and wife were careful how they budgeted and spent their income; their household was run very _____.

3. The _____ red tape raised my blood pressure several notches for I could not understand why it should take so long for the administrators to act on my application.

4. The _____ age of the fossil was inferred from the layer of the rock deposit where it was found.

5. When women command the controlling positions in a society, that arrangement may be called a/an _____.

6. Secret meetings were set up by the _____ to plot an overthrow of the government in power.

7. They realized that they would have to _____ after they looked at their credit card statement.

8. José acted like a/an _____, expecting everyone to cater to his whims.

9. _____ leaders expect that their opinions and demands will be accepted without question.

10. Theirs was a/an _____ form of government in which men held all the positions of authority.

11. We live in a/an _____ republic where we send representatives to the seats of government.

12. The people in charge of the government procedure were permitted to carry on a/an _____ operation without anyone supervising them.

Strategy Box 10-B—Recognizing Word Elements That Communicate Ideas about Measuring, Writing, and Viewing

The English language relies on some endings that communicate considerable meaning about the ways we measure, write, and view things around us. See Table 10.2 for a listing. Like the combining elements you just studied, these endings are Greek roots, but because in English we use them mainly at the ends of words, we often think of them as suffixes. To interpret these endings, use the two-step strategy given earlier in this chapter.

Before reading on, study Table 10.2. With a highlighting marker, color the element found at the end of each word example. Then hypothesize the meaning based on the parts you recognize.

Table 10.2   Special Endings That Come from Greek Roots—Measuring, Writing, and Viewing

Ending	Meaning	Examples
-meter	instrument for measuring	barometer, diameter, perimeter, odometer
-metry	art or science of measuring	geometry, optometry, trigonometry
-graph	instrument for writing, writing	telegraph, photograph, autograph, holograph, cardiograph
-graphy	art or science of writing	biography, cartography, photography, topography
-gram	thing that is written	diagram, telegram, hologram, cardiogram
-scope	instrument for viewing, viewing	periscope, stethoscope, microscope, telescope

Word Study Module 10-B—Endings That Communicate Measuring, Writing, and Viewing

Pronounce the featured words, highlight the meaningful ending on each, study the definitions and examples, and then in your mind make up a sentence using each word.

✦   1. **ba rom e ter** (bə rom′ i tər), *n.,* instrument for measuring atmospheric pressure, typically used in weather forecasting.

   ***Related word:* bar o me tric,** *adj.*

   Contexts: When the barometer began to fall, I knew we were in for a storm. A rise in the barometric pressure is an indicator of better weather ahead.

✦   2. **pe rim e ter** (pə rim′ i tər), *n.,* in mathematics, the length of the closed curve that encloses a geometric shape such as a circle; in general, the surrounding edge of an area.

   Contexts: I used a piece of string to measure the perimeter of the circle. I walked the perimeter of my property looking for markers to indicate where my land ended.

✦✦

Highlighted Word Element

peri-, a Greek prefix meaning "around."

Words with the element: *periphery, peripheral, periscope*

✦✦

✦   3. **op tom e try** (op tom′ i trē), *n.,* profession that involves examining eyes and measuring for corrective lenses.

   ***Related word:* op tom e trist,** *n.*

   Contexts: Because my friend was interested in human biology but could not afford to go to medical school, he decided that a career in optometry was for him. After graduating from college, he had to go to a special school to study to become an optometrist.

✦✦

Highlighted Word Element

opti-, a Greek element meaning "visible."

Words with the element: *optic, optical, optician.*

✦✦

✦ 4. **sym met ric al** (sə met′ rəc əl), *adj.,* characterized by having its two opposite sides nearly identical. (Reminder: The prefix *sym-* means "same.")

>   *Related word:* **a sym met ric al,** *adj.* (Reminder: The prefix *a-* means "not.")

>   *Contexts:* A face that is symmetrical is really not so interesting as one that has variations on each side.
>   The artist designed the space to be asymmetrical with one side being different from the other.

✦ 5. **au to bi o graph i cal** (ô′ tō bi ə graf′ ə kəl), *adj.,* related to accounts of one's life that a person writes about one's self.

>   *Related word:* **au to bi og ra phy,** *n.*

>   *Contexts:* As part of my application I had to include an autobiographical account of my life up to that point.
>   Having read the author's autobiography, I better understood why she wrote as she did.

✦ 6. **bib li og ra phy** (bib′ lē og′ rə fē), *n.,* list of books relative to a topic.

>   *Related word:* **bib li o graph i cal,** *adj.*

>   *Contexts:* My professor requires a bibliography at the end of each paper that I write. A bibliographical citation should include the name of the author, the book, and publisher, as well as the city where the publisher is located and the date of publication. An annotated bibliography also includes a very brief description of the book.

✦ 7. **graph ic** (graf′ ik), *adj.,* related to a written representation; vivid or sharply detailed.

>   *Related word:* **graph i cal ly,** *adv.;* **graph,** *n.*

>   *Contexts:* In his opening paragraph of his mystery story, the writer described the crime scene in graphic detail. The speaker described the incident so graphically that I felt I had been there myself.
>   I created a graph showing increases in weight over the past ten years based on information the researcher supplied me.

✦ 8. **mon o graph** (mon′ ə graf), *n.,* short book, or treatise, on a single topic, especially a technical one. (Note the use of the prefix *mono-,* meaning "one.")

>   *Context:* As part of the course requirements, the students had to read a monograph that detailed the relationships between the causes and the events they were considering.

✦ 9. **gram ma ti cal** (grə mat′ i kəl), *adj.,* conforming to the rules of good expression, or of grammar. (Note: A grammarian studies the way language works and is used.)

Related word: **gram mar,** *n.* or *adj.;* **un gram mat i cal,** *adj.*

Contexts: My English teacher taught us several grammatical constructions that were entirely new to me. I realized from the grammar lesson that I had been using some ungrammatical expressions.

✦   10. **mon o gram** (mon′ ə gram), *n.,* letters, usually the initials of one person's or organization's name.

Context: I had my monogram affixed to my luggage.

✦   11. **scope** (skōp), *n.,* range or area of a person's awareness, influence, thoughts, actions; area covered by a subject or activity.

Contexts: The scientist limited the scope of her investigation to focus on the most significant question.
Reading a scientific monograph is beyond the scope of his ability.

✦   12. **tel e scope** (tel′ ə skop′), *n.,* instrument for viewing something located at a great distance, so far away that the eye cannot see details unaided.

Related word: **tel e scop ic,** *n.*

Contexts: The university has a telescope through which the astronomers on the faculty can observe the heavenly bodies.
I affixed a telescopic lens to my camera in order to pick up detail located at a distant point.

Word Study Activities Module 10-B— Making Meaning with Words

10-B-1 Words in Meaningful Sentence Contexts: From the list, select the word that best fits the overall meaning of each sentence. Write that word in the blank. Use each option only once. Use your Know-for-sure/Process-of-elimination test-taking strategy.

a. autobiographical	d. grammatical	g. monograph	j. scope
b. barometer	e. graphic	h. optometry	k. symmetrical
c. bibliography	f. monogram	i. perimeter	l. telescope

1. A perfect circle is _____; if you cut it exactly across the middle, you end with two identical pieces.

2. My friend is a/an _____ perfectionist; as an English teacher, she knows the way English should be handled and she uses the language precisely at all times.

3. In her book, the author provides a/an _____ description of the Battle of Bull Run.

4. Before going out in their sailboat, my friends check their _____ to be sure the weather will remain good for sailing.

5. Before I die, I want to write a/an _____ account of my life.

6. I walked around the _____ of the football field looking for the glasses that I had lost when I had walked there previously.

7. One of the books that I included in my _____ at the end of my article was a biography of Benjamin Franklin.

8. The astronomer scanned the heavens with a/an _____ to track the path of the approaching comet.

9. The scholar wrote a short _____ in which he examined in detail the pros and cons of a democratic system of government.

10. I recognized the equipment as belonging to my father because I saw his

_____ on it.

11. In the study of _____, a person learns how to measure the eye and prescribe lenses to remediate vision problems.

12. The sociologist broadened the _____ of her studies to include several additional questions for investigation.

10-B-2 Definitional Study: Write the appropriate word on the line in front of the definition to which it best relates.

1. **autobiographical**   _____   a. instrument for measuring atmospheric pressure

2. **barometer**   _____   b. instrument for viewing heavenly bodies

3. **bibliography**   _____   c. vivid and detailed

4. **grammatical**   _____   d. initials

5. **graphic**   _____   e. study of lenses for correcting vision defects

6. **monogram**   _____   f. same on two sides

7. **monograph**   _____   g. path along the edge of

8. **optometry**   _____   h. list of books

9. **perimeter**   _____   i. related to an account of one's life

10. **scope**   _____   j. short book on a specific topic

11. **symmetrical**   _____   k. area, or range

12. **telescope**   _____   l. related to precise or correct use of language

10-B-3 Picturing: Draw a picture or diagram that shows some aspect of the meaning of each of these words. Be creative in your visualizations.

1. telescope

2. perimeter

3. bibliography

4. monogram

5. symmetrical

6. asymmetrical

10-B-4 Truth or Falsity: Decide whether each of these statements is more likely to be true or more likely to be false. Write True or False on the line.

1. A bibliography is generally composed of a single entry. _____

2. A person writes one's own autobiography, whereas a person writes somebody else's biography. _____

3. A monogram is more than likely to be a single letter. _____

4. A symmetrical vase has the same shape on both sides. _____

5. Scientists use a microscope to scan the heavens and a telescope to look at tiny objects that are nearby. _____

6. A graphic description is generally hard to figure out. _____

7. In investigating the grammatical aspects of a communication, a linguist studies the overall meaning of it and not the way the language is used in it. _____

8. A barometer is used to study the temperature of a region. _____

9. A monograph generally focuses on a single topic. _____

10. Optometry is the study of the best conditions under which to measure the universe.

_____

11. To find the perimeter of a square, one multiplies the length of an edge by the number four. _____

12. Scientists generally limit the scope of their investigations so that they can find answers to their key questions. _____

Reading with Meaning Module 10-C— Learning about the Tricky Ways We Use Language

Read the following short passage using context and your knowledge of word elements to make meaning with the highlighted words.

Negative Connotation, Euphemisms, and Doublespeak

When you hear the word *bureaucracy,* do you think of standing in long lines, filling in needlessly lengthy forms, meeting utterly ridiculous deadlines and requirements, being shuffled from one desk or office to another, and waiting on hold while music drones in the background? For many of us, the word *bureaucracy* clearly has unhappy associations. In short, the word bears a negative **connotation,** or meaning.

Some words are like that; they **conjure** up negative rather than positive pictures. For example, think about these words, all of which relate to a particular body build: *slim, thin, scrawny*. Does one of these three words carry a negative connotation for you? Does one come across most positively? Is one relatively **neutral** in the emotional **wallop** it carries? Probably you answered these questions by rating *scrawny* as carrying a negative connotation, *slim* as bearing a positive connotation, and *thin* as a relatively neutral word.

Because people have built up negative feelings toward some English words, over time we have developed expressions that may be less **objectionable**—at least when we begin to use them. For example, we use the word *toilet* as the name for a particular piece of equipment and we talk of "going to the toilet." Using such an expression, however, presents a rather graphic picture of the activity to be performed, which is not acceptable as part of polite conversation. Rather we turn to euphemistic substitutes such as "the restroom," "the powder room," "the girls' or boys' room." We use these **euphemisms** to avoid unpleasantness. You probably can think of other examples, some of which—like this one—relate to private functions of the body.

Sometimes, too, we use euphemisms to cast an activity or object in a more favorable light so as to achieve a personal objective. Have you heard advertisements for "previously owned vehicles"—or "used cars," if we are speaking more directly? When we employ language in this way, especially with the intent to deceive, we move out of the **realm** of euphemism and enter the realm of **doublespeak.** For example, military commanders at times resort to doublespeak when they describe the bombing of an area (which conjures up a picture of death and destruction) as "providing air support."

When we listen and read, we must be aware that words carry emotional meanings. We must also be alert for instances in which a speaker or writer deliberately uses language to communicate a personal point of view or even a **bias.** Only then can we arrive at our own conclusions rather than accepting someone else's words verbatim.

Word Study Activities Module 10-C— Working with Context Clues

10-C-1 Context Clues: Write the word from the left column on the line in front of the word at the right that best communicates its meaning.

1. **connotation** _____   a. punch

2. **conjure** _____   b. prejudicial slant

3. **neutral** _____   c. region or area

4. **wallop** _____   d. expression used to cast something in a more positive light

5. **objectionable** _____   e. expression used with the intent to cover up or deceive

6. **euphemism** _____   f. emotional content of a message

7. **realm** _____   g. cause to appear

8. **doublespeak** _____   h. unpleasant

9. **bias** _____   i. neither negative nor positive

10-C-2 Sentence Completion: Write sentences starting with the given phrases and including one or more of the words you have been learning in this module.

1. As I listen, I

2. His words made me think

3. Feelings are

4. As I read, I

10-C-3 Review of Word Elements: Study the boldfaced part of each word. Then write the meaning of the element and your predicted meaning of the word. Check your predictions in your dictionary.

Word	*Meaning of Boldfaced Element*	*Predicted Meaning of the Word*

1. **theo**logy

2. **demo**graphy

3. **matri**mony

4. **patri**otic

5. **bio**graphy

6. **opti**cs

7. **peri**scope

Confusing Words—*Imply* and *Infer*

Two verbs that many people misuse are *imply* and *infer*. These words are closely related in meaning, which may be the cause of the confusion. Read these sentences in which *imply* and *infer* appear and see if you can figure out when to use one and when to use the other.

• I took offense at my professor when he implied that I was not giving the course all my attention. I inferred from his remarks that he did not have a very high estimation of me.

• From what my friend said, I inferred that she had dated my boyfriend, although she did not come right out and say that. She had only implied that a relationship existed between them.

What is the distinction here? To imply is to say something rather indirectly—to hint. In implying, a person does not come right out and say something but rather "beats around the bush." To get the meaning, the listener or reader must figure it out for himself or herself by putting pieces of the message together. To infer, then, is to figure out. In short, speakers and writers imply, or hint; listeners and readers infer, or figure out.

Related words are *implication* and *inference*. An implication is an indirect indication—a hint. An inference is rather like a conclusion that we draw based on indirect references or evidence. We talk about the implications of a message. We talk about making inferences based on what we have heard or read.

Try out these distinctions by inserting *imply, implying, implied, infer, inferring, inferred, implication,* or *inference* in the blanks. You do not have to use all these words; you may use a word more than once.

1. "Are you _____ that I gained my position through inappropriate

   means?" the man shouted. "I resent that _____."

2. From what the student said, I _____ that he was none too happy with his
   grade.

3. I made an _____ based on all the evidence at hand.

4. I was annoyed because her rebuke _____ that I had cheated her.

PART V

BASIC ROOTS AND WORD ELEMENTS

11

Roots—Talking, Writing, Sensing, Knowing

◆◆

Objectives: In Chapter 11, you will develop the ability to

- explain relationships among words derived from the same root by talking about such words as *scribe, describe,* and *prescription* that contain *scrib-,* meaning "to write";

- interpret roots that relate to saying and writing, such as *dict-, vok-, loqu-, log-, scribe-, doc-, nomen-, verb-,* listed in Table 11.1;

- comprehend and use the following words featured in Module 11-A:

advocate	edict	inscription	provocative
dictatorial	eloquent	nominated	verbose
documentation	indoctrinated	prologue	vindicated

- recognize the prefix *ad-* featured in Module 11-A and attach the meaning "to" or "near" to it;

- interpret roots that relate to seeing, hearing, knowing, and feeling, such as *aud-, vid-, spect-, opti-, cred-, sci-, mne-, anim-,* listed in Table 11.2;

- comprehend and use the following words featured in Module 11-B:

animated	credentials	evident	incredible	scientific
conscience	credibility	inanimate	optical	spectacle
conscious	disrespectful	inaudible	revision	visualize

  amnesty (*power word*)

- recognize the prefix *in-* meaning "not" and the prefix *con-* meaning "together" featured in Module 11-B;

- recognize compound words such as *milestone* and *cornerstone* and use your knowledge of the component words to unlock their meaning; and

- distinguish between the words *perspective* and *prospective.*

A word is not a crystal, transparent and unchanged; it is the skin
of a living thought and may vary greatly in color and content
according to the circumstances and the time in which it is used.

—Oliver Wendell Holmes

Interesting Words to Think About—
Scribble, Scribe, Script, and Other Related Words

Some people think of the early marks that children make with pen or pencil as scribble—marks on paper that do not mean anything. That, after all, is what the dictionary says that scribble is. Recently, however, researchers have begun to study the marks that young children make on paper; they have discovered that those marks are really not scribble after all. To youngsters the marks they are making on paper mean something. To researchers those marks prove that children possess considerable understanding of the way writing works. For instance, the children's marks may show understanding of linearity, directionality, and even creativity in telling a story. Keep that in mind when next you see a sample of young children's writing.

Scribble is a great word, for it has an interesting etymology and is related to so many other words. *Scribble* can be traced through medieval Latin to the old Latin word *scribere,* meaning "to write." Even to this day you can see the commonality between the old Latin word and today's *scribble.*

What are some other words that can be traced back to *scribere* and are built from the root meaning "to write"? Here are some nouns and their meanings:

- **scribe,** *n.,* a person who copies manuscripts; one who writes things down.
- **script,** *n.,* handwriting; manuscript of a book or play.
- **manuscript,** *n.,* handwritten, typed, or computer-generated draft of a book or play; the draft before the final printed document.

Here are some verbs and some nouns and adjectives derived from those verbs:

- **inscribe,** *v.,* write or engrave words on a surface;

    inscription, *n.,* that which is inscribed on a surface.
- **transcribe,** *v.,* set down in writing, sometimes from shorthand notes;

transcript, *n.,* written or typed copy, copy of anything;

transcription, *n.,* the act of transcribing, or copying; sometimes used as a synonym for *transcript.*

- **prescribe,** *v.,* lay down as a rule, order as a treatment;

  prescript, *n.,* that which has been laid down, a rule or order;

  prescription, *n.,* a written order, especially for medicine, the act of prescribing, or ordering;

  prescriptive, *adj.,* set in place by law or by custom.

- **describe,** *v.,* tell or write about the characteristics of;

  description, *n.,* act of telling or writing about;

  descriptive, *adj.,* using description;

  descriptively, *adv.,* including a lot of description of the characteristics of.

- **conscript,** *v.,* made to serve by government action;

  conscription, *n.,* the act of forcing people to serve.

- **subscribe,** *v.,* enroll to receive a service or product, usually for money to be paid;

  subscription, *n.,* the act of enrolling at a fee;

  subscript, *n.,* a number or letter written underneath or below—in the formula for water H_2O, the 2 is a subscript. (And don't forget about the word *postscript.*)

Shared by all these words is an etymology that goes back to the old Latin word *scribere.* Whenever you see the root *scrib-* in an English word today, you are on safe ground if you hypothesize that the word has something to do with writing. The differences in meaning lie in the affixes—the prefixes and suffixes—that are attached to the root. But the heart of the matter is that your knowledge of the root can help you unlock the meanings of a host of words.

Collaborative Search and Discover

- You know the word *bibliography.* Look it up in a dictionary to discover the main root contained within the word. What is it? What does it mean? What other words can you find in the same location in the dictionary that can be traced to the same Latin source?

- Study Figure 11.1 With a marker, highlight the segment that is derived from the Latin word *mittere.*

Strategy Box 11-A—Root Awareness

Keeping alert for affixes—prefixes and suffixes—you know is a valid word-study strategy. Keeping alert for roots, or central, meaningful parts of words is also helpful. In English, you find two kinds of roots—**base words** and **combining roots.**

Figure 11.1   A Web of *Mit-/Mis-* Words

A base word is one that can stand alone as a word. In *premix,* following the prefix is the simple base word *mix,* meaning to combine or join together. Putting that meaning together with the meaning of the prefix that you already know, you can safely suggest that to premix is to put things together ahead of time.

In contrast, a combining root cannot stand alone as an English word. It comes from (or is derived from) another language such as Latin or Greek and requires the addition of a prefix and/or suffix to function as an English word. One combining root is *loqu-* or *locut-,* which is derived from (or comes from) Latin and generally means "to speak." A large number of English words are formed from this combining root. You already have studied the word *loquacious,* an adjective that means "very talkative." Here are a few others: *eloquent, elocution, colloquial,* and *collo-*

quium. You may want to check these out in your dictionary and see how their meanings relate to the idea of speaking.

A strategy for working with roots has these steps:

- Step 1: Strip the affixes off the word and consider the meaning of those beginning and ending parts.
- Step 2: Study the remaining base and see if you recognize its meaning.
- Step 3: Relate the meanings of the affixes, or the prefixes and suffixes, to the meaning of the root. Hypothesize the meaning of the total word.

See Table 11.1 for some combining roots related to talking and writing. You will be considering some of these in Module A of Chapter 11. With a marker, highlight the root in each exemplar word.

Table 11.1   Roots Related to Talking and Writing

Root	Meaning	Examples
dict-	say	dictionary, dictator, contradict
voc-, vok-	call	vocal, vocalize, advocate, evoke
locut-, loqu-	speak	eloquent, elocution, loquacious
log-, -logue	speak, choose	prologue, epilogue
scrib-	write	inscription, scripture, script
doc-	teach	doctrine, doctorate, indoctrinate
nomen-	name	nominate, nomenclature, nominal, nominee
verb-	word	verbalize, verbose, verbatim

Collaborative Search and Discover

Think of one word that you already know that is formed from each of these roots; share it with a peer and record the word in your word study notebook. Checking a dictionary will help you do this.

Word Study Module 11-A—
Roots about Talking and Writing

Pronounce the featured words, highlight the combining root within each, study the definitions and examples, and then in your mind make up a sentence using each word.

◆ 1. **dic ta to ri al** (dik′ tə tôr ē əl), *adj.*, given to laying down the law and issuing orders; domineering and overbearing.

> *Related words:* **dic tate,** *v.;* **dic ta tor ship,** *n.*

> *Contexts:* I really resented my father's dictatorial manner; he felt that he could tell me exactly what I should do, leaving me no space for making my own decisions. Each time he would dictate to me, my resentment would grow. It is difficult to live within a dictatorship.

◆ 2. **e dict** (ē′ dikt), *n.,* an order, generally a public one issued by someone of power in a government.

> *Contexts:* The monarch issued an edict forbidding any frivolous activity on the holy day.

◆ 3. **vin di cate** (vin′ də kāt), *v.,* clear from suspicion of wrongdoing, exonerate.

> *Related word:* **vin di ca tion,** *n.*

> *Contexts:* I know that when the judge hears all the evidence, her verdict will vindicate me. The thought of complete vindication after so many months of living beneath a cloud of suspicion makes my heart leap.

◆ 4. **in scrip tion** (in skrip′ shən), *n.,* letters and words written or engraved on a surface, especially on a stone or metal surface.

> *Related word:* **in scribe,** *v.*

> *Contexts*: I read the inscription that is engraved at the top of the Lincoln Memorial in Washington, D.C. It had been inscribed there when the Memorial was erected.

◆ 5. **ad vo cate** (ad′ və kāt), *v.,* speak or write in favor of a particular position or action; (ad′ və kit), *n.,* one who speaks or writes in favor of a particular position.

> *Related word:* **ad vo ca cy,** n.

> *Contexts:* The governor advocated spending more money on higher education. She became a strong advocate of this cause. As a result of her continuing advocacy, the legislature passed a bill allocating a large grant to the state university.

◆ 6. **pro vo ca tive** (prə vok′ ə tiv), *adj.,* irritating to the point of raising people's ire; calling forth action such as laughter or anger.

Related words: **pro voke**, *v.;* **pro vo ca tion**, *n.*

Contexts: The executive's behavior was always provocative. No matter what the issue or the problem, and without provocation, he would get nasty. His action would provoke others to retaliate.

◆◆

Highlighted Word Element

ad-, a Latin prefix meaning "to," "near."

Words with the element *ad-: address, addict, affirm.* (Note: This prefix changes when it is affixed to various roots. For example, when it is affixed to a root starting with the letter *f,* it becomes *af-,* as in the word *affirm;* when it joins a root starting with the letter *c,* it becomes *ac-,* as in the word *accommodate.*)

◆◆

◆ 7. **el o quent** (el′ ə kwent), *adj.,* vividly expressive and fluent in speaking.

   Related words: **el o quence**, *n.;* **el o quent ly**, *adv.*

   Contexts: The senator was an eloquent speaker who could arouse an audience to tears. It was his eloquence that accounted for the fact that he had been re-elected four times. On the anniversary of D-Day, he spoke eloquently of the sacrifices soldiers had made for their country.

◆ 8. **pro logue** (prō′ log), *n.,* introduction to a poem or novel; an introductory event.

   Related word: **ep i logue**, *n.*

   Contexts: When I read the prologue, I knew that I would not rest until I had finished the story. As I read the epilogue, I realized that the author was indeed a master of the writing craft, for he had held my attention from his beginning words until the end.

◆ 9. **doc u men ta tion** (dok′ yə men tā′ shən), *n.,* written or printed paper that provides irrefutable proof of something; the act of providing such proof.

   Related words: **doc u ment**, *v.* or *n.;* **doc u men ta ry**, *n.*

   Contexts: In order to enter the country, I had to provide documentation proving that I was who I said I was. The document that I used was my birth certificate. It documented that I was born in Iowa in 1979.
   I enjoy watching documentaries on television, for I have found that I learn so much about the world from them.

◆ 10. **in doc tri nate** (in dok′ trə nāt), *v.,* teach someone in such a way that he or she accepts a point of view without analyzing it.

Related word: **in doc tri na tion**, *n.*

Contexts: Because I knew that the group would try to indoctrinate me, I did not fall for their line. We must all be aware that indoctrination does occur; we must be analytical as we listen to others' points of view.

✦ 11. **ver bose** (vər bōs′), *adj.*, wordy.

Related word: **ver bos i ty**, *n.*

Contexts: My colleague is the most verbose person I have ever met; she talks endlessly. At some point, I begin to react negatively to her verbosity, wondering if she ever will stop talking and let me express my opinion.

✦ 12. **nom i nate** (nom′ ə nāt), *v.*, propose a person for a job or to stand for election.

Related word: **nom i nee**, *n.*

Contexts: I was proud to nominate my friend to stand election for the position of president of our club. Having become a nominee, he campaigned hard.

Word Study Activities Module 11-A—
Making Meaning with Words

11-A-1 Words in Meaningful Sentence Contexts: From the list, select the word that best fits the overall meaning of each sentence. Write that word in the blank. Use each option only once. Apply your Know-for-sure/Process-of-elimination test-taking strategy.

a. advocate	d. edict	g. inscription	j. provocative
b. dictatorial	e. eloquent	h. nominated	k. verbose
c. documentation	f. indoctrinated	i. prologue	l. vindicated

1. I had faith that eventually I would be _____ for I knew that I was innocent of any wrongdoing.

2. In the _____ of her poem, the author established the mood that she would maintain throughout the body of the piece.

3. As part of basic training, the troops were _____ so that they believed strongly in the mission on which they were about to embark.

4. Before leaving the country, be sure you have sufficient _____ so that you have no trouble on reentry.

5. Some people seem naturally _____; in contrast, I am quieter, more of a listener than a talker.

6. When I was _____ for secretary of our class, I withdrew my name for I am not fond of taking minutes.

7. To succeed as a politician in today's world of television, one must be a/an _____ speaker.

8. When the patriarch announced his _____, the citizenry rebelled.

9. The matriarch of the family tended to be _____; she believed that it was her responsibility to tell others what to do.

10. The professor resented the _____ manner of the student; that student would always disagree just to start an argument.

11. The _____ on the coin read, "E pluribus unum."

12. She was a/an _____ of suffrage for women, and she campaigned endlessly for her cause.

11-A-2 Definitional Study: Write the word from the left column on the line in front of the word or phrase in the right column that defines it.

1. **advocate**   _____   a. opening lines

2. **dictatorial**   _____   b. calling forth anger or laughter

3. **documentation** _____   c. words engraved in stone or metal

4. **edict**   _____   d. teach in a way that prevents one from thinking for himself or herself

5. **eloquent**   _____   e. wordy

6. **indoctrinate**   _____   f. name a person to run for office

7. **inscription**   _____   g. write or speak strongly for

8. **nominate**   _____   h. papers that support a claim

9. **prologue**   _____   i. characterized by beauty of speech

10. **provocative**   _____   j. bossy

11. **verbose**   _____   k. clear of suspicion of wrongdoing

12. **vindicate**   _____   l. directive handed down by a ruler

11-A-3 Truth or Falsity: Write True or False on the line to indicate the truth or falsity of the statement.

1. Words on a tombstone are considered to be an inscription. _____

2. Most people react negatively when an edict is handed down that prevents their doing what they want. _____

3. To be nominated is to be placed in office. _____

4. A prologue is the opposite of an epilogue. _____

5. To be provocative is to be cool, calm, and collected. _____

6. To be vindicated is the hope of innocent people. _____

7. Sometimes people who are verbose do not give others an opportunity to speak.

_____

8. Documentation of one's identity is required today if a person wants to travel by air.

_____

9. Advocates of a cause keep their ideas to themselves. _____

10. Most people resent those who operate in a dictatorial fashion. _____

11. To resist indoctrination, one must be analytical and stop to realize what the indoctri-

nator is trying to do. _____

12. Generally, an eloquent speaker bores us. _____

11-A-4 Roots and Their Meanings: Select the meaning of the root by starring the most appropriate option.

1. **scribe-**   a. write   b. say   c. call   d. cry
2. **dict-**   a. write   b. say   c. call   d. cry
3. **locut-**   a. look   b. lie   c. light   d. speak
4. **nomen-**   a. thought   b. feeling   c. name   d. lie
5. **verb-**   a. be   b. action   c. word   d. want
6. **-log**   a. speak   b. write   c. hear   d. feel
7. **vok-**   a. vote   b. live   c. hear   d. call
8. **doc-**   a. try   b. play   c. cure   d. teach

In the margin next to each root, write down a word containing it.

Strategy Box 11-B—Root Awareness, Part II

English has derived other roots from Greek and Latin that communicate meanings related to sensing and knowing. Keep alert for these roots: *aud-, vis-, spec-, opti-, cred-, sci-, anim-*. Table 11.2 lists these roots with their meanings and examples. Highlight the roots as you see and hear them in the examples in Table 11.2.

Table 11.2   Roots Related to Sensing and Knowing

Root	Meaning	Examples
aud-, audit-	hear	audition, inaudible, auditorium
vid-, vis-	see	visualize, video, visor, evident, invisible, revise, supervise, envy
spec-, spect-	look	spectacular, inspection, spectator, prospective
opti-	eye	optical, optician, optometrist
cred-	believe, trust	incredible, credited, credentials, incredulous
sci-	know	scientific, conscious, conscience, conscientious
mne-	remember	amnesty, mnemonic
anim-	mind, feeling, life	animated, inanimate, animal

Collaborative Search and Discover

Think of one word that you already know that is formed from each of the roots in the table and share it with a peer. Record the word in your notebook. Checking a dictionary will help you do this. Just look up some of the examples in the table and you will spot a derivative nearby.

Word Study Module 11-B— Roots That Tell about Sensing and Knowing

Pronounce the featured words, highlight the combining root within each, study the definitions and examples, and then in your mind make up a sentence using each word.

✦   1. **in au di ble** (in ô′ də blə), *adj.,* not able to be heard.

   ***Related words*: in au di bly,** *adv.;* **au di ble,** *adj.*

◆◆◆

Highlighted Word Element

in-, a Latin prefix meaning "not."

Words with the element: *insincere, incapable, ineligible.*

◆◆◆

Contexts: Because the man was speaking in a large auditorium without a microphone, his voice was inaudible to those sitting in the rear. Also his voice was inaudibly weak, which compounded the problem. When we finally got the microphone set up, his voice became audible; even I could hear it as I sat in the back.

✦   2. **revision** (ri vizh′ ən), *n.,* the act or process of changing something; literally, the act of reseeing something.

> *Related word:* **re vise,** *v.*

> *Contexts:* Revision is an important part of writing; after getting your ideas down, you should check to see if you need to revise them in any way.

✦   3. **vis u al ize** (vizh′ ū ə līz), *v.,* form a mental image of something.

> *Related word:* **vis u al,** *adj.*

> *Contexts:* I found it difficult to visualize what the speaker was describing; I could not form a mental picture of it.
> I am a visual learner; I learn best when I have pictures to support a verbal message.

✦   4. **ev i dent** (ev′ ə dənt), *adj.,* easy to understand or see.

> *Related words:* **ev i dence,** *n.;* **ev i dent ly,** *adv.*

> *Contexts:* To me it was clearly evident that the man was not telling the truth. The evidence that he gave did not in any way fit the facts. Evidently, he thought we were all stupid and would believe anything he said.

✦   5. **op ti cal** (op′ tə kəl), *adj.;* dealing with the eye and the sense of sight.

> *Related words:* **op tic,** *adj.* **op ti cian,** *n.;* also see **op tom e try** in Chapter 10.

> *Contexts:* When I needed new glasses, I went to an optical shop. An optician who worked there helped me to pick out well-styled frames.
> The optic nerve carries impulses from the eye to the brain.

✦   6. **dis re spect ful** (dis′ ri spekt′ fəl), *adj.,* lacking in courtesy (or respect) toward one's superiors or elders.

> *Related words:* **dis re spect ful ness,** *n.;* **dis re spect ful ly,** *adv.;* **re spect ful,** *adj.*

> *Contexts:* The student's disrespectful attitude landed her in considerable trouble. Her professor would not tolerate disrespectfulness. When the student talked disrespectfully to him during class, the professor asked her to leave. Most students are respectful of their professors.

✦   7. **spectacle** (spek′ tə kəl), *n.,* public display, generally large in nature; sometimes carries a negative connotation as in the phrase, "to make a spectacle of oneself." (Note: **Spectacles,** the plural form, means "set of eyeglasses.")

Related words: **spec ta tor,** *n.;* **spec tac u lar,** *adj.*

Contexts: The New York City Fourth of July fireworks display is a spectacle not to be missed. As a spectator, I stood in awe as the night sky lighted up with a multitude of colors. This was one of the most spectacular things I have ever seen.

✦ 8. **cre den tials** (kri den′ shəlz), *n.,* professional résumé, papers listing important background information, especially information related to education and past employment.

   Contexts: Before starting to search for a job, you should begin to compile your credentials.

✦ 9. **cred i bil i ty** (kred′ ə bil′ ə tē), *n.,* quality or state of being believable (or credible).

   Contexts: The politician's statement lacked credibility because he offered no evidence to support it.

✦ 10. **in cred i ble** (in kred′ ə bəl), *adj.,* difficult to believe; seemingly too extraordinary to warrant belief.

   Related words: **in cred i bly,** *adv.;* **in cre du li ty,** *n.* (See also *incredulous* in Chapter 8.)

   Contexts: My economics professor has an incredible command of her subject. She also is an incredibly talented speaker.
   When I heard her excuse, I was incredulous; the look of incredulity on my face must have communicated to her how I felt, for she immediately revised her story.

✦ 11. **con science** (kon′ shəns), *n.,* sense of right and wrong, inner feeling that tells one that an act is right or wrong.

   Related words: **con sci en tious,** *adj.;* **con sci en tious ly,** *adv.*

   Contexts: The senator's conscience would not let her vote for a bill in which she did not totally believe.
   The clerk was a conscientious worker who came on time and stayed beyond his allotted hours. He approached every task conscientiously, giving it his very best.

✦✦✦

Highlighted Word Element

con- or **com-,** a Latin prefix meaning "together."

Words with the element: *consider, conspire, conduct, compromise.*

✦✦✦

✦   12. **con scious** (kon′ shəs), *adj.,* aware of what is going on around one; able to feel; intentional

> *Related word:* **con scious ness,** *n.*

> *Contexts:* The patient was conscious during the operation; he could hear what was going on around him. He lost consciousness just after the crash, probably from a blow to the head.
> As she began her speech, the girl was conscious of her father sitting in the front row, proud of her success.

✦   13. **sci en ti fic** (sī′ ən tif′ ik), *adj.,* of or pertaining to the study of natural events and phenomena.

> *Related word:* **sci ence,** *n.*

> *Contexts:* The first scientific investigation that the young woman attempted took place in her freshman biology class. She so enjoyed the mental stimulation that she decided she would make science her life's work.

◆◆◆

Power Words Related to Remembering

am nes ty, a noun that means "general pardon for past criminal acts against the government" (from the Greek root *mne-* meaning "memory").

Related words: **am ne sia, mne mon ic.**

Contexts: The federal government granted a general amnesty to all those who paid their back taxes by the end of the year.
My friend suffered from amnesia as a result of her accident.
A mnemonic device is an aid to the memory. Some people use mnemonic devices to help them remember details; for example, one way to remember that *dessert* is spelled with a double *s* is to recall that dessert is something extra at the end of a meal.

◆◆◆

✦   14. **an i ma ted** (an′ ə mā′ tid), *adj.,* filled with lots of life and spirit; made to appear alive.

> *Related word:* **an i ma tion,** *n.*

> *Contexts:* The youngster was so animated that I could not take my eyes off him. He moved with such animation that I felt that I should join him in his activity.

✦   15. **in an i mate** (in an′ ə mit), *adj.,* not having the characteristics of a living organism; appearing lifeless or as if dead.

> *Contexts:* A teddy bear may be an inanimate object, but to a child that toy is a dear and living friend.

Word Study Activities Module 11-B—
Making Meanings with Words

11-B-1 Words in Meaningful Sentence Contexts: From the list, select the word that best fits the overall meaning of each sentence. Write that word in the blank. Use each option only once.

a. animated	d. credentials	g. evident	j. incredible	m. scientific
b. conscience	e. credibility	h. inanimate	k. optical	n. spectacle
c. conscious	f. disrespectful	i. inaudible	l. revision	o. visualize

1. I had a/an _____ discussion with my professor in which we were both equally excited about the ideas we were considering.

2. Because of my interest in the natural world, I decided to pursue _____ studies.

3. I did not mean to be _____, but somehow the lawyer thought that I was when I questioned his _____.

4. Given my friend's strong _____, I was incredulous when I learned that she had not won the position she sought.

5. The criminal had absolutely no _____. He could commit a crime without feeling any remorse afterward.

6. Because my mother had a/an _____ problem, she had to wear corrective lenses. She went to an optician to be fitted for a pair of spectacles.

7. The sound of the telephone ringing was _____ because someone had lowered the volume on the buzzer.

8. The youngster was unaware of the _____ she made of herself when she threw a temper tantrum in the supermarket.

9. Sometimes the _____ of a paper takes longer than the actual writing of it.

10. "Try to _____ yourself in this dress on a hot day," the salesperson suggested as she tried to convince me to buy the dress to take south with me for my winter holiday.

11. The prosecutor had a/an _____ memory. He could remember every case that he had ever tried.

12. During the operation, I was only _____ at the very beginning; after that, I was really "out of it."

13. It was clearly _____ that the speaker was unprepared. She rambled and stammered her way through her half-hour presentation.

14. If you walk along the major avenue in Barcelona, you will see mimes standing as still as if they were _____ objects.

11-B-2 Synonyms and Definitions: Write the word from the left column on the line at the right in front of the word or phrase that has about the same meaning. Use the process of elimination to help you.

1. **animated**   _____   a. create a picture in the mind

2. **conscience**   _____   b. public display

3. **conscious**   _____   c. act of changing

4. **credentials**   _____   d. without life

5. **credibility**   _____   e. aware

6. **disrespectful**   _____   f. clear

7. **evident**   _____   g. full of life

8. **inanimate**   _____   h. unable to be heard

9. **inaudible**   _____   i. related to the memory

10. **incredible**   _____   j. having to do with the eyes

11. **optical**   _____   k. related to study of natural events

12. **revision**   _____   l. beyond belief

13. **scientific**   _____   m. general pardon

14. **spectacle**   _____   n. sense of right and wrong

15. **visualize**   _____   o. lacking in courtesy toward

16. **amnesty**   _____   p. résumé

17. **mnemonic**   _____   q. believability

11-B-3 Question Writing: Starting with the beginning words given here, write questions that contain one or more of the words featured in this module.

1. Have you ever

2. Are you

3. Can you

4. Do you

5. When did you

6. Why do you

7. Where will you

11-B-4 Roots and Their Meanings: Select the meaning of the root by starring the most appropriate option.

1. **aud-**	a. see	b. hear	c. cry	d. hurt
2. **anim-**	a. animal	b. anger	c. life	d. belief
3. **spect-**	a. look	b. lie	c. lean	d. like
4. **opti-**	a. eye	b. ear	c. nose	d. mouth
5. **cred-**	a. create	b. give	c. believe	d. want
6. **vid-**	a. open	b. find	c. believe	d. see
7. **sci-**	a. give	b. live	c. hear	d. know

In the margin next to each root, write down a word containing it.

Reading with Meaning Module 11-C—
Learning to Interpret Compound Words

Read the following passage to find out about a special kind of word—a compound word. Use the context and your knowledge of roots and affixes to make meaning with words that are new to you.

Milestone, Cornerstone, *and Other Stony Words*

Driving along a turnpike or parkway, you may have noticed posts along the side with numbers that **progressively** get larger or smaller as you go on. These are mile markers, and they are placed **precisely** one mile apart. Going at sixty miles per hour, you pass a marker each minute of your drive.

In the old days, the markers were made of stone, and numerals that indicated the mile marks were inscribed upon them. **Thus**, they were called *milestones*. On some highways still today, you will find markers that are **literally** milestones, because the mile-marking numerals are engraved in stone.

Milestone is a **compound word** made up of two little words: *mile* and *stone*. In times gone by, speakers simply put the two words together to come up with a new word to use in reference to the stone highway markers. And today, although the markers are **typically** not made of stone, we continue to call them *milestones*.

We sometimes use **milestone** in a more figurative, **abstract** way to mean a key event, point, or item. For example, in a recent TV advertisement, a salesperson described some "videos with songs that were milestones in the career of Frank Sinatra." In this case, the milestones were not **literally** stones marking miles. They were key points in the life of this singer.

In the same vein, you can identify milestones in your life—your graduation from high school, your meeting of a significant other, your discovery of something important, your graduation from university. You could well draw a timeline on which you plot such milestones in your life. You can also identify milestones in the history of the world, in scientific study, and in the arts.

A similar type of word is *cornerstone,* which is made of *corner* and *stone*. Literally, a **cornerstone** is a stone set at the corner and base of a building. Sometimes, the stone is filled with **memorabilia** that are representative of the period in which the building was constructed and recall the times when the building was constructed. The laying of a cornerstone is an event of significance, with major community leaders and the public in attendance.

Just as milestone has a figurative use, so does *cornerstone*. We speak figuratively of the Constitution as the cornerstone of the American democracy and the Magna Carta as the cornerstone of British freedom. We say that belief in Allah is the cornerstone of the Muslim faith. Of ourselves, we may say that our "significant other" is the cornerstone of our lives.

Word Study Activities Module 11-C—
Working with Compound Words and Context Clues

11-C-1 Compound Words:

1. Check three related compound words in the dictionary: *touchstone, capstone,* and *lodestone*. What is the literal meaning of each? What is a more abstract application? Respond in your word study notebook.

2. Look up any two or three of these compound words in a dictionary and be able to explain how they are used: *keynote (n., v.); highlight (n., v.); highroad (n.); furthermore (adv.); paperwork (n.); paperweight (n.); nearsighted (adj.); farsighted (adj.); blackmail (v.).* Record in your notebook.

3. Reread the opening section of this module. Find at least three other compound words and identify the component parts. Find one hyphenated word and identify the component parts. Record in your notebook.

11-C-2 Context Clues: Star the word or phrase that is closest in meaning to the word or prefix at the left.

1. **progressively**   a. stepwise   b. thought-provokingly   c. formally   d. generally

2. **precisely**   a. exactly   b. typically   c. progressively   d. literally

3. **thus**   a. and   b. as a result   c. because   d. but

4. **literally**   a. actually   b. concretely   c. exactly   d. formally

5. **compound word**   a. word that contains a suffix
   b. word that contains a prefix
   c. word that contains both a suffix and a prefix
   d. word that is made from two words

6. **typically**   a. progressively   b. literally   c. figuratively   d. generally

7. **milestone**   a. engraved mile-marker
   b. stone found in a mill
   c. stone placed at the corner of a building
   d. lucky stone

8. **abstract**   a. figurative   b. concrete   c. precise   d. typical

9. **cornerstone**   a. engraved mile-marker
   b. stone found in a mill
   c. stone placed at the corner of a building
   d. lucky stone

10. **memorabilia**   a. objects that have bad memories associated with them
    b. books that jog the memory
    c. an object that causes one to forget
    d. objects that recall past times

11. **the prefix *in-***   a. together   b. to or near   c. not

12. **the prefix *con-***   a. together   b. to or near   c. not

13. **the prefix *ad-***   a. together   b. to or near   c. not

11-C-3 Writing Sentences and Paragraphs: In your notebook, write several sentences about a milestone in your life. In your sentences use the words *milestone, typically,* and *thus,* as well as any other of the words featured in the selection that fit logically.

Confusing Words—*Prospective* and *Perspective*

Do you know the difference between the words **prospective** and **perspective?** Do you use these words correctly?

Read these sentences and see if you can perceive the difference between the two:

- To get a clear perspective, you must step back and look at the entire scene.
- From his perspective, I was the one who had erred; from my perspective, he was the one in the wrong.
- My mother counseled me to keep things in perspective.
- When you are being interviewed by a prospective employer, you must maintain your poise, think before you speak, and then speak clearly.
- The woman looked over her prospective daughter-in-law and decided her son had made a wise choice.

Perspective serves as a noun in each of the sample sentences. In the first sample, *perspective* means "view." You can figure that out by using your substitution strategy. In the second sentence, *perspective* means "viewpoint"—a meaning very similar to that found in the first sentence. In the third sentence, the phrase *to keep things in perspective* means "to view all aspects of a situation rather than to focus on any one element."

In contrast, *prospective* serves as an adjective in the last two sentences. In both cases, *prospective* means "likely to become." Your prospective employer is one who is likely to become your boss. A prospective daughter-in-law is one who is likely to become a daughter-in-law.

Apply your understanding by inserting either the word *perspective* or *prospective* in each blank.

1. I went to the conference to meet some _____ customers.

2. Because I was angry, I knew I had to back off and get a different _____ on the issue.

3. To keep things in _____ , I took a day off from my studies and went out with my friends.

4. The _____ parents took classes on baby care.

12

Roots—Active Living

◆◆◆

Objectives: In Chapter 12, you will develop the ability to

- explain relationships among the words *introvert, extrovert*, and *versus*, derived from the same root—*vert-/vers-;*
- recognize and interpret the roots *duct-, ject-, pon-, press-, rupt-, tract-, firm-*, as in Table ·12.1;
- visualize words in terms of meaningful units—prefixes, roots, suffixes—and create word towers that clarify these units;
- comprehend and use the following words highlighted in Module 12-A:

abduct	composite	disruptive	intractable	repressive
affirm	confirmation	impressionable	oppression	retract
component	corrupt	interject	rejection	subdue

- recognize and interpret the prefixes *ab-* and *re-* featured in Module 12-A (a review objective);
- recognize and interpret the roots *cap-, cede-, fac-, junct-, port-, struct-, tens-, ven-, fort-*, which are listed in Table 12.2;
- comprehend and use the following words featured in Module 12-B:

concession	conventional	extensive	indestructible	secede
constructive	deportation	facsimile	portfolio	successive
convene	disjointed	fortitude	receptive	tendency
intensity (*power word*)				

- recognize and interpret the prefix *se-*, meaning "apart," featured in Module 12-A;
- interpret figurative language in reading and avoid clichés in writing; and
- distinguish between *precede* and *proceed* as well as derivatives of these everyday words.

> **A** powerful agent is the right word. . . . The difference between
> the right word and the almost right word is the difference
> between lightning and the lightning bug.
>
> —Mark Twain

◆◆◆

Interesting Words to Think About—
Introvert versus *Extrovert*

Are you an introvert or are you an extrovert? Regardless of the way you answer, you owe your ability to talk about yourself in these terms to a basic Latin root—*vert-* or *vers-,* that means "to turn." You also owe it to two prefixes you have already encountered in this text—*intro-* or *intra-,* meaning "within," and *extro-* or *extra-,* meaning "outside."

The root *vert-* in conjunction with *intro-* and *extro-* identify the characteristics of introversion and extroversion. Introverts turn their attention inward and are especially concerned with their own thoughts and feelings rather than with what is happening around them. Introverts are less likely to be **loquacious** and outgoing. In contrast, extroverts turn outward and seek out people with whom to interact. Extroverts are likely to be the life of the party. Introverts are likely to be looking on from the sidelines, analyzing what is going on. In some cases, introverts are the thinkers, given to **introspection;** extroverts are the doers.

Obviously, we all have elements of introversion and extroversion within us, but when we categorize ourselves as either introverts or extroverts, we are highlighting our primary orientation. From that perspective, to talk about introversion *versus* extroversion is not exactly the way to do it. Instead we should talk about introversion *and* extroversion.

What does *versus* mean? It, too, is derived from the same Latin root meaning "to turn." **Typically,** we use it to suggest the idea of "an alternative to" or "in contrast to" or even "against." Here are some expressions in which we use *versus:* Brown versus the Board of Education (a legal court case), honesty versus **deceit,** you versus me. Sometimes we abbreviate *versus,* and so you will see it as Brown *vs.* the Board of Education. You probably recognize the Latin noun-ending *-us* on *versus;* it is the same ending we talked about in Chapter 5 when we encountered it at the end of *hippopotamus.*

Once you become aware of the meaning of the root *vert-/vers-,* you can use your knowledge to decipher the meaning of lots of other words. Here is a list of some of the members of the *vert-/vers-* word family. As you can see, this is one big clan.

adversary	diversion	traverse
adverse	divert	universal
adversity	extroversion	universe
advertise	extrovert	university
advertisement	introversion	versatile
averse	introvert	verse
aversion	inverse	version
avert	invert	versus
controversial	invertebrate	vertebra
controversy	irreversible	vertex
conversation	perverse	vertical
converse	perversion	vertigo
convert	pervert	vortex
convertible	reverse	
diverse	reversibility	
diversify	subversive	
diversity	transverse	

Collaborative Search and Discover

* Based on your knowledge of *uni-* (one) and *vert-* (to turn), hypothesize why we call a university by that name and why we call the universe by that name. Respond in your word study notebook.

* In this passage are some words you have already studied. What do these words mean? Write a synonym or definition next to each:

deceit

introspection

loquacious

typically

Strategy Box 12-A—Roots That Communicate Active Living

There are any number of roots derived from Latin and Greek that communicate ideas about living an active life filled with turning, carrying, leading, seizing, drawing, driving, building. Table 12.1 lists a few that you will focus on in Chapter 12, Module A. Use a marker to highlight the root in each sample word in the table.

At this point, too, it may be helpful to review your strategies for handling prefixes, suffixes, and roots and put them together in one composite strategy. The steps in a composite strategy are as follows:

Step 1: Focus on the front of the word and ask: "Are there any prefixes that I know that are clues to the meaning of the word?"

Step 2: Focus on the root and ask: "Is this word derived from a root that I recognize?"

Step 3: Focus on the end of the word and ask: "Are there any suffixes that help me to figure out how this word is working in the sentence—as a noun, adjective, verb?"

By applying this composite strategy, you may see words not as strings of individual letters but as a series of meaningful units or parts. Study the following word tower to see how becoming aware of prefixes, roots, and suffixes can help you to see meaning within them. The words in the tower are all built with the Latin root *duct-* or *duc-,* meaning "to lead."

ab DUC tion

con DUCT or

con DUIT

de DUCE

DUCH ess

DUKE

pro DUC tiv ity

re pro DUC tion

sub DUE

via DUCT

Table 12.1   Roots That Let You Talk about Your Active Lifestyle

Root	Meaning	Examples
duc-, duct-	lead	induction, deduce, subdue, reduction
ject-	throw	eject, rejectable, projection, interject
pon-, posit-, pose-, pound-	place, put	postpone, component, exponent, deposition
press-	press	oppression, repressive, depress
rupt-	break	erupt, corruption, disruption
tract-	drag, draw	protractor, retract, intractable, tractor
firm-	firm, strong	confirmation, firmament, affirm, infirmity

Word Study Module 12-A—Roots That Tell about Active Living

Pronounce the featured words, with a marker highlight the combining root within each, study the definitions and examples, and then in your mind construct a sentence using each word.

◆   1. **ab duct** (ab dukt′), *v.,* carry away by force.

> *Related word:* **ab duc tion,** *n.*

> *Contexts:* The Vikings abducted their English captives taking them to Denmark as slaves.
> The abduction of the Sabine women by the men of Rome is part of the legend told about the founding of Rome.

◆◆◆

Highlighted Word Element

ab-, abs-, a-, a Latin prefix meaning "away, from." Note: This prefix never changes when it is affixed to a root starting with a consonant, so try not to mix it up with the prefix *ad-,* meaning "to," which sometimes changes when affixed to a root that starts with a consonant as in the word *accommodate.*

Words with the element *ab-* or *a-: abdicate, abduct, abhor, abortion, abound.*

Words with the element *ad-: admit, accede, arrange.*

◆◆◆

✦ 2. **sub due** (səb doo′), *v.,* conquer, overcome by force; tone down or soften.

> *Contexts:* The army was called in to subdue the rebels.

> (See Chapter 1 for the word *conducive,* Chapter 7 for the word *deduce;* both are derivative of the root *duct-.)*

✦ 3. **in ter ject** (in′ tər jekt′), *v.,* add in between or insert.

> *Related word:* **in ter jec tion,** *n.*

> *Contexts:* I tried to interject a comment, but everyone else was so loquacious that I—more introverted—could not get anyone's attention.
> His interjection of an anecdote from time to time broke up the monotony of his speech.

✦ 4. **re jec tion** (ri jek′ shən), *n.,* act of refusing to accept or recognize.

> *Related words:* **re ject′,** *v.;* **re′ ject,** *n.*

> *Contexts:* Because the girl was a particularly sensitive person, the rejection by her friends struck her to her very core. I had to reject the job offer because I lived too far away.

✦✦

Highlighted Word Element

re-, a Latin prefix meaning "again, back"; it also intensifies the meaning of the root.

Words with the element *re-: reduce, recompose, repress.*

✦✦

✦ 5. **com po nent** (kəm pō′ nənt), *n.,* element or piece that makes up something larger.

> *Contexts:* One component of the problem had been resolved; however, other components had not, which meant that further negotiations were necessary.

✦ 6. **com pos ite** (kəm poz′ it), *n.,* item or entity made up of distinct components.

> *Related words:* **com pose,** *v.;* **com po si tion,** *n.*

> *Contexts:* The drawing was a composite made from many individual drawings. I studied its composition and came to the conclusion that it lacked an overall design.
> The girl tried to compose a letter expressing her remorse, but she could not find the words to say she was sorry.

✦ 7. **im pres sion a ble** (im presh′ ə nə bəl), *adj.,* easily influenced or impressed.

> *Related words:* **im press,** *v.;* **im pres sion,** *n.;* **im pres sive,** *adj.*

Contexts: The teenager was at an impressionable stage in her life, so that when she dated an older man she easily fell under his negative influence. He was able to impress her with his poise and wealth. He made such a strong impression on her that she dropped out of high school to run off with him.

The lawyer had an impressive set of credentials, so that he was able to get an even better position than he already held.

✦ 8. **re pres sive** (ri pres′ iv), *adj.,* tending to put down or keep down, especially in a harsh manner.

> *Related words:* **re press,** *v.;* **re pres sion,** *n.*

Contexts: The communist government in the U.S.S.R. after World War II is known today for its repressive acts against its own people. To repress any thoughts contrary to the party line, the leaders abducted those who spoke out and sent them to Siberia. A government founded on repression eventually will fall, although it may take time.

✦ 9. **op pres sion** (ə presh′ ən), *n.,* cruel treatment or persecution by someone usually of greater power or authority.

> *Related words:* **op press,** *v.;* **op pres sive,** *adj.;* **op pres sors,** *n.*

Contexts: Finally, the people rose up against the oppression that had existed in their homeland so long. They would no longer allow their leaders to oppress them. They had suffered severely as a result of the oppressive acts that their leaders had committed. The oppressors were punished.

✦ 10. **cor rupt** (kə rupt′), *adj.,* dishonest or wicked, often influenced by bribery and "horsetrading."

> *Related words:* **cor rupt,** *v.;* **cor rup tion,** *n.;* **cor rup ti ble,** *adj.;* **in cor rup ti ble,** *adj.*

Contexts: On the city council were several corrupt individuals who made decisions based not on the needs of the people but on the way the decisions would affect them personally. Through their activities, they corrupted the entire system. Eventually, corruption reigned across the city.

Some people are easily corruptible for they have no ethical principles. Others who have a set of principles to guide them are incorruptible.

✦ 11. **dis rup tive** (dis rup′ tiv), *adj.,* causing a breaking up, causing some chaos.

> *Related words:* **dis rupt,** *v.;* **dis rup tion,** *n.*

Contexts: The audience became so disruptive that the invited speaker stopped his presentation and left the podium.

The young woman did everything she could to disrupt the discussion. This kind of disruption is unfair to other participants.

✦ 12. **re tract** (ri trakt′), *v.,* take back, especially take back a statement; draw back in.

Related word: **re trac tion,** *n.*

Contexts: The politician agreed to retract his statement that cast his opponent in a negative light. He published his retraction in the newspaper.
The snail retracted its body into its shell when it sensed a predator nearby.

◆ 13. **in trac ta ble** (in trak′ tə bəl), *adj.,* stubborn; difficult to manage or control.

Contexts: Because her husband was so intractable and always wanted his own way, the woman finally left him.

◆ 14. **con fir ma tion** (kon′ fər mā′ shən), *n.,* verification, statement that verifies.

Related word: **con firm,** *v.*

Contexts: The student received confirmation in the mail that she had been accepted at the university. A letter had been sent to confirm the job offer.

◆ 15. **af firm** (ə fûrm′), *v.,* declare or state as the truth.

Related words: **af fir ma tion,** *n.;* **af fir ma tive,** *adj.*

Contexts: The new citizen stood up to affirm that she loved her adopted country and supported its constitution. When she was asked whether she believed in democracy, she replied in the affirmative. She made her affirmation with more than one hundred others who had taken the oath of citizenship on the same day.

Word Study Activities Module 12-A—
Making Meaning with Words

12-A-1 Words in Meaningful Sentence Contexts: From the list, select the word that best fits the overall meaning of each sentence. Write that word in the blank. Use each option only once. Use your Know-for-sure/Process-of-elimination test-taking strategy.

a. abduct	d. composite	g. disruptive	j. intractable	m. repressive
b. affirm	e. confirmation	h. impressionable	k. oppression	n. retract
c. component	f. corrupt	i. interject	l. rejection	o. subdue

1. To say the Pledge to the Flag is to _____ our allegiance to our country.

2. The journalist refused to _____ his statement for he knew he had evidence to support it.

3. I could stand their _____ of my ideas only so long; then I simply got up and walked away.

4. I was missing one _____; until I found it, I could not assemble the equipment.

5. When the terrorist tried to _____ her in order to hold her as a hostage, he was caught in the act.

6. Finally the man's associates uncovered evidence of his _____ dealings and fired him.

7. The boy, who was at a/an _____ age, got into trouble when he began to travel with a wild crowd.

8. When I wanted to _____ my opinion, no one would listen although I had listened considerately to theirs.

9. During the Holocaust, the rabbi was a victim of overwhelming _____.

10. No matter what I said, my father was _____; he would not budge from his original position.

11. The police were able to _____ the violent criminal.

12. The author received written _____ that Prentice Hall had accepted her book for publication.

13. The telecast was a/an _____ of several other programs.

14. The loud music was a/an _____ element that made it difficult for the student to concentrate on his assignment.

15. In a/an _____ environment, few ideas surface for people fear reprisals.

12-A-2 Crossword Puzzle: Complete the crossword puzzle in Figure 12.1 by using the words featured in this module. If you have trouble, turn to the opening page of Chapter 12 where the words from Module 12-A are listed.

12-A-3 Related Words in Meaningful Sentence Contexts: From the list, select the word that best fits the overall meaning of each sentence. Write that word in the blank. Use each option only once.

a. abduction	d. confirm	g. incorruptible	j. reject	m. retraction
b. affirmative	e. disrupt	h. oppressive	k. repress	n. tract
c. compose	f. interjection	i. reaffirm	l. subdued	

1. The _____ of four nuns to serve as hostages horrified the world.

2. After being punished, the young boy appeared _____.

3. After fifty years of marriage, the couple decided to _____ their vows.

4. Few people are totally _____. Mother Theresa was one of them.

5. The father bought a _____ of land far out in the country in the hope that its value would increase by the time his children were in college.

Figure 12.1   A Crossword Puzzle of Words with Roots Related to Active Living

ACROSS
  3 Carry off by force
  4 Verification
  8 Part or constituent
element
  12 Pull back
  13 Easily influenced
  14 Something made up of
individual parts

DOWN
  1 Tending to keep or
put down
  2 Conquer, overcome
  5 Persecution, cruel
and harsh treatment
  6 Stubborn
  7 Tending to bring
disorder

  8 Dishonest
  9 Declare formally
  10 Act of turning down of
something or someone
  11 Insert in an abrupt
way

6. The change to Daylight Savings Time will _____ the airlines' normal
   Saturday night schedule.

7. The government tried to _____ any expression of disagreement.

8. I will _____ a letter in which I will affirm my belief in your innocence.

9. Because he was in agreement, the governor answered in the _____.

10. The newspaper failed to print the man's _____, so no one knew that he had changed his story.

11. The heat was so _____ that I had no energy to do my work.

12. His _____ was lost in the outburst that occurred; nobody heard what he was trying to say.

13. When my mother called the airline to _____ our reservation, she learned that our names were listed for the nine o'clock flight rather than the flight leaving at eight.

14. My brother decided to _____ the offer of a summer job; instead he went to school to earn six additional credits.

12-A-4 Root Review: Next to each root, write its meaning. Then in your word study notebook make a word tower built for each one, following the model tower for DUCT/ DUC given in the strategy box of Module 12-A.

1. PRESS
2. TRACT
3. POSE
4. JECT

Strategy Box 12-B— More Roots That Communicate Active Living

Keep in mind the strategy you learned earlier in Chapter 12 of visualizing words in terms of prefixes, roots, and suffixes. One root that you will study in Module B is *ced-*, from a Latin word meaning "to go." Remember that *pre-* means "before," *con-* means "together," *re-* means "back," and *se-* means "apart." Highlight the root in the words here; then hypothesize the meaning of each based on the component parts, recording your answers in your notebook:

CEDE

pre CEDE

con CEDE

con CES   sion

re   CEDE

re   CES   sion

re   CES   sion   al

se	CEDE		
se	CES	sion	
se	CES	sion	ist

Table 12.2 lists some other common roots. With a marker, highlight the root in each sample word.

Table 12.2   More Roots to Use in Talking about Active Living

Root	Meaning	Examples
cap-, cip-, capt-, cept-	take, seize	capture, recipient, except
ced-, ces-	go, yield	cede, precede, concede, recede, recession, concession
fac-, fic-, fact-, fect-	made, do	factory, facsimile, benefactor, factual, perfect, effective
junct-, join-	join	conjunction, injunction, joint, adjoining, disjointed, adjuncts
port-	carry	portal, portfolio, comport, deport
struct-	build	instruction, reconstruct, destructive
tens-	stretch, strive	contend, tendency, extension
ven-, vent-	come	intervene, prevention, invent
fort-	strong	fortress, fortify, fortitude

Word Study Module 12-B—
More Roots That Tell about Active Living

Pronounce the featured words, focusing on the syllables. With a marker, highlight the combining root within each, study the definitions and examples, and then in your mind make up a sentence using each word.

✦   1. **re cep tive** (ri sep′ tiv), *adj.*, ready and willing to take in, or to receive something, especially ideas.

Related word: **re cep tion,** *n.*

Contexts: I found the student was receptive to my suggestion that he review his paper for possible misspelling. His positive reception of the idea made me believe that he was really interested in learning how to revise his writing.

I attended a social reception at a leading hotel in the area.

✦ 2. **con ces sion** (kən sesh′ ən), *n.,* act of giving in on or agreeing to a point that was previously not acceptable.

Related word: **con cede,** *v.*

Contexts: The only concession that the professor would make was to allow the students to submit their papers by late afternoon rather than in the morning. The students could not get him to concede more than that.

✦ 3. **se cede** (si sed′), *v.,* withdraw in a formal way from a union, especially from a country, association, or other organization.

Related word: **se ces sion,** *n.*

Contexts: When the Southern states tried to secede from the United States, the Civil War began. The Northern states would fight before accepting a secession that would lead to a division of the nation into two segments.

◆◆◆

Highlighted Word Element

se-, a Latin prefix meaning "apart."

Words with the element: *secession, secret, seduce, sedition.*

◆◆◆

✦ 4. **suc ces sive** (sək ses′ iv), *adj.,* following without interruption, following one after another in sequence, or order.

Related word: **suc ces sion,** *n.*

Contexts: On four successive occasions, the student failed to turn in an assignment. There had been a succession of instructors into the class—a sequence of one after another—which may have accounted for the student's failure to keep up with his assignments.

✦ 5. **fac sim i le** (fak sim′ ə lē), *n.,* exact copy or duplicate, especially of a document such as a birth certificate.

Related word: **fax,** *n.* or *v.*

Contexts: I did not send an original; I sent a facsimile instead. Today we talk about "faxing" a document to someone. That means we send the document via electronic means over telephone lines. In short, we send a fax.

✦ 6. **dis joint ed** (dis join′ tid), *adj.,* lacking in order, out of joint, incoherent.

Contexts: I was concerned about the disjointed way in which he organized his affairs. I had never seen anyone manage his day to day activities in such a disjointed manner.

✦ 7. **port fo li o** (pôrt fō′ lē ō), *n.,* a case for carrying papers or drawings; the components of such a case.

Contexts: When the man went for his job interview, he took along a portfolio of items to document his prior experiences doing tasks similar to those he would do if he got the position.

✦ 8. **de por ta tion** (dē pôr tā′ shən), *n.,* act of being banished from a country, expulsion from a country.

Related words: **de port,** *v.;* **de port ee,** *n.*

Contexts: Deportation is the ultimate outcome when a visitor from another country is discovered working without a green card. The visitor who disobeys the law is liable to be deported. One who is deported is called a deportee.

✦ 9. **in de struc ti ble** (in′ di struk′ tə bəl), *adj.,* so strong or well made that it cannot be destroyed, unbreakable.

Related words: **des truc tive,** *adj.;* **de struc ti ble,** *adj.*

Contexts: The destructive child broke every toy he received; in his hands nothing was safe, even something advertised as indestructible.
    The large building proved to be easily destructible; when the demolition experts placed dynamite at key locations in it and set off the explosives, the building came tumbling down.

✦ 10. **con struc tive** (kən struk′ tiv), *adj.,* serving a worthwhile purpose, helpful.

Related word: **con struc tive ly,** *adv.*

Contexts: The editor gave the author constructive criticism that helped her to improve her writing. If offered without malice, criticism given constructively can be helpful and bring positive results.

✦ 11. **ex ten sive** (ik sten′ siv), *adj.,* large in range or amount.

Related words: **ex tend,** *v.;* **ex ten sion,** *n.*

Contexts: The old house required extensive renovations before anyone could inhabit it. The new owners constructed an extension in the rear that included a solarium and a new kitchen. To do this, they had to extend the house by twenty feet.

◆◆◆

Power Word with the Same Root

intensity, a noun that means "very great power, force, emphasis." It is formed from the Latin root *tens-,* meaning "strive or stretch" and the prefix *in-,* which here intensifies the meaning of the root.

Related words: intense, intensify, intensive, intent.

Contexts: The hurricane came rolling in with such intensity that it blew off every roof in the area. As the storm intensified, it became more dangerous. The winds were so intense that I could not hear my mother call to me.

I was so intent on what he was saying that I forgot to take notes.

To do well requires intensive study—study in which you delve deeply into the subject.

◆◆◆

◆ 12. **ten den cy** (ten′ dən cē), *n.,* inclination to behave or act in a certain way.

> *Related word:* **tend,** *v.*

> *Contexts:* The preacher had a tendency to pause before saying something of special import, or significance. He also tended to pause after saying it.

◆ 13. **con vene** (kən vēn′), *v.,* meet for a purpose; gather or assemble as a group.

> *Related word:* **con ven tion,** *n.*

> *Contexts:* The association will convene in St. Louis to elect its new officers. At the national convention, many leading authorities in the field will speak.

◆ 14. **con ven tion al** (kən ven′ shə nəl), *adj.,* customary, established as the norm through general usage or custom.

> *Related word:* **un con ven tion al,** *adj.*

> *Contexts:* The conventional view is that the parent knows best; the unconventional view is that the child knows much more than the parent realizes.

◆ 15. **for ti tude** (fôr′ ti tōōd′), *n.,* strength to endure pain and misfortune with bravery; courage.

> *Contexts:* No matter how dire the situation got, my mother always faced it with fortitude. I only wish I had her fortitude.

Word Study Activities Module 12-B— Making Meaning with Words

12-B-1 Words in Meaningful Sentence Contexts: From the list, select the word that best fits the overall meaning of each sentence. Write that word in the blank. Use each option only once.

a. concessions   d. conventional   g. extensive   j. indestructible   m. secede

b. constructive   e. deportation   h. facsimile   k. portfolio   n. successive

c. convene   f. disjointed   i. fortitude   l. receptive   o. tendency

1. The young woman was not at all _____ to the suggestions I offered; she turned them down because they were contrary to her own perceptions.

2. Life on the prairie during the last half of the nineteenth century required great _____ if one were to survive the hardships.

3. The representatives had to _____ for an extra two hours to get all their work completed.

4. Each representative arrived at the meeting with a/an _____ packed with relevant papers.

5. The man, who had earlier entered the country illegally, faced immediate _____ when he was apprehended.

6. On three _____ Thursday afternoons, the professors convened to talk about the goals of the university.

7. Each one wanted the statement of goals to be exactly as he or she had phrased them. No one would make any _____.

8. The only document that I had was a _____. This was insufficient for the immigration service wanted an original, not a copy.

9. The woman wrote the most _____ examination paper the teacher had ever heard; there was no logic to it at all.

10. I began to think my car was _____, for it kept on going mile after mile no matter how I treated it.

11. The student had a/an _____ to be argumentative. Typically she would start her remarks by saying, "I think you are wrong."

12. The assigned term paper required _____ research in the library.

13. The _____ grading system is one in which the best papers receive As and the poorest papers receive Fs.

14. The people who lived in that area wanted to _____ from the common-wealth, but they did not have the power to do that.

15. The professor would allow only _____ comments after a student had presented an oral report. Participants in the seminar could not be destructive in their approach to others.

12-B-2 Definitional Study: Star the word or phrase that is closest in meaning to the first term.

1. **concession**   a. act of agreeing to something   b. act of pulling away from
c. act of stating something   d. act of trying to comprehend

2. **constructive**   a. easy   b. helpful   c. meaningful   d. forceful

3. **convene**   a. state   b. join   c. meet   d. stay

4. **conventional**   a. typical   b. irregular   c. harmful   d. helpful

5. **deport**   a. carry out   b. banish   c. weigh   d. enter a port

6. **disjointed**   a. lacking in organization   b. lacking in harmony
c. lacking in enjoyment   d. lacking in money

7. **extensive**   a. given more time   b. great in quantity or size
c. hidden from sight   d. related to the past

8. **facsimile**   a. facts   b. copy   c. original   d. already sent

9. **fortitude**   a. strength of body or mind
b. castle constructed of stone
c. embankment of stone
d. a period of time consisting of two weeks

10. **indestructible**   a. unbreakable   b. colorless   c. formless   d. undesirable

11. **portfolio**   a. collection of people   b. collection of papers
c. collection of seaports   d. collection of ships

12. **receptive**   a. open to ideas   b. connected to a telephone
c. received via TV   d. able to be understood

13. **secede**   a. enter into   b. pull back from
c. serve as mediator between   d. withdraw from

14. **successive**   a. following in order   b. getting better and better
                       c. getting worse and worse   d. successful

15. **tendency**   a. delicate nature   b. hurtful spot
                       c. inclination   d. stubbornness

16. **intensity**   a. discontentedness   b. great power
                       c. inappropriate behavior   d. stubbornness

12-B-3 Related Words in Meaningful Sentence Contexts: From the list, select the word that best fits the overall meaning of each sentence. Write that word in the blank. Use each option only once.

a. concede   d. deport   g. extension   j. intensify   m. tend
b. constructively   e. destructible   h. fax   k. secession   n. unconventional
c. convention   f. destructive   i. succession   l. unreceptive   o. intensity

1. The government intended to _____ him for he had entered the country illegally.

2. My mentor would not _____ that I was right. I knew, however, that the research supported my point of view.

3. Because time was limited, I decided to _____ the document to him so that it would arrive within seconds of my sending it.

4. The police intend to _____ the search for the criminal because he is so dangerous.

5. I _____ to believe whatever my mother says for she is the epitome of truth.

6. Because my tutor had _____ criticized my first draft, my final report was one of the best papers I had ever written.

7. The taxpayer received a/an _____ of the deadline so that he did not have to file the papers on the given date.

8. Because the class reacted with such _____ to the suggestion that members hand in their papers a week earlier than previously proposed, the professor kept to the assigned deadline.

9. The English professor would not accept papers with _____ usages of English. He believed that every paper should adhere to the normal conventions of language use.

10. The British recently changed the royal _____. Now older daughters of a monarch can succeed to the throne before younger sons.

11. My father was totally _____ to my idea that I should use his newer car for the evening rather than my own piece of antiquity.

12. Because her husband had a/an _____ personality, she knew she was in danger and left home while he was away.

13. The _____ of the five largest countries from the alliance left the alliance without the strength to function successfully.

14. The organization held its annual _____ in New Orleans.

15. The building was easily_____ for it had not been built with sufficient supporting beams.

12-B-4 Root Review: Next to each root, write its meaning. Then in your word study notebook make a word tower built around each root following the model tower for **CEDE** given in the strategy box of Module 12-B. You may start by using some of the sample words in Table 12.2.

1. PORT
2. TENS
3. STRUCT
4. FORT
5. FACT
6. JOINT

Reading with Meaning Module 12-C—
Learning about Figurative Language and Clichés

Read the following passage to learn about idioms and their relation to clichés. Use the context and your knowledge of roots and affixes to make meaning with words that are new to you.

Language "Gone Bad"

Have you heard these expressions? What do they mean to you?

• iron out the wrinkles

• see the handwriting on the wall

• paint the town red

• die a thousand deaths

• eat your heart out

Each is an **idiom**—an expression that does not mean exactly what it says and that you must, therefore, interpret **figuratively** rather than **literally** word for word. When you iron out the wrinkles, you do not literally use an iron to press out the creases; rather you get rid of the problems that stand in the way of your realizing a plan. When you see the handwriting on the wall, you do not actually look at letters and words written there; instead you come to realize that your position is not a particularly advantageous one and you probably bow out. When you paint the town red, you do not buy paint and a brush; rather you enjoy a great evening of reveling. When you die a thousand deaths, you do not leave this world forever; what you do is become very embarrassed. And finally, when you eat your heart out, you do not make a meal off your heart; what you do is suffer from jealousy.

The English language is filled with idioms like these. People use them all the time in everyday communications. Can you think of others?

Unfortunately we have used some idiomatic expressions so often that they have become **clichés;** using them, we communicate almost nothing. Most masters of the written language avoid clichés. They realize that they must use language in original ways if they are to write with style, precision, and clarity. Here are a few expressions to avoid:

- caught red-handed
- bring home the bacon
- face the music
- put on the dog
- turn over a new leaf
- shot in the arm
- wash your hands of

What does each mean idiomatically? What could you write instead of relying on each of these idioms?

Other clichés are not really idioms—expressions that you must interpret figuratively rather than literally. They are simply overused phrases that you should try to avoid. Here are some examples: sly as a fox, wise as an owl, happy as a lark, burn the midnight oil, blushing bride, fools rush in. The first three of these are **similes**—comparisons that rely on the phrase "as a." You probably know other similes that are equally overworked: quiet as a mouse, fit as a fiddle, red as a beet.

Word Study Activities Module 12-C—Figurative Language and Clichés

12-C-1 A Talking Point: Talking with a friend, decide on the figurative meaning of the idioms in the list in the passage that begins "caught red-handed." Then brainstorm other idioms that you know.

12-C-2 A Second Talking Point: Decide why the phrase "gone bad" is within quotation marks in the title of the passage.

12-C-3 Context Clues: Define these terms based on their use in the passage you just read.

1. idiom

2. literal use of language versus figurative use

3. simile

4. cliché

12-C-4 Prefix Review: Highlight the prefixes at the beginnings of these words. Then indicate the meaning of the prefix and decide on the meaning of the component word.

1. recede

2. adhere

3. abstract

4. secure

5. precede

6. postpone

Confusing Words—*Precede* and *Proceed*

Some people confuse the words *precede* and *proceed*. Do you know the difference? Let us talk about them.

Both words are derived from the root you already met in Module 12-B: *ced-*, which means "to go or to yield." The key to understanding the difference is noting the prefix. You know that the prefix *pre-* means "before." With that in mind, you can hypothesize rather easily that *precede* means "to go before." You talk about one event preceding, or coming before, another. You talk about precedents or prior decisions—particularly judicial decisions—on which we base current decisions. You talk about one person taking precedence over another—or ranking ahead of another because of his or her position or status. In each of these related words, there is an element of "going before."

In contrast, *proceed* starts with the prefix *pro-*, which means "forward." Here the root *ced-* has changed in spelling, with the result being *ceed,* but still with the meaning "to go." Simply put the two parts together: *proceed* means "to go forward." You talk about proceeding on your way, or getting yourself going. You talk also about reading the proceedings—the official document in which are recorded the events that occurred during a meeting (i.e., the minutes). You speak also about having a procedure for doing something—a particular way of performing a task.

In sum, the clue is the prefix. To review, *pre-* means "before"; *pro-* means "forward." *Precede* means "go before." *Proceed* means "go forward." Decide which word or derivative fits in each of these blanks.

1. We needed a new _____ for checking out library books, for the old one no longer worked.

2. I got a copy of the _____ of the meeting so that I could learn what went on.

3. On the _____ day, I had lost my portfolio.

4. The full professors always _____ the associate professors in the graduation procession.

5. We tried to follow the _____ set by the older members on prior occasions, but for us it did not work.

6. "His question takes _____ over yours, for he has been waiting longer to be heard," the moderator told me.

13

Basic Elements—The Environment and Life

◆◆

Objectives: In Chapter 13, you will develop the ability to

- explain the importance of Latin and Greek roots in the English language by talking about relationships between such words as *latitude* and *longitude;*
- identify and interpret word elements that deal with environmental relationships as listed in Table 13.1—*astro, tele-, spher-, sol-, lun-, terra-, geo-, aqua-, hydra-, photo-, thermo-, termi-, temp-, chron-, anno-;*
- visualize words in terms of their elements rather than in terms of individual letters;
- comprehend and use the following words featured in Module 13-A:

  asterisk   solar   aquatic   interminable   chronic
  astronomical   terrain   dehydrate   terminate   chronology
  spherical   terrestrial   thermal   contemporary   perennial
  zenith and nadir *(power words)*

- identify and interpret word elements that deal with biological relationships as listed in Table 13.2—*anthro-, archae-, zoo-, vor-, herb-, carn-, tox-, corp-, gen-, cycl-, pseud-, pod-;*
- comprehend and use the following words featured in Module 13-B:

  anthropologist   devour   toxic   corporal   cyclical
  archaeology   voracious   degenerate   incorporate   cyclone
  zoological   intoxicated   generation   pseudonym   carnage
  monsoon and typhoon *(power words)*

- explain about the purpose of jargon in professional areas and read knowledgeably in the sciences as a result of your understanding of the elements from which terminology is derived; and
- distinguish among *adapt, adopt,* and *adept.*

> Words often corrupt and modify the meanings they are supposed to keep intact, but liability to infection is a price paid by every living thing for the privilege of living.
>
> —John Dewey, *How We Think,* 1933

◆◆◆

Interesting Words to Think About—*Latitude, Longitude,* and Other Terms from the Globe

When astronaut John Glenn orbited the earth three times in 1962 and over a hundred times in 1998, he viewed the earth's continents and terrain, oceans and seas, polar ice caps, and lights of cities such as Perth, Australia, spread out gloriously before him. What a splendid sight to behold!

What he did not see, however, were the lines of latitude and longitude and the legal boundaries that most of us visualize as part of planet Earth. Of course, these lines are only imaginary ones that geographers superimpose upon the earth to help us to locate our position and chart our movements. Latitude and longitude exist in the human mind and on the maps and globes through which we represent our planet.

Lines of latitude, or parallels, circle the earth from east to west. We use them to plot locations and measure distance north and south of the equator. The equator at 0° latitude divides the planet into northern and southern hemispheres that are of equal size. *Latitude* and *equator* are particularly appropriate terms to use here. *Latitude* comes from a Latin word meaning "side"; you can reason the way in which that meaning relates to these east-west lines. You already know that *equator* begins with the prefix *equi-,* which means "equal."

You may be familiar with the related word *lateral,* derived from the same Latin root. *Lateral* is an adjective that means "located at or on the side." Fish have lateral as well as dorsal fins. You may also recognize the noun-forming suffix *-tude* that you met earlier in this textbook on such words as *fortitude, multitude,* and *platitude.*

You find *-tude* also as a suffix on *longitude.* Lines of longitude, or meridians, run from pole to pole. We use these lines to measure distances and locate places east and west. Again, *longitude* is a particularly good word to use here because it is derived from a Latin word meaning "long." Longitudinal lines are long, actually about 2,403 miles in length. 0° longitude is the prime meridian for we start numbering the lines of longitude there. The prime meridian runs through Greenwich, England. If you go there, you can straddle the prime meridian, literally placing one foot in the eastern hemisphere and one foot in the western hemisphere.

Just talking about the way geographers use latitude and longitude to measure their way around and across the world makes us realize how many English words—especially scientific words—come from Latin and Greek. Here is a list of words from this passage that have interesting origins:

Word	*Element*	*Meaning of Element*	*Source*
latitude and lateral	later-	side	Latin
terrain	terra-	earth	Latin
longitude	long-	long	Latin
astronaut	astro-	star	Greek
	naut-	ship	Greek
hemisphere	hemi-	half	Greek
	spher-	sphere	Greek
geographer	geo-	earth	Greek
	graph-	writing	Greek
equator	equi-	equal	Latin
prime	prime-	first	Latin
meridian	meri-	middle	Latin
superimpose	super-	over/above	Latin
	im-	on	Latin
	pos-, pon-	place	Latin

As you continue your college studies, you will be taking courses in both the social and natural sciences. In these courses, you will encounter considerable terminology that has been derived from Latin and Greek elements. In this chapter you will become acquainted with some of these roots that are frequently used in the sciences.

Collaborative Search and Discover

Study a globe and locate other lines that we use to talk about geographic relationships: Arctic Circle, Antarctic Circle, Tropic of Cancer, Tropic of Capricorn. Check the meanings of these terms in your dictionary and be ready to talk about why we have named these particular lines of latitude.

Strategy Box 13-A—Becoming Aware of Word Elements That Deal with Environmental Relationships

By now you should be viewing words in terms of the elements of which they are composed. This is a prime strategy for handling terminology in the sciences: Highlight meaningful elements in a term, think about their meaning, and then put the meanings of the elements together to predict the meaning of the term.

In Table 13.1 are some interesting elements that you may enjoy investigating. Highlight with a marker the meaningful element or elements in each sample word.

Table 13.1   Elements That Deal with Environmental Relationships

Element	Meaning of the Element	Sample Words
astro-	star	asterisk, astronomy, astronaut
tele-	distant, afar	telephone, telegraphic, telecommute
spher-	ball, sphere	hemisphere, spherical, atmosphere
sol-	sun	solar, parasol, solarium
lun-	moon	lunar, lunatic, lunacy
terra-	earth	terrestrial, terrarium, territory, terrain
geo-	earth	geometry, geographer, geologist
aqua-	water	aquatic, aquarium
hydra-	water, hydrogen	dehydrate, hydrant, hydrolysis
photo-	light	photosynthesis, photograph
thermo-	heat	thermal, thermostat, thermosphere
termi-	end	term, terminal, terminate, interminable
temp-	time	temporary, contemporary, temporal
chron-	time	chronology, chronic
anno-	year	annual, millennium, annals

Word Study Module 13-A—Land, Sea, and Sky

Pronounce the featured words. With a marker, highlight the meaningful element in each. Then think about the meaning of the words themselves in light of the element or elements they bear.

◆ 1. **as ter isk** (as′ tə risk′), *n.*, star-shaped symbol * used to indicate a reference to a footnote or to highlight an item.

> *Contexts:* The writer placed an asterisk after each item that she wanted to draw to the attention of her readers.

◆ 2. **as tro nom i cal** (as′ trə nom′ i kəl), *adj.*, immense, unbelievably large; related to astronomy.

> *Related words:* **as tro nom i cal ly**, *adv.;* **as tron o my**, *n.;* **as tron o mer**, *n.*

> *Contexts:* The cost of sending human beings to the moon was astronomical. The entrepreneur asked an astronomically high price for the property I wanted to buy.
> An astronomer studies the universe beyond the earth. Astronomy is the study of the universe beyond the earth.

◆ 3. **spher i cal** (sfîr′ i kəl), *adj.*, shaped like a ball, globular.

> *Contexts:* The gold vase was spherical in shape; as a result, it looked like a bright sun as it sat on my window ledge.

◆ 4. **so lar** (sō′ lər), *adj.*, related to the sun.

> *Contexts:* The older woman held a parasol over her head to protect herself from the solar rays.

◆◆◆

Power Words

ze nith, *n.*, from the Arabic, the highest point, the peak; also the point on the heavenly sphere directly above an observer;

na dir, *n.*, from the Arabic, the lowest point, the bottom; also the point on the heavenly sphere opposite the zenith

Contexts: The executive was at the zenith of her career when she learned that she had a terminal illness.
The man believed that he had arrived at the nadir of his life when his wife died in an automobile accident.
(Note: Make word cards with *zenith* and *nadir* as suggested in Chapter 2. Look at them from time to time.)

◆◆◆

✦ 5. **ter rain** (tə rān′), *n.*, physical characteristic of the land in a particular area; the ground.

    Contexts: Because the terrain was rocky, we had to be careful not to trip.

✦ 6. **ter res tri al** (tə res′ trē əl), *adj.*, of or relating to the earth or the earth's inhabitants.

    Related word: **ex tra ter res tri al,** *adj.*

    Contexts: At times we should broaden our outlook from terrestrial matters and think about extraterrestrial space.

✦ 7. **a quat ic** (ə kwot′ ik), *adj.*, of or related to water.

    Related word: **a qua,** *adj.*

    Contexts: The young man took up scuba diving because he enjoyed adventuring in an aquatic environment.

    She bought a new aqua suit; it was a light bluish green, the color of the Mediterranean Sea.

✦ 8. **de hy drate** (dē hī′ drāt), *v.*, loss of water by plants and animals.

    Related word: **de hy dra tion,** *n.*

    Contexts: I feared that my body would dehydrate since I had walked very far in the heat without drinking any water.

    Dehydration can occur when one has lost body fluids as a result of an intestinal disorder.

✦ 9. **ther mal** (thûr′ məl), *adj.*, of or relating to heat, especially producing or conserving it.

    Related word: **ther mal ly,** *adv.*

    Contexts: When I went skiing in Vermont, I bought a set of thermal underwear to keep me warm.

✦ 10. **in ter mi na ble** (in tûr′ mə nə bəl), *adj.*, lengthy as related to time and to the point of causing boredom.

    Related word: **in ter mi na bly,** *adv.*

    Contexts: After what seemed like an interminable wait, I finally got to see the doctor. Since I had waited an interminably long time, I was nervous and highstrung.

✦ 11. **ter mi nate** (tûr′ mə nāt′), *v.*, bring to an end.

    Related word: **ter mi nal,** *adj.*

    Contexts: I decided to terminate my agreement with my agent for he had not upheld his side of our bargain.

The older man had a terminal illness; he was not expected to live longer than a month.

✦ 12. **con tem po rar y** (kən tem′ pə rer′ ē), *adj.,* belonging to or related to the same time; related to the present time, modern.

    Related word: **con tem po ra ries,** *n.*

    Contexts: Washington and Adams were contemporary statesmen; they both lived during the eighteenth century. Sometimes we say that people living at the same time are contemporaries.

    Ruth selected contemporary furniture, whereas I picked out more traditional pieces.

✦ 13. **chron ic** (kron′ ik), *adj.,* of a long period of time, related to a habit or disease that lasts for a long time.

    Related word: **chron i cal ly,** *adv.*

    Contexts: Sally suffers from chronic indigestion; she is always "popping" antacids. She is also chronically late, which may be a contributing factor to her stomach disorders.

✦ 14. **chro nol o gy** (krə nol′ ə jē), *n.,* order of events in time.

    Related word: **chron o log i cal,** *adj.*

    Contexts: The lawyer led the witness step by step through the events that she had observed to be sure that the members of the jury understood the chronology.

    On the test, I had to put the events leading up to the Revolutionary War in chronological order.

✦ 15. **per en ni al** (pə ren′ ē əl), *adj.,* lasting indefinitely or without end, appearing over and over, active through the year or over many years.

    Related word: **per en ni al ly,** *adv.*

    Contexts: A perennial concern in my cousin's family is whether there will be enough money to cover the family's obligations. My cousin worried perennially about the debts she was amassing.

Word Study Activities Module 13-A—
Making Meaning with Words

13-A-1 Words in Meaningful Sentence Contexts: From the list, select the word that best fits into the overall meaning of each sentence. Then write that word in the blank. Use each option only once. Apply your Know-for-sure/Process-of-elimination test-taking strategy.

a. asterisk	d. solar	g. aquatic	j. interminable	m. chronic
b. astronomical	e. terrain	h. dehydrate	k. terminate	n. chronology
c. spherical	f. terrestrial	i. thermal	l. contemporary	o. perennial

1. As winter drew near, the man got out his _____ underwear so that he would be prepared for the cold weather ahead.

2. Jane realized that she was beginning to _____ when her lips became very dry.

3. After a/an _____ wait, I finally got in to see the doctor; by then my headache, which had become a/an _____ disorder, was banging my forehead unmercifully.

4. The earth is basically _____ in shape; it is an immense ball of matter that revolves around the sun.

5. In the margin, I placed a/an _____ to remind myself to go back to reread what I felt was a significant point.

6. The Joneses installed pipes on their roof so that they could heat water circulating through the pipes with _____ energy.

7. My _____ concern has become my car; every day of every month for the past two years I have wondered whether my old Chevy would start.

8. The doctor asked the patient to review the _____ of her prior illnesses that led up to her current one.

9. The shark is a/an _____ being that is well adapted to its environment.

10. Because the _____ was even, I could walk quickly without fear of tripping.

11. The charges that Jean incurred when she went to the hospital were so _____ that she thought there must be a mistake.

12. Thomas knew that he had to _____ his relationship with Jennie when she told him that the gift he had given her was not expensive enough.

13. Deer are _____ beings; fish, in contrast, are aquatic beings.

14. Jackie's tastes are very _____, whereas Janet's tastes are more traditional.

13-A-2 Synonym Study: Match the words in the left column with the word or phrase in the right column that is closest in meaning by writing the word from the left column in front of its equivalent at the right.

1. **asterisk**   _____ a. related to heat

2. **astronomical**   _____ b. related to the sun

3. **spherical**   _____   c. very high

4. **solar**   _____   d. surface of the land

5. **terrain**   _____   e. having the shape of a ball

6. **terrestrial**   _____   f. order of events in time

7. **aquatic**   _____   g. lasting indefinitely

8. **dehydrate**   _____   h. occurring or living at the same time

9. **thermal**   _____   i. end

10. **interminable**   _____   j. lengthy, lasting a long time

11. **terminate**   _____   k. lose water

12. **contemporary**   _____   l. related to water

13. **chronic**   _____   m. related to the earth

14. **chronology**   _____   n. related to a longlasting habit or disease

15. **perennial**   _____   o. a star-shaped symbol

13-A-3 Same or Different: On the line at the right, write either Same or Different, depending on whether the pair of words carries the same or different meanings.

1. terminate/end   _____

2. aquatic/terrestrial   _____

3. chronic/periodic   _____

4. astronomical/very high   _____

5. spherical/ball-shaped   _____

6. interminable/endless   _____

7. terrain/ocean   _____

8. terrestrial/extraterrestrial   _____

9. thermal/icy   _____

10. contemporary/modern   _____

11. dehydrated/waterlogged   _____

12. solar/lunar   _____

13. chronological/illogical   _____

14. asterisk/circle   _____

15. perennial/intermittent   _____

16. nadir/zenith   _____

13-A-4 Reviewing Roots: What is the meaning of each of these roots? Write the meaning next to each and then list one word built with that root. Do not list any of the fifteen words featured in this module.

Root	*Meaning*	*Word Sample*
1. astr-		
2. sol-		
3. therm-		
4. chron-		
5. anno-		
6. temp-		
7. lun-		
8. aqua-		

Strategy Box 13-B—Becoming Aware of Word Elements That Deal with Biological Relationships

In Table 13.2 are some interesting elements that you may enjoy investigating. Highlight with a marker the meaningful element or elements in each sample word. Remember to view multisyllable words in terms of meaningful units as in the two word towers given here:

	in	CARN	ate		HERB			
re	in	CARN	a	tion	HERB	al		
		CARN	al		HERB	al	ist	
		CARN	age		HERB	a	rium	
		CARN	i	val	HERB	a	ceous	
		CARN	i	vore	HERB	i	vore	
		CARN	i	vor	ous	HERB	i	vor	ous

Table 13.2   Life-Related Word Elements

Element	Meaning of the Element	Sample Words
anthro-	human being	anthropology, anthropologist, philanthropy
archae-, arche-	ancient, primitive, beginning	archaeology, archaeologist
zoo-	animal	zoo, zoology, zoologist
vor-	devour, eat	voracious, devour, carnivore
herb-	grass	herbal, herbivore, herbaceous
carn-	flesh	carnal, carnage, carnivore
tox-	poison	toxin, toxic, antitoxin
corp-, corpor-	body	corporal, corpuscle, corpulence, incorporate
gen-	kind, race	generation, degenerate, regenerate
cycl-	circle, wheel	cyclical, motorcyle, circle
pseud-	false	pseudopod, pseudonym
pod-	foot	podiatrist, pedal, pedestrian, pedestal

Word Study Module 13-B—Life and Life Forms

Pronounce the featured words. With a marker, highlight the meaningful element in each. Then think about the meaning of the words themselves in light of the element or elements they bear.

✦ 1. **an thro pol o gist** (an′ thrə pol′ ə jəst), *n.,* one who systematically studies the origin and development of humankind, especially physical, cultural, social, and behavioral developments.

   Related words: **an thro po log i cal,** *adj.;* **an thro pol o gy,** *n.*

   Contexts: Margaret Mead was a noted anthropologist. She conducted in-depth anthropological studies in Samoa. As a result, many people became aware of the importance of anthropology as a field of investigation.

✦ 2. **ar chae ol o gy** or **ar che ol o gy** (är′ kē ol′ ə jē), *n.,* systematic study of the remains of past human life, such as graves, artifacts, and buildings.

Related words: **ar chae o log i cal,** *adj.;* **ar chae ol o gist,** *n.*

Contexts: Jeff decided to study archaeology because he was intrigued by civilizations of the past and wanted to investigate them. As part of his studies, Jeff went on several archaeological digs in Turkey. His career goal was to become an archaeologist.

✦ 3. **zo ol o gy** (zō ol′ ə jē), *n.,* branch of biology that investigates animal life as distinct from botany, which is the branch of biology that investigates plant life.

Related words: **zo o log i cal,** *adj.;* **zo ol o gist,** *n.*

Contexts: Karen majored in zoology because she was a pre-med student and felt that the study of animal forms and structures would give her a good background. In her zoological studies, she learned about all animal species. She was fortunate to study with several noted zoologists.

✦ 4. **de vour** (di vour′), *v.,* eat, consume completely, destroy, take in with great eagerness.

Related word: **de vour er,** *n.*

Contexts: In fairy tales, the dragon is the devourer. It scours the land looking for prey to devour.

My friend Edith devours one mystery novel after another. Her appetite for this kind of book is insatiable.

✦ 5. **vo ra cious** (vô rā′ shəs), *adj.,* having an insatiable appetite for, greedy.

Related word: **vo ra cious ness,** *n.*

Contexts: John's father is a voracious reader; he reads two or three books each week. John has never been able to understand his father's voraciousness in this regard, for he himself has trouble concentrating when he reads.

✦ 6. **in tox i ca ted** (in tok′ si kā′ tid), *adj.,* drunk, excited.

Related word: **in tox i ca tion,** *n.*

Contexts: Just a few drinks of liquor caused Julie to become intoxicated. Drinking too much alcohol can result in intoxication.

Life itself tended to intoxicate him; he would bubble over with joy as he marveled about the wonders of nature all around. Life for him was an intoxicant.

✦ 7. **tox ic** (tok′ sik), *adj.,* causing death, harmful.

Related words: **tox ic i ty,** *n.;* **tox i col o gy,** *n.*

Contexts: Although for years lead was put into most paint, today we know that it is a toxic substance. Its toxicity is so great that children can get very sick from ingesting paint fragments.

Toxicology is the study of the nature and effects of poisons.

✦ 8. **de gen er ate** (di jen′ ər āt′), *v.*, decline, deterioriate, fall apart.

> *Related words:* **de gen er a tive,** *adj.;* **de gen er a tion,** *n.*

> *Contexts:* We began to see our uncle degenerate before our eyes as his cancer became more life-threatening. It is difficult to watch a person get weaker and weaker as a result of a degenerative condition such as Lou Gehrig's disease. Our uncle's slow degeneration was difficult for him to accept.

✦ 9. **gen er a tion** (jen′ ə rā′ shən), *n.*, a group of contemporaries, those living at the same time; act or process of producing something, especially offspring.

> *Related word:* **gen er ate,** *v.*

> *Contexts:* I find it difficult to believe that I am now of the older generation in my family. Our generation was the first to see space travel become a reality.
> He tried to generate income by investing in the stock market, but he lost more than he gained.

✦ 10. **cor po ral** (kôr′ pər əl), *adj.,* of or related to the body.

> *Related word:* **corpse,** n.

> *Contexts:* Today, corporal punishment is against the law.
> The medical examiner's job was to examine the corpse to determine the cause of death.

✦ 11. **in cor po rate** (in kôr′ pə rāt′), *v.,* include, organize officially as a corporation, or business firm.

> *Contexts:* The chairperson tried to incorporate the suggestions of the members of the committee in the final report that he had to write. The women decided to incorporate their business rather than continue to function simply as a partnership.

✦ 12. **pseu do nym** (soo̅′ də nim), *n.,* false name assumed by an author, pen name.

> *Contexts:* Some authors write not only under their own name but also under a pseudonym.

✦ 13. **cy clic** (sī′ klik), *adj.,* related to circles, recurring in repeated patterns.

> *Related word:* **cy cle,** *n.*

> *Contexts:* Some stocks on the stock market seem to rise and fall in a cyclic pattern. The idea, of course, is to buy at the low and sell at the high. Scientists have observed many cycles in nature. The rock cycle and the water cycle are just two.

✦ 14. **cy clone** (sī′ klōn′), *n.,* a violent storm center characterized by heavy, whirling winds.

> *Contexts:* The cyclone destroyed everything in its path.

◆◆

Power Words

mon soon, *n.,* from the Arabic by way of Portugese and Dutch, a wind system that affects large areas of the earth and produces the intense wet season in India and southern Asia.

ty phoon, *n.,* from the Cantonese, a severe tropical storm, especially one occurring in the western Pacific and the China Sea; comparable to a hurricane in the Americas.

Contexts: During the wet monsoon season, great rains poured down on the coastal regions of India and caused flooding.
   A small ship caught in a typhoon is in severe trouble.

◆◆

◆ 15. **car nage** (kär′ nij), *n.,* huge loss of life, especially from killing during battle, slaughter of large numbers of human beings.

   Contexts: The carnage on the battlefields of Gettysburg is too horrible to conceive; thousands and thousands of Union and Confederate soldiers lost their lives.

Word Study Activities Module 13-B—Making Meaning with Words

13-B-1 Words in Meaningful Sentence Contexts: From the list, select the featured word that best fits into the overall meaning of each sentence. Then write that word in the blank. Use each option only once.

a. anthropologist	d. devour	g. toxic	j. corporal	m. cyclical
b. archaeology	e. voracious	h. degenerate	k. incorporate	n. cyclone
c. zoological	f. intoxicated	i. generation	l. pseudonym	o. carnage

1. The entrepreneurs decided to _____ their business in Delaware since they got a tax advantage there.

2. My cousin is of my _____; my aunt is of an earlier one.

3. I know Phil has a/an _____ appetite, for at a buffet he piles his plate high with food and refills it several times.

4. The _____ under which he writes is Grant Mark, a reversal of his real name—Mark Grant.

5. When Raymond was in Turkey, he visited the ruins of ancient civilizations that he had studied in college when he took a course in _____.

6. After Mr. Ramos bought his home, he discovered that previously the yard had been a _____ waste dump. He knew that poisons could be still in and on the ground, and so he moved out as soon as he could.

7. During the _____, the strong winds destroyed houses, uprooted trees, and lifted cars high into the air.

8. Actually the _____ caused by the storm was greater than the loss of life that resulted from the earlier rebellion.

9. My favorite biological science is _____ studies; I have always been intrigued by the diversity of animal forms we find in the world.

10. The job of a chairperson is to ensure that the discussion does not _____ into a free-for-all in which participants hurl insults at one another.

11. During the fraternity party, Matt became _____; as a result, he became obnoxious, was insulting to others, and had to be taken back to his dorm.

12. Maggie decided she wanted to be a/an _____ because she was intrigued with the diversity in cultural traits she saw among societies across the world.

13. The lions were able to _____ completely the carcass of the gazelle that they had killed.

14. Whipping is a form of _____ punishment that is punishable by law.

15. The seasons are _____ in nature; they pattern in the same way from year to year.

13-B-2 Crossword Puzzle: Solve the puzzle in Figure 13.1 by inserting the words featured in Module 13-B. Use the words as listed on the opening page of Chapter 13 to guide you.

13-B-3 Truth or Falsity: Read each statement. Decide whether each is more likely to be true or more likely to be false. Write True or False on the line based on your decision.

1. One must not ingest toxic materials. _____

2. Everyone has a pseudonym. _____

3. Corporal punishment is encouraged in American society. _____

4. A cyclone is rather like a powerful hurricane. _____

5. Anthropologists are really zoologists. _____

6. Archaeologists are most interested in things of the past. _____

7. We all enjoy being with people when they are intoxicated. _____

Figure 13.1   A Crossword Puzzle with Words about Life

ACROSS
2 Those who live contemporaneously
4 Formally form into a business, include
6 Study of the remains of past human life
10 Study of animal forms and functions
11 Huge loss of life
14 One specializing in study of the origin and development of humankind

DOWN
1 Consume completely
3 Related to the body
4 Drunk or very excited
5 Violent storm
7 Decline
8 Pen name
9 Greedy
12 Recurring in a pattern
13 Poisonous

8. Illness can cause the degeneration of bone mass. _____

9. Some hormones work in a cyclic manner. _____

10. The carnage of battle overwhelms most people. _____

11. Voraciousness is a positive trait that we enjoy in our friends. _____

12. Your parents are members of a generation older than yours. _____

13. Those with a voracious appetite tend to devour very little meat. _____

14. English has incorporated words from many languages into its lexicon. _____

15. In zoology emphasis is on the study of plants, whereas in botany emphasis is on the study of animal forms and processes. _____

16. A typhoon is a tropical storm comparable to a hurricane. _____

17. In India, the monsoon brings flooding to coastal regions. _____

13-B-4 Review of Word Elements: Next to each element, write its meaning and a word built with it. Pick one element and in your notebook, make a word tower that shows internal word relationships as per the samples in the Strategy Box.

1. gen-

2. corp-

3. zoo-

4. pseud-

5. cycl-

6. anthro-

7. archae-

8. vor-

Reading with Meaning Module 13-C—Learning about Jargon

Read the following passage to learn about jargon and about the way it affects your college or university studies.

The Jargon of the Sciences

Members of professional groups, such as archaeologists, anthropologists, zoologists, ecologists, and the like, have their own *jargon,* or terminology, that they use to talk about **phenomena** within their area of specialization. As a person pursues studies within an area, he or she must master the **jargon:** He or she must learn to talk the specialized language that members of that profession use.

For example, if you should take a course in **ecology** (the study of environmental interrelationships), you will encounter such terms as *carnivore, herbivore,* and *omnivore.* You probably can figure out the meanings of these three terms. A carnivore is a flesh-eating animal. As you may remember, *carn-* is an element derived from the Latin; it means "flesh." *Vor-* is an element that means "to devour." And there you have the meaning of *carnivore!* When you think of carnivores, think of lions, hyenas, and crows.

In the same way, you can figure out the meaning of *herbivore;* you see in that word the Latin roots *herb-,* meaning "grass," and *vor-.* Obviously an **herbivore** is a plant-eater—no meat for this grazer! When you visualize an herbivore, you picture cows, deer, and gazelle.

And what about the **omnivore?** Can you figure out what it eats? Can you figure out to which category you belong? You will find the answers to these questions by considering the meaning of *omni-.*

Words such as *carnivore, herbivore,* and *omnivore* are part of the jargon of ecology. If you take studies in ecology, you will have to learn to use these terms as well as lots of others—*biome* and *photosynthesis* to name just two. Knowing how to look at terms with a knowledgeable eye will help you master their meanings. For example, you see in *biome* the element *bio-* that you know means "life." A biome is an area controlled by climatic conditions; examples include desert, grassland, tropical forest, arctic tundra. Your knowledge of *bio-* helps you remember the meaning, for in the examples you can see a relationship between the climate and life forms found within a biome.

Similarly, you can see in *photosynthesis* the element *photo-* and the word *synthesis.* Since you know that *photo-* means "light" and *synthesis* means "putting together," just from the word itself you get the idea that in *photosynthesis* things are being put together and light is an important factor. Obviously, such a definition is imprecise, but based on your word analysis strategy, you are starting with a foundation of basic understanding.

You may be wondering why each area of study has its specialized jargon. You may be asking, "Why can't ecologists just talk about plant-eaters, flesh-eaters, and eaters of everything? Why can't they talk about climatic regions? Why can't they talk about plants making their leaves through a light-activated process? Why must they introduce complicated terminology?" However, in the end, the terms make study easier; they allow communication among scientists based on words with agreed-upon meanings. The outcome is less confusion and fewer chances of mistaken meanings.

Word Study Activities Module 13-C—Getting Meaning from Context and Word Elements

13-C-1 Predicting Meaning: Give the meaning of each of these terms based on their use in the passage:

1. jargon

2. ecology

3. phenomena

4. herbivore

5. omnivore

13-C-2 Reviewing Word Elements: Give the meaning of each of these elements. Then write down one word that contains that element. Think about how the meaning of the element relates to the meaning of the term.

1. photo-

2. omni-

3. bio-

4. carn-

5. herb-

13-C-3 Reviewing Power Words: Here are the definitions of the power words from the chapter. On the line at the right (following the first letter clues), write the word:

1. lowest point   1. n_____

2. highest point   2. z_____

3. hurricane in the western Pacific   3. t_____

4. wet season in India   4. m_____

Write a sentence in which you use the words for lowest and highest points.

Confusing Words—*Adapt, Adopt,* and *Adept*

Here are three words that some people confuse: *adapt, adopt, adept*. What does each mean?

Adapt is a verb that means "to make suitable, to adjust." We talk about animals adapting to their environment and about people adapting to a new situation or job. We also talk about adapting a novel so that it can become the screenplay for a film. An adaptation is a change made in response to a force of some kind. Some adaptations we may have had to make are changing our life style when our income goes down and changing the way we walk if we have had a serious accident. A person who reacts easily to change is said to be "adaptable."

Adopt also functions as a verb. It means "to take as one's own, especially to take a child as one's own." In parliamentary circles, *adopt* means "to accept formally." We talk of adopting a child or an idea. We also talk about adopting a motion during a meeting. *Adoption* is the noun built from the verb and means "the process of taking as one own." We can say that the adoption was formally approved.

In contrast, *adept* functions as an adjective and means "highly skilled." A person can be adept at avoiding unpleasantness; he or she can be adept at playing the piano. Typically, we use the word *adept* in conjunction with the word *at;* a person is *adept at* . . . . There is also an adverbial form: *adeptly*. We can remark that the lawyer adeptly avoided being pinned down to an exact answer.

Try placing *adapt* and *adaptation, adopt* and *adoption, adept* and *adeptly* in the following sentences:

1. Because Joe could not _____ to the college dorm scene, he decided he would live at home and commute to school.
2. After the girl was turned down by the sorority, she decided to _____ a new approach to friendships.
3. Mary quickly became _____ at making friends in her classes and in the dorm.
4. The professor _____ turned aside the student's sarcastic question and answered in an objective way.
5. The author's story was an _____ of a longer novel that he had written many years before.
6. The student's _____ of her professor's point of view occurred only after she had analyzed it thoroughly.

14

Basic Elements—The Self in Society

◆◆

Objectives: In Chapter 14, you will develop the ability to

- perceive and explain relationships among words that are built from the root *spir-*, such as *aspiration, inspiration,* and *expiration;*

- recognize and interpret word elements that relate to the person as listed in Table 14.1 *(psycho-, auto-, sol-, natal-, fid-, spir-, hol-, sanct-, sac-, valeo-);*

- visualize words in terms of their elements rather than in terms of individual letters;

- comprehend and use the following words featured in Module 14-A:

psychological	solitude	infidelity	sanctimonious	sacrilege
automatic	renaissance	aspire	sanction	valiant
desolate	bona fide	conspiracy	consecrate	validate

  semper fidelis (*power phrase*)   holocaust (*power word*)

- recognize and interpret word elements that relate to the way people interact as listed in Table 14.2 *(jud-, reg-, jur-, greg-, viv-, grand-, lev-, grav-, fini-);*

- comprehend and use the following words featured in Module 14-B:

judicious	rectify	segregation	grandeur	gravity
prejudice	perjury	revitalize	alleviate	definitive
deregulate	egregious	vivid	leverage	infinitesimal

  apartheid and pariah (*power words*)

- explain about literary allusion and interpret allusions as you encounter them in reading; and

- distinguish between *eminent* and *imminent.*

> By the time we reach college and find that we are almost ready
> to take our place in public affairs, we become more concerned
> about our language. We want to feel confident
> in our pronunciation and our choice of words.
>
> —Porter Perrin, *Writer's Guide and Index to English,* 1965.

◆◆

Interesting Words to Think About— *Aspiration, Inspiration, Expiration,* and Other Words of the Spirit

What are your aspirations for your future? Do you dream of getting an excellent job, enjoying good friendships, and having time for fine vacations? Do you see yourself scaling high mountains and achieving great goals?

Dictionaries generally define *aspiration* as "the act of desiring a lofty object, having a high goal, seeking earnestly after something worthwhile." Etymologists suggest that the English word *aspiration* has three parts: the Latin prefix *ad-,* meaning "toward," the Latin root *spir-* from the Latin word *spirare,* meaning "to breathe upon," and the suffix *-ion,* meaning "the act of." Putting those meanings together gives you a pretty fair picture of what is involved in aspiring toward a goal.

Several other English words are derived from the Latin root *spir-.* One of them is the word *inspiration.* You are inspired when you are filled with wonderful thoughts that encourage you to go forward. Something that is inspirational propels you to do good deeds. To speak inspiringly is to speak in a way that arouses others to try harder. One who speaks inspiringly is an inspirer. You probably know someone who has inspired you at some point to try your very best. In each of these forms of the word *inspiration,* the prefix *in-* means "in, within, toward." The literal meaning of *inspire* is "to breathe toward," which comes rather close to the dictionary definition—an influence that arouses efforts to do well.

Then there is the word *expiration.* Because the prefix *ex-* means "out," *expiration* carries the meaning of "coming to an end." Literally, it means "breathing out." We expire when we die, and a license can expire if not renewed. But when we exhale (or breathe out), we are also expiring.

Other words are similarly built from the Latin root *spir-.* When you combine the prefix *con-,* which means "together," with *spir-,* the result is *conspire.* You conspire when you work secretly with someone to plot a course of action. What you are literally doing when you conspire is "to breathe together." The result is a conspiracy, which in the end can land you in trouble. If you do conspire, you could become a conspirator or even a co-conspirator.

What makes *spir-* interesting is that it is the base of the word *spirit*. We talk of the human spirit, spirits that haunt the woods, and highly spirited people. People of the Christian faith speak of the "Holy Spirit." You may want to think about how the idea of breath and breathing relates to these ways of using the word *spirit*.

Collaborative Search and Discover

- Study these words: *median, medium, mediate, immediate*. What base root do you see in each? Look up the words in a dictionary to find the meaning of the base root. Then use the meaning of the root to explain the meaning of each of the words. Respond in your word study notebook.

- Study these words: *naval, navigate, navigable, unnavigable*. What base root do these words share? Look up the words in a dictionary to find the meaning of the root. Then use the meaning of the root as well as your knowledge of prefixes and suffixes to explain the meaning of the words. Respond in your notebook.

- Study these words: *refer, reference, confer, conference, transfer, infer, inference*. What base root do these words share? In your word study notebook, create a word tower with them. Then look up the words in a dictionary to find the meaning of the root, and use the meaning of the root as well as your knowledge of prefixes and suffixes to explain the meaning of each word.

- Brainstorm other words that are built with *spir-*. In your notebook, create a word tower of *spir-* derivatives.

Strategy Box 14-A—Elements That Relate to the Person

In Table 14.1 are some basic elements upon which the English language builds numerous words that relate to fundamental beliefs about life and living. As you study the table, apply your strategy for perceiving words in terms of meaningful elements. With a marker, highlight the major root in each sample word.

One of the elements in Table 14.1 is *val-*, which means "to be strong." Here is a word tower that shows the interrelationships of some words derived from that Latin root and helps you to become more aware of the meaningful units that make up these words:

Prefix	Root	Suffixes	
	VAL	ue	
	VAL	or	
	VAL	u	able
a	VAIL		

e	VAL	u	ate
equi	VAL	ent	
pre	VAL	ent	
in	VAL	id	ate
con	VAL	es	cent
de	VAL	ue	

Table 14.1   Elements That Relate to the Person

Element	Meaning	Sample Words
psycho-, psych-	mind, soul	psychology, psychotic, psychosomatic, psyche
auto-	self	automatic, autonomous, autocracy
sol-	alone	sole, solitude, desolate
natal-	birth	prenatal, native, natural, renaissance
fid-	faith	bona fide, confide, confidential, infidel
spir-	breathe	inspirational, respire, conspire
hol-	whole	holocaust, holy
sanct-	holy	sanctify, sanction, sanctuary
sac-	sacred	sacrosanct, sacred, sacrificial
val(eo)-	valor	valor, valiant, validate

Word Study Module 14-A—The Person

Pronounce the featured words. With a marker, highlight the meaningful element in each. Then think about the meaning of the words themselves in light of the element or elements they bear.

✦   1. **psy cho log i cal** (sī′ kə loj′ i kəl), *adj.*, related to the mind and the emotions, of or related to the study of the mind and the emotions.

      Related words: **psy cho log i cal ly,** *adv.;* **psy chol o gy,** *n.*

      Contexts: Because Marie was confused about her life, she took a series of psychological tests so that she could better understand herself and her goals.

Psychologically she had a problem, for she pictured herself far differently from the way she really was.

Most people benefit from studying psychology in college because they get a better understanding of their own motivation.

◆ 2. **au to ma tic** (ô′ tə mat′ ik), *adj.,* acting in a mechanical, independent way without thought or without human control.

> *Related words:* **au to mate,** *v.;* **au to ma tion,** *n.*

> *Contexts:* The professor's response was automatic for she had answered the same question many times before.

> The pilot switched to automatic controls once the plane was over the ocean.

> Many tasks that the human hand previously controlled are now automated and controlled by computers. Automation of this kind has a "downside"; jobs are being lost to machines.

◆ 3. **des o late** (des′ ə lit), *adj.,* deserted without human inhabitants, barren, forlorn.

> *Related word:* **des o late,** *v.*

> *Contexts:* The man lived in a desolate area far away from any other people. The land was desolate; nothing grew for miles around.

> After hearing about the death of her friend, the child was desolate.

> The typhoon desolated the land, destroying every building in its path.

◆ 4. **sol i tude** (sol′ i to͞od′), *n.,* state of being alone and away from others.

> *Related words:* **sol i tary,** *adj.;* **sole,** *adj.*

> *Contexts:* At the end of an eventful day, some people want a bit of solitude to recover from the hustle and bustle of the workplace.

> The naturalist sat in solitary quiet by the window surveying the terrain spread before him. He was the sole person in the room, and he appreciated his solitude.

◆ 5. **ren ais sance** (ren′ ə säns′), *n.,* period of rebirth, especially in art and learning. **Renaissance,** the period of great learning in Europe that extended from the 1300s to the 1500s.

> *Contexts:* The professor experienced a personal renaissance when she spent the summer in Florence, Italy, and was able to visit the art museums and the great cathedral that is there. During the Renaissance, many cathedrals were built across Europe.

◆ 6. **bon a fide** (bo′ nə fīd′), *adj.,* genuine, sincere, made in good faith.

> *Contexts:* When we bought the painting, we thought it was a bona fide original by Matisse; instead we discovered it was a reproduction.

> I believed that he had made a bona fide attempt to change his life style. As a result, I took his statement as the truth.

✦   7. **in fi del i ty** (in′ fi del′ i tē), *n.,* marital unfaithfulness, lack of loyalty in general.

> *Related word:* **in fi del,** *n.*

> *Contexts:* Infidelity seems to be more commonplace today than in the past, but I still believe in the sanctity of marriage vows.
>   An infidel is a nonbeliever; people of one religion at times call people of other religions "infidels" because they do not have the same faith.

◆◆◆

Power Phrase

semper fidelis, always faithful—this is the motto of the United States Marine Corps. The word *fidelis* contains the Latin root *fid-,* meaning "faith," as does the English word *infidelity.*

◆◆◆

✦   8. **as pire** (ə spīr′), *v.,* strive to great ends, hope for.

> *Related word:* **as pi ra tions,** *n.*

> *Contexts:* Some people aspire to greatness; others have few dreams for the future.
>   Jerry had very low aspirations because he had had such a sorrowful child-hood.

✦   9. **con spir a cy** (kən spîr′ ə sē), *n.,* a secret plot or plan to do wrong.

> *Related words:* **con spire,** *v.;* **co con spir a tor,** *n.*

> *Contexts:* The members of the conspiracy were caught before they could implement their plot to destroy the industrial complex. They were indicted as co-conspirators because they had plotted together. The plotters had conspired for several months as they put together their horrible plan.
>   Events seemed to conspire against me for no matter what I attempted, everything went wrong.

✦   10. **sanc ti mo ni ous** (sangk′ tə mō′ nē əs), *adj.,* feigning, or putting on, an air of righteousness or holiness.

> *Related words:* **sanc ti mo ni ous ly,** *adv.;* **sanc ti mo ny,** *n.*

> *Contexts:* The speaker assumed a sanctimonious manner that really irritated me because I knew of his infidelity. He looked sanctimoniously at me as if to say, "My behavior is better than yours." This kind of sanctimony is galling when one knows that the speaker is a hypocrite.

✦   11. **sanc tion** (sangk′ shən), *v.,* authorize or allow; *n.,* penalty for noncompliance.

Related word: **sanc tion a ble,** *adj.*

Contexts: My conscience would not permit me to sanction that kind of untruthful behavior on the part of my colleagues even though it would have benefited me.

The Congress voted to continue sanctions against South Africa until that country reversed its apartheid policies.

✦ 12. **con se crate** (kon′ si krāt′), *v.,* declare as holy, set apart as sacred.

Related word: **con se cra tion,** *n.*

Contexts: A large group of people gathered at the place where the battle had been fought to consecrate the land as a sacred and permanent memorial to all who had died there. Abraham Lincoln was a speaker at the consecration of Gettysburg.

✦ 13. **sac ri lege** (sak′ rə lij), *n.,* disrespectful treatment of something holy, intentional act of disrespect for something sacred.

Related word: **sac ri le gious,** *adj.*

Contexts: The destruction of the cathedral by the invading hordes was a sacrilege. No one could understand or condone such a sacrilegious act.

✦ 14. **val iant** (val′ yənt), *adj.,* brave, courageous.

Related words: **val iant ly,** *adv.;* **val or,** *n.*

Contexts: The soldiers' valiant acts during the battle were recognized later when they were awarded the Medal of Honor.

The colonists fought valiantly for freedom. Today, some of us find it difficult to understand such personal valor for we rarely see bravery of this magnitude.

✦ 15. **val i date,** (val′ ə dāt), *v.,* make legal, give the force of law.

Related words: **val id,** *adj.;* **val i da tion,** *n.;* **in val i date,** *v.*

Contexts: The students had to have their IDs validated before they could enroll for second semester classes. They got their validation by having their current ID cards stamped at the registrar's office.

To work in the United States, noncitizens must have a valid green card. Working illegally can invalidate a noncitizen's entry visa.

✦✦

Power Word

hol o caust, *n.,* great destruction, especially by fire. The **Holocaust,** the mass killing of Jewish people in Germany and surrounding countries during World War II. The word *holocaust* comes from the Greek *holo-* meaning "whole," and *caus-* meaning "to burn." Something that is caustic causes burns.

Contexts: The Holocaust is a blot on humanity that makes one question whether people are truly civilized.

✦✦

Word Study Activities Module 14-A— Making Meaning with Words

14-A-1 Words in Meaningful Sentence Contexts: From the list, select the word that best fits into the overall meaning of each sentence. Then write that word in the blank. Use each option only once.

a. psychological	d. solitude	g. infidelity	j. sanctimonious	m. sacrilege
b. automatic	e. renaissance	h. aspire	k. sanction	n. valiant
c. desolate	f. bona fide	i. conspiracy	l. consecrate	o. validated

1. Matt's response to his neighbor's distress was _____; without a thought, he offered his help.

2. In the _____ of her room, Melissa was able to think through her problems and make a decision regarding them.

3. Because the young woman could not forgive her husband's _____, which to her was a sin, she divorced him.

4. Professor Williams had _____ reasons for assigning an F to the student's paper.

5. José respected his mother for her _____ attempts to keep the family together after his father's death.

6. The city of Baltimore experienced a/an _____ after the rebuilding of its port area.

7. I realized that there was a/an _____ in the making when I saw several groups of people whispering on street corners during the hours around midnight.

8. His _____ attitude rubbed us the wrong way because we knew that he was not so honest as he pretended to be.

9. Before venturing into the _____ area at night, the young man checked his map and made certain that he knew precisely where he was going.

10. If you _____ to be a dentist, you must get good grades in biology.

11. The young woman went into the health center for a/an _____ evaluation because she had suffered from depression for several weeks.

12. The rabbi will _____ the land on which the synagogue will be erected.

13. The parole board refused to _____ the prisoner's early release from jail; as a result, he was incarcerated for another six months.

14. I needed to get my parking permit _____ so that I could park my automobile close to the classroom building.

15. Dumping garbage in a graveyard is a/an _____; this kind of act shows disrespect for the dead.

14-A-2 Definitional Study: Write a word from the left column on the line in front of the phrase at the right that best gives its definition.

1. **psychological** _____   a. genuine

2. **automatic** _____   b. rebirth

3. **desolate** _____   c. great destruction

4. **solitude** _____   d. courageous

5. **renaissance** _____   e. made legal

6. **bona fide** _____   f. strive toward

7. **infidelity** _____   g. of or related to feigned righteousness

8. **aspire** _____   h. declare as holy

9. **conspiracy** _____   i. state of being alone

10. **consecrate** _____   j. allow

11. **sacrilege** _____   k. acting in a mechanical way

12. **sanctimonious** _____   l. of or related to the mind or emotions

13. **sanction** _____   m. marital unfaithfulness

14. **valiant** _____   n. deserted, without human inhabitants

15. **validated** _____   o. disrespectful treatment of holy things

16. **holocaust** _____   p. secretive plan to commit a bad act

14-A-3 Related Words: Star the word or phrase closest in meaning to the one at the left.

1. **conspire** a. breathe in b. give hope to c. plot secretly d. die

2. **valor** a. bravery b. valley site c. material that is sticky d. interest on money

3. **holocaust** a. something very sacred b. something that is caustic c. horrendous destruction d. religious leader

4. **infidel**
   a. thoughtless person
   b. nonbeliever
   c. concerned person
   d. nonsmoker

5. **invalid**
   a. not legal   b. not well   c. not brave   d. not happy

6. **aspirations**
   a. hopes for the future
   b. secret plots
   c. concerns about the past
   d. love affairs

7. **coconspirators**
   a. those who live together
   b. those who plot together
   c. those with common concerns
   d. those who go to school together

8. **sanctions**
   a. act of consecrating something
   b. holy acts
   c. penalties for noncompliance
   d. objects that will not float

9. **psychology**
   a. study of peoples of the past
   b. study of society
   c. study of animal forms
   d. study of the mind and emotions

10. **sacrilegious**
    a. related to holy living
    b. related to disrespectful treatment of holy things
    c. related to religious rites and ceremonies
    d. related to those who minister to the sick and needy

11. **desolate** (v)
    a. dissolve a solid in a liquid
    b. destroy everything in its path
    c. provide opportunity for peaceful living
    d. show disrespect for religion

12. **solitary**
    a. related to solutions
    b. alone
    c. related to one's salary
    d. slow to function

13. **sanctimony**
    a. high-and-mighty attitude, especially one related to one's own goodness
    b. act of becoming married
    c. use of money to help others who are less well off
    d. process of making others feel desolate

14. **consecration**
    a. act of gathering to pay respects to the dead
    b. act of declaring a place holy
    c. act of paying respect to one's elders
    d. act of showing remorse for evil acts

15. **automate**
    a. make self-operating
    b. make a person more independent
    c. teach a person the skills to operate a car
    d. drive a hard bargain

14-A-4 Word Elements and Relationships: Record the meanings of these word elements. Then in your notebook, construct a word tower based on each of them. To get started, use the words in Table 14.1. Check the dictionary for other related words.

1. **psych-**

2. **fid-**

3. **nat-**

Strategy Box 14-B—Elements That Relate to Living and Interacting with Others

In Table 14.2 are some basic elements upon which the English language builds numerous words that relate to the way people live and interact with one another. As you study the table, apply your strategy for perceiving words in terms of meaningful elements. With a marker, highlight the root in each sample.

One of the elements in Table 14.2 is *fini-,* which means "end." Here is a word tower that shows the interrelationships of some words derived from that Latin root.

Prefix	Root	Suffix
in	FIN	ite
	FIN	ite
de	FIN	ite
in de	FIN	ite
de	FIN	itive
	FIN	ish

Table 14.2   Elements That Relate to the Way People Live and Interact with One Another

Element	Meaning	Sample Words
jud-, judic-	rule	judicial, prejudice, adjudicate, judge
reg-, rect-	rule or straighten	regulate, deregulation, irregular, rectify
jur-	swear	jury, perjury, jurisdiction

Table 14.2   Elements That Relate to the Way People Live and Interact
with One Another (*cont.*)

Element	Meaning	Sample Words
greg-	flock or herd together	congregate, segregation, egregious
viv-	live	vivid, vivacious, revive, survive
grand-	great	grand, aggrandizement, grandiose, grandeur
lev-	light	alleviate, elevate, leverage
grav-	heavy	gravity, grave, aggravate
fini-	end	infinite, infinitesimal, definite

Word Study Module 14-B—Living and Interacting

Pronounce the featured words. With a marker, highlight the meaningful element in each. Then think about the meaning of the words themselves in light of the element or elements they bear.

✦ 1. **ju di cious** (jū dish′ əs), *adj.,* exhibiting good sense or wiseness, sensible, wise.

   ***Related words:* ju di cious ness,** *n.;* **ju di cious ly,** *adv.*

   Contexts: Mr. Stern decided that it would not be judicious for him to choose only one of his sons to represent him; instead he assigned both men equal responsibilities.

   My father's judiciousness made people respect him and come to him for advice. He decided judiciously not to aggravate us by choosing one before the other; he treated us fairly in every way.

✦ 2. **prej u dice** (prej′ ə dis), *n.,* opinion formed without analyzing the facts, unfair judgment, unfounded bias, irrational hatred of a group of people; also *v.,* affect unfairly and injuriously.

   ***Related word:* prej u di cial,** *adj.*

   Contexts: The old TV character, Archie Bunker, was a creature of prejudice; he made prejudicial decisions about everyone and everything.

   "I do not mean to prejudice your decision," I told my friend, "but these are facts you must consider in making it."

✦ 3. **de reg u late** (dē reg′ yə lāt′), *v.,* decontrol, stop controlling, especially when done by a governmental body.

   ***Related words:* de reg u la tion,** *n.;* **reg u late,** *v.*

Contexts: When the government decided to deregulate the airline industry, everyone believed that prices for air travel would go down. Unfortunately after deregulation, prices escalated. Do you think that the government will try to regulate that industry again?

✦ 4. **rec ti fy** (rek′ tə fī), *v.,* set right, correct.

   Related word: **ir rec ti fi a ble,** *adj.*

   Contexts: Although the president tried to rectify the situation, he could not set things right because conditions were so dire. The situation was irrectifiable.

✦ 5. **per ju ry** (pûr′ jə rē), *n.,* deliberate giving of false testimony under oath.

   Related word: **per jure,** *v.*

   Contexts: Perjury is a crime against the state. One should never commit perjury. To perjure oneself is to open oneself to criminal charges.

✦ 6. **e gre gious** (i grē′ jəs), *adj.,* outstandingly bad.

   Related word: **e gre gious ly,** *adv.*

   Contexts: My professor could not accept such egregious behavior from a student, so she asked the young man to leave the class. He behaved so egregiously that his classmates were astounded.

✦ 7. **seg re ga tion** (seg′ ri gā′ shən), *n.,* act or process of separating some items or people from other ones, isolation.

   Related words: **seg re gate,** *v.;* **seg re ga tion ist,** *n.*

   Contexts: Some prisons practice a form of segregation; they separate youthful offenders from hardened criminals.
   In some religions during services, the women are segregated from the men.
   For years the segregationists ruled in parts of the United States and in countries such as South Africa.

✦✦✦

Power Words

a part heid (ä pärt′ hīt), *n.,* racial segregation as previously practiced in South Africa (a word with African and Dutch origins).

pa ri ah (pə rī′ ə), *n.,* social outcast; outcast member of a low caste, or social group, in India (from a Tamil word originating in India).

Contexts: Many countries placed economic sanctions on South Africa because of that country's past policy of apartheid.
   The girl felt like a pariah when her previous friends would no longer associate with her.

✦✦✦

✦ 8. **re vi tal ize** (rē vīt′ i līz′), *v.,* give new life to, bring new vigor to.

Related word: **re vi tal i za tion,** *n.*

Contexts: Many states are attempting to revitalize their inner cities by encouraging the development of new malls, theater districts, and the like. In many cases, revitalization is working, for the shops and theaters are bringing more people into the inner cities.

✦ 9. **viv id** (viv′ id), *adj.,* bright and distinct, sharp in color.

Related words: **viv id ly,** *adv.;* **viv id ness,** *n.*

Contexts: Carl paints with vivid colors and sharp lines. His paintings vividly portray the excitement of life. He depicts the world with a vividness that is distinctive.

✦ 10. **gran deur** (gran′ jər), *n.,* greatness, majesty, splendor, dignity.

Related word: **gran di ose,** *adj.*

Contexts: The grandeur of the Blue Mosque in Istanbul is beyond description.

When my sister came to me with her grandiose plans for the reception, I had to tell her that people would think she was putting on airs if she went through with them.

✦ 11. **al le vi ate** (ə lē′ vē āt), *v.,* make less severe or more bearable, relieve, lessen.

Contexts: Carrie's friend tried to alleviate her distress by taking her out to dinner, but to no avail.

✦ 12. **lev er age** (lev′ ər ij), *n.,* power to act with effectiveness.

Contexts: Because the patriarch had considerable prestige in the organization, he was able to use that as leverage to achieve change. His position gave him leverage to do what he wanted.

✦ 13. **grav i ty** (grav′ ə tē), *n.,* seriousness; weightiness; also the force that causes objects to move toward the center of a heavenly body such as the earth.

Related words: **grav i tate,** *v.;* **grav i ta tional,** *adj.*

Contexts: The doctor explained to my mother the gravity of her condition.

Gloria has such a dynamic personality that at a party everyone seems to gravitate toward her until she is the center of a converging group.

Gravity is what gives weight to bodies on the earth. Astronauts must operate in space without gravitational forces pulling them down; as a result, they float about.

✦ 14. **de fin i tive** (di fin′ i tiv), *adj.,* sure, precise, certain.

Related words: **de fin i tive ly,** *adv.;* **de fin i tive ness,** *n.*

    Contexts: In this case, we have no definitive answers; we really do not know which option is better.

    The personnel officer asked me to answer definitively, but I would not until I had sounded out other prospects.

    I rather liked my husband's definitiveness for it gave me a sense of security to know that he was so sure that we had chosen the right course.

✦ 15. **in fin i tes i mal** (in′ fin i tes′ ə məl), *adj.,* very, very small; so tiny it cannot be measured.

    Contexts: The microchip designer moved the object an infinitesimal amount, but amazingly that move made a big difference in the chip's overall function.

Word Study Activities Module 14-B—
Making Meaning with Words

14-B-1 Words in Meaningful Sentence Contexts: From the list, select the word that best fits into the overall meaning of each sentence. Then write that word in the blank. Use each option only once.

a. judicious	d. rectify	g. segregation	j. grandeur	m. gravity
b. prejudice	e. perjury	h. revitalize	k. alleviate	n. definitive
c. deregulate	f. egregious	i. vivid	l. leverage	o. infinitesimal

1. Although the change my mother made was _____, it made a significant difference in the long run.

2. A cold shower will _____ a person after he or she has spent a long, hot day at work.

3. I knew that I had made a/an _____ error when I received a summons from the courts.

4. When I have a cold, I take some medicine to _____ the congestion in my head.

5. As I stood overlooking the canyon, I was awed by its _____.

6. A/An _____ application of makeup can turn a pale person into a delightful picture.

7. Gwen was indicted for _____ because she had lied under oath during a murder trial.

8. There was a time in the United States that _____ of the races was the norm. Thankfully that time is behind us.

9. The youngster realized the _____ of his situation when the police took him into custody for shoplifting.

10. The repair person leaned back to get greater _____ so that he could pull the beams apart.

11. Tillie did everything she could to help her husband overcome his _____ toward those who differed from him in their religious beliefs.

12. When Wendy proffered her invitation for Thanksgiving dinner, she wanted me to give her a/an _____ answer so that she could be certain of the number of people who would be coming to her house.

13. I tried to _____ the mistake in grammar that I had made on the invitations, but unfortunately it was too late; they had already been mailed.

14. Little Frankie gave a/an _____ account of what had occurred during the accident; his account was so graphic that I felt that I had been there with him

15. When the members of Congress tried to _____ the automobile industry, they ran into unexpected problems, for the controls they lifted had been in place for a long time.

14-B-2 Crossword Puzzle: Complete the crossword puzzle in Figure 14.1 by using the words from Module 14-B and the power words of the chapter. If you have trouble solving the puzzle, look at the list of Module 14-B words on the page that opens Chapter 14.

14-B-3 Writing Sentences: Write five sentences. In each use at least one word featured in Module 14-B: *judicious, rectify, segregation, grandeur, gravity, prejudice, perjury, revitalize, alleviate, definitive, deregulate, egregious, vivid, leverage, infinitesimal.* Model your sentences after those in 14-B-1.

1.

2.

3.

4.

5.

Figure 14.1   A Crossword Puzzle with Words about Living Together

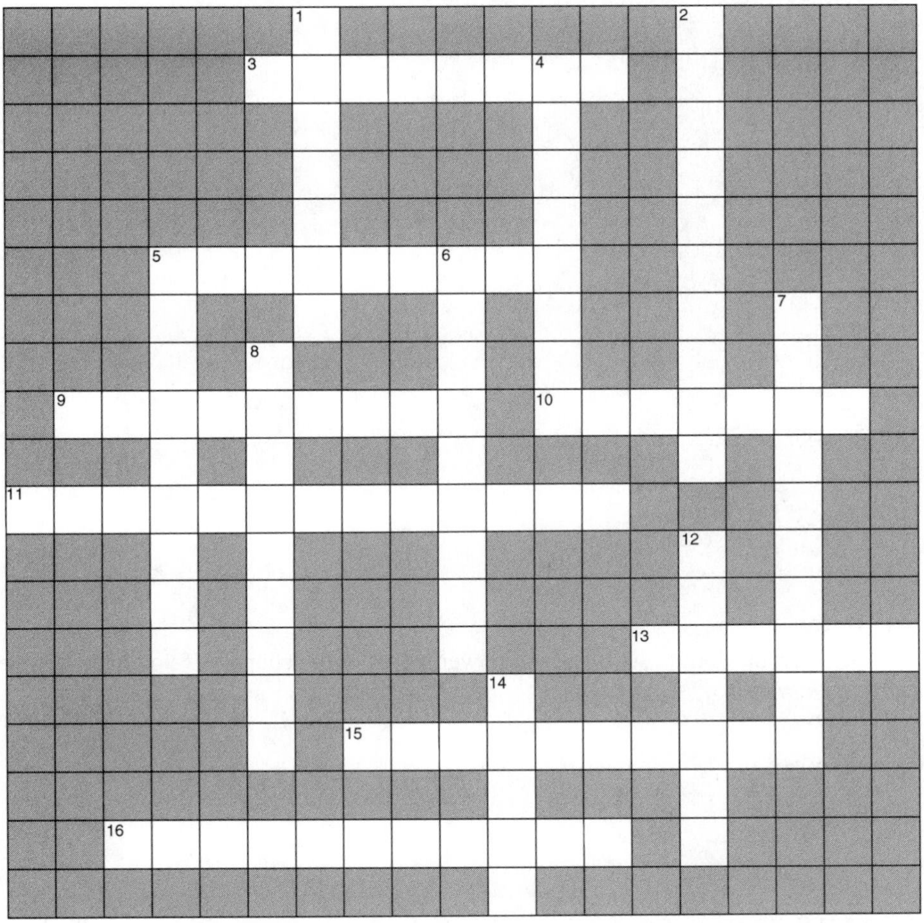

ACROSS
3 Power to operate
5 Racial segregation in
South Africa
9 Bias
10 Correct
11 Very, very small
13 Social outcast

15 Renew, give new life to
16 Separation

DOWN
1 A lie under oath
2 Decontrol
4 Splendor, greatness,
condition of being grand

5 Relieve, lessen
6 Outstandingly bad
7 Certain, sure
8 Wise
12 Seriousness, weight-
iness
14 Bright, distinct

14-B-4 Review of Key Word Elements: Review the meaning of each of these elements by writing its meaning in the space provided. Then write down two words built from each element and highlight the element with a marker.

Element	Meaning	Examples

1. viv-

2. greg-

3. reg-

4. jur-

5. rect-

6. fini-

7. grand-

8. lev-

9. grav-

14-B-5 Truth or Falsity: Decide which of these statements is more likely to be true and which more likely to be false. Write Tue or False on the line provided.

1. A vivid picture uses muted colors such as pale pinks and blues. _____

2. When an area experiences revitalization, it gets new vigor. _____

3. Most of us appreciate being treated judiciously. _____

4. To sense the gravity of a situation is to realize how unimportant it is. _____

5. When someone perjures himself, he is lying under oath. _____

6. To err egregiously is to make a simple mistake. _____

7. Most people today have no respect for those who are racial segregationists. _____

8. One way to alleviate the pain of a burn is to apply ointment to the surface. _____

9. To reply definitively is to reply with certainty or sureness. _____

10. An infinitesimal amount is a very large one, so large it cannot be imagined. _____

11. Most of us are uncomfortable when we are with people who have strong prejudices. _____

12. When deregulation of an industry occurs, the government puts more controls in place. _____

13. An irrectifiable mistake is one that can be easily corrected. _____

14. When a person needs more leverage in a situation, he or she is already very powerful. _____

15. Our response to grandeur when we behold it is awe. _____

16. Most of us enjoy being pariahs. _____

17. Apartheid is a form of segregation. _____

Reading with Meaning Module 14-C—
Learning to Interpret Literary Allusions

Read the following passage to learn about literary allusion.

Opening Pandora's Box

Have you ever heard someone refer to Pandora's box? The person may have said something like this: "I knew that with my **initial** remarks I had opened a **Pandora's box** when members of the audience began raising controversial questions, others stamped their feet, and others walked out." What does a speaker or writer mean when he or she makes a reference such as this to a Pandora's box?

You may recall the ancient myth about Pandora, the woman who was given a box and warned not to open it. The woman's curiosity, however, was greater than her common sense; she opened the box and out flew the troubles of the world. As the myth explains, those troubles remain with the world even today. Thus, when a person **refers** to Pandora's box, he or she is alluding to that mythical woman and suggesting that in some way the situation about which he or she is talking is **comparable** to the situation in which Pandora released trouble into the world. This kind of indirect reference to a story that is part of our cultural **heritage,** or traditions handed down from generation to generation, is called a **literary allusion.**

Mythology is a **repository** from which writers sometimes draw their literary allusions. Writers may allude to Midas—the king with the golden touch; the Trojan horse in which the enemy hid to emerge after dark; Icarus who melted his wings by flying too close to the sun; Atlas who supported the world on his shoulders; or Hercules who was a hero of exceptional strength. In the later case, we even have an adjective, *Herculean,* that we use to communicate the idea of great strength. Obviously, to comprehend the allusion, you must know the piece of literature from which the writer derived it.

Writers also tap into other stories for their literary allusions. Tall tales such as those about Paul Bunyan and Babe the Blue Ox can supply material for allusions. So can children's tales such as Beatrix Potter's Peter Rabbit stories and the Pollyanna series. Of course, some authors allude to longer, sophisticated stories. The plays of Shakespeare, for example, have supplied their share of allusions as when people talk about a person being a Lady Macbeth–type or another person being sunk in a Hamlet-kind of depression. The more you have read the more likely you will be able to comprehend what authors are trying to communicate through these kinds of allusions.

Word Study Activities Module 14-C—
Getting Meaning from the Context

14-C-1 Defintional Study: In items 1–7, star the meaning of each of these words or phrases based on their use in the passage; then answer the question in item 8.

1. **initial**   a. letters   b. opening   c. monogram   d. thoughtless

2. **refer to**   a. make mention of   b. name someone as a reference
                      c. explain   d. clarify

3. **comparable to**   a. opposite to   b. similar to
                            c. superior to   d. inferior to

4. **literary allusion**   a. image in a mirror that reflects what one is thinking
                                b. mirage that one imagines that one sees
                                c. indirect reference to a story
                                d. story written in the past tense

5. **allude to**   a. refer directly and clearly to
                        b. explain fully about
                        c. clarify the reasons for
                        d. refer indirectly to

6. **heritage**   a. what is handed down from one generation to the next
                       b. what is part of the genetic code
                       c. books, in general
                       d. buildings inherited from one's family

7. **repository**   a. place where things are kept or stored
                       b. place for taking a rest
                       c. place for meeting people, especially single people
                       d. place for asking questions

8. What does a writer mean when he or she says that "a person opened a Pandora's box"?

14-C-2 Writing an Explanation: In your own words explain what is meant by the term *literary allusion*. Then tell why you may have trouble interpreting some allusions.

Confusing Words—*Eminent* and *Imminent*

Do you know the difference between *eminent* and *imminent?* Let us study these words that confuse some of us. Consider these sentences:

- Grace went to an eminent surgeon, one who was noted in his field.
- The surgeon was eminently qualified to perform microsurgery.
- We stood on the street corner waiting to see the president of the United States for we had been told that his arrival was imminent.
- When we saw black clouds massing on the horizon, we knew a storm was imminent. When we saw lightening in the sky and rain falling in sheets, we knew the storm had struck.

Did you figure out that *eminent* means "high in rank or performance"? An eminent surgeon is one who is highly respected in his or her field, head and shoulders above others. In contrast, when you say that something is *imminent,* you mean that it is about to occur, that it can occur at any moment, but it has not happened yet. *Imminent* is often used in reference to a storm or an arrival.

Try the words in these sentence contexts:

1. I went to the lecture to hear an _____ astronomer talk about her investigations. She was _____ qualified on the topic for she had written several articles as well as a major textbook.

2. Although Rob heard that a storm was _____, he went out to play golf. He was on the golf course when the storm hit.

A related word is *preeminent*. Based on your knowledge of the prefix *pre-* and the word *eminent,* hypothesize the meaning of *preeminent*. Then check it in a dictionary.

Photo Credits

Page 1: Gary Conner/PhotoEdit
Page 43: Alinari/Art Resource, N.Y.
Page 85: Tony Freeman/PhotoEdit
Page 145: PhotoDisc, Inc.
Page 211: Laima Druskis/Pearson Education/PH College

Topical Index

Roots and Combining Forms

anim-, mind, feeling, life, 223
anno-, year, 258
anthro-, human being, 265
aqua-, water, 258
-arch, one who rules, 193
archae-, arche-, ancient, primitive, beginning, 265
-archy, rule by, 191–193
astro-, star, 257–258
aud-, audit-, hear, 223
auto-, self, 194, 278

bene-, good, 51
bi-, two, 128
bio-, life, 197, 272

cap-, cip-, capt-, cept-, take, seize, 144, 224
cardi-, heart, 7
carn-, flesh, 265, 272
caus-, burn, 281
ced-, ces-, go or yield, 244, 253
cent-, ten, 128
chron-, time, 118, 158
cogni-, know, 93
commun-, common, general, 67–68
corp-, corpor-, body, 265
cosm-, universe, order, 34
-cracy, rule by, 191–193
-crat, one who advocates rule by, 193
cred-, believe, trust, 152, 223
culpa-, guilty, 49
cycl-, circle, wheel, 265

deci-, decim-, 128
demo-, people, 191
di-, two, 128
dic-, dict-, say, 94, 217

digni-, worthy, 168, 180
doc-, teach, 217
duc-, duct-, lead, 236–237

ego-, self, 11

fac-, fic-, fact-, fect-, make, do, 244
fer-, bear, carry, 277
fid-, faith, 278, 280
fini-, end, 285
firm-, firm, strong, 50, 237
fort-, strong, 7, 244

gen-, kind, race, 265
geo-, earth, 27, 197, 257–258
-gram, thing that is written, 201
grand-, great, 286
-graph, instrument for writing, writing, 201, 257
-graphy, art of science of writing, 201
grav-, heavy, 286
greg-, flock or herd together, 286

hemi-, half, 257
her-, to stick, 110, 166
herb-, grass, 265, 272
hol-, whole, 278, 281
homo-, same, 24
hydra-, water, hydrogen, 258

ject-, throw, 237
junct-, join-, join, 244
jud-, judic-, rule, 285
jur-, swear, 285

lat-, side, 257
lev-, light, 286

lingua-, tongue, 9
locut-, loqu-, speak, 216, 173
log-, -logue, speak, choose, 217
long-, long, 257
loqui-, speak, 168, 173
lude-, play, 124
lun-, moon, 258

macro-, very large, 128
magni-, large, 128
male-, bad, 51
matri-, matro-, matr-, mother, 195
maxi-, large, 128
medi-, middle, 168, 179, 277
meter-, instrument for measuring, 201
metry-, art or science of measuring, 201
micro-, small, 128
milli-, thousand, 126–127
mini-, very small, 128
mit-, send, or let go, 216
mne-, remember, 223, 226
modi-, measure, 168, 181
mono-, one, 128, 191
mort-, death, 52
multi-, many, 127

natal-, birth, 278
naut-, ship, 257
nomen-, name, 217
nomy-, science or system governing, 193
novem-, nov-, nine, 128

oct, octav-, eight, 128
-ology, study of or science of, 193
omni-, all, 128, 272
opti-, visible, eye, 202, 223
optimus-, best, 168, 174

pan-, all, 128, 132
patri-, patr-, father, 196
pax-, peace, 59
-phobia, abnormal fear of, 29
phone-, sound, 24
photo-, light, 258, 272
pod-, foot, 265
poly-, many, much, 128
pon-, posit-, pos-, pound-, place, put, 237, 257
port-, carry, 244
pot-, power, 131
press-, press, 237
prim-, one, first, 83, 128, 257
pseud-, false, 265

psycho-, psych-, mind, soul, 278

quadr-, four, fourth, 128
quint-, five, 128

reg-, rect-, rule or straighten, 285
rupt-, break, 237

sac-, sacred, 278
sanct-, holy, 278
sci-, know, 223
-scope, instrument for viewing, viewing, 201
scrib-, write, 215, 217
semi-, partly, 128
sept-, seven, 128
sext-, sex-, six, 128
signi-, sign, 168, 181
sol-, alone, 278
sol-, sun, 258
spec-, spect-, look, 223
spher-, sphere, 257–258
spir-, spirit, 276, 278
struct-, build, 244

tele-, distant, far, 258
temp-, time, 258
tens-, stretch, 244, 247
termi-, end, 258
terra-, earth, 50, 99, 257–258
theo-, god, 192
thermo-, heat, 258
tox-, poison, 265
tract-, drag, draw, 237
turb-, to disturb, 160
tri-, three, 128

uni-, single, 128

valeo-, val-, be strong, valor, 277–278
ven-, vent-, come, 244
verb-, word, 217
vid-, vis-, see, 223
viv-, live, 286
voc-, vok-, call, 217
volv-, roll, 138
vor-, devour, eat, 265, 272

zoo-, animal, 265

Prefixes

Suffixes

-**able, -ible,** inclined to, tending to, 136, 151
-**acy,** quality or state of being, 172
-**al,** pertaining to, 149–150
-**ant,** pertaining to, 150
-**ary, -arium,** place for, 171
-**ary,** having the characteristic of, pertaining to, 150
-**ate,** make, 169,170, 178
-**ate,** pertaining to, 151

-**dom,** full of, 171

-**ence, -ency, -ance, -ancy,** state of being full of, 172
-**ent,** pertaining to, 150
-**er, -or,** one who works in, 171

-**ful,** full of, having the characteristic of, 148, 150

-**gon,** angle, angled figure, 135

-**ic,** pertaining to, 150
-**ician,** one who works at, 171
-**id,** inclined to, tending to, 151
-**ify,** make, 178
-**igate,** make, drive, 178
-**ile,** pertaining to, 150
-**ine,** pertaining to, 151
-**ish,** full of, having the characteristic of, 150
-**ism,** belief in, 171

-**ist,** one who works in or believes in, 171
-**itous, -icious,** inclined to, tending to, 151
-**itude,** quality or state of, 171, 256
-**ity,** quality or state of, 171
-**ive,** inclined to, tending to, 151, 170
-**ize,** make, 178

-**less,** without, 92, 151

-**ment,** state or condition of, means of action for, 171

-**ness,** full of, 171

-**olent, -ulent,** full of, having the characteristic of, 148, 150
-**or,** one who works in, 168–170
-**ory,** inclined to, tending to, 151
-**ose,** full of, having the characteristic of, 148
-**ous,** full of, having the characteristic of , 38, 148, 150

-**some,** full of, having the characteristic of, 150

-**tion, -sion,** state or condition of, act of, 168, 169, 170, 171, 276

-**uous,** inclined to, tending to, 151

-**y,** inclined to, tending to, 151

Word Index